READING
The News

READING
The News

A PANTHEON GUIDE

TO

POPULAR CULTURE

Robert Karl Manoff and Michael Schudson
EDITORS

PANTHEON **B**OOKS,
NEW YORK

ACKNOWLEDGMENTS

The editors gratefully acknowledge the support of the Gannett Center for Media Studies and the New York University Center for War, Peace, and the News Media. Gannett Center fellowships to James W. Carey and Michael Schudson helped support the writing of their chapters; grants to the NYU Center from the Carnegie Corporation of New York and the Maryanne Mott Charitable Trust helped underwrite that of Robert Karl Manoff. The editors would also like to thank Tom Engelhardt for his creative and skillful editorial assistance.

Library of Congress Cataloging-in-Publication Data

Reading the news.

    1. Journalism.   I. Manoff, Robert Karl.
II. Schudson, Michael.
PN4731.R43 1987   070   86-42639
ISBN 0-394-54362-9
ISBN 0-394-74649-X (pbk.)

Designed by Robert Bull

Manufactured in the United States of America

9 8 7 6 5 4 3 2

Contents

READING
The News

Reading the News

ROBERT KARL MANOFF
AND MICHAEL SCHUDSON

"**E**very newspaper reporter should answer the questions, What? Who? Where? When? Why? and should do it in the first paragraph as nearly as possible. This is the first and greatest commandment in the matter of journalistic style and the penalty for breaking it is the wastebasket and swift oblivion."

This advice to reporters, now nearly a century old, has become not only the first commandment but the second nature of American journalism. The "five *W*'s and an *H*" (the *H* for How?) are still part of the journalism-school catechism, and editors still expect a news story lead to address them. But these questions hide within their simplicity and their apparent common sense a whole framework of interpretation from which reporters—even the best and most "objective" reporters—operate, and necessarily so. After all, the world does not submit directly to blunt interrogation. Nor, in actual practice, do reporters demand that it should. Newspaper reporters rarely race to the scene to directly witness a news event. (Even when they do, as Leon Sigal observes, objective reporting requires that they derive the information they use more from authoritative sources than from their own observations.) Normal practice is that the reporter calls up a reliable "source" after the event to get a story; or, in another normal routine, the source calls up the reporter before an event set up specifically for the press to report on it.

From the beginning, then, there is interaction between what the world is and how it gets reported. Reporting is inevitably a part of a double reality, both separate from the world it tells stories about and a constituent of that world, an element of the story. The reporter not only relates stories but makes them.

This, of course, is heresy within the world of journalism. You report, you do not manufacture. You ask your who, what, when, where, why, and how; get the answers; and come on home. But how—and this is the central line of questioning the essays in this book take up—does the reporter know when to ask the basic journalistic questions, and who to ask them of? How does the reporter know when the questions have been answered? Who counts as a newsworthy "who"? What facts or events qualify as reportable responses to the question "what"? Even with the apparently simplest questions of all, "when" and "where," how does the reporter know if an answer is really sufficient? In the ideology of journalism, a dateline tells all—"Washington, D.C., April 18. At the White House today . . ." But the fact is that news stories—even wire service stories—scarcely ever stop there. The where in this instance is, as it happens, a metaphor for who—the president. The president is often a metaphor for "the nation" and the United States is all too often a metaphor for some larger geopolitical creature, say, the "free world." And why is Washington, D.C., news? In part because the major news organizations made a political and budgetary decision to send more of their reporters to Washington than to Milwaukee. Ordinarily, we might scarcely argue with such a judgment; but sometimes, as Daniel Hallin shows, the decision to focus on Washington has fateful consequences—as when the press reports stories about El Salvador or Nicaragua out of Washington rather than out of San Salvador or Managua.

There is a structure to the reporting and the writing of the news that is never taught in the journalism schools, never mentioned by the city editor to the novice. The reporter who asks "what" is expected to operate with an understanding of what a fact is and what an event is that is never made explicit and, as Carlin Romano suggests, never could be; the reporter who asks "who" is supposed to develop a sense of what "whos" in the world are legitimate sources for and subjects of news. If you ask "when," you necessarily incorporate a particular version of history, however foreshortened; if you ask "where," you call up an already inscribed political geography, no matter how unconscious it may be. No "why" or "how" gets asked without some assumption about what counts in the press as an explanation. In short, the apparently simple commandment questions of journalism presuppose a platform for inquiry, a framework for interpreting answers, a set of rules about who to ask what about what.

The essays in this book hold that these platforms, frameworks, and rules organize the kind of news we read (not the only kind of news that might be written), and trace them to political and economic structures, occupational routines of daily journalism, and literary forms that journalists work with. All of the essays pay some close attention to what it's like to be a newspaper reporter, what kinds of organizational pressures a reporter faces. News gathering is often, as Michael Schudson writes in his essay, "a matter of the representatives of one bureaucracy picking up prefabricated news items from representatives of another bureaucracy."

These essays examine the social, economic, and political constraints under which journalists work. They also examine the literary or narrative structure of news writing that itself acts as a constraint on what journalists can produce. As several of the essays demonstrate through close readings of news stories, some events or trends in the world are likely to get reported not because powerful interests push them forward but because their dramatic or narrative structure make them obtrusive and, to a storytelling, story-writing reporter, irresistible ("Guest Drowns at Party for 100 Lifeguards").

These are not topics journalists themselves like to dwell on. If reporters are aware of underlying ideology and unspoken limitations in their professional norms and values, it is not an awareness they find comfortable. Fearing the fate of dancers who look at their feet, they prefer to get on with the business of journalism. Or like Wily Coyote, they race so furiously along the precipice of news gathering that they are unaware when they reach thin air above an abyss—or they are aware and believe they can keep going so long as they do not look down. (Sometimes journalists are like the couple traveling on holiday who, stopping for gas, are asked by the attendant if they haven't missed their turnoff some miles back. Oh, yes, we did, they say, but we have been making such good time.)

Journalism, like any other storytelling activity, is a form of fiction operating out of its own conventions and understandings and within its own set of sociological, ideological, and literary constraints. To recognize that journalists try to be "objective" in no way contradicts this. It is, instead, evidence that journalists have a strong sense of formal constraints on their work, one of which is the set of rules, procedures, and traditions that define what "objectivity" means and when (not always) to invoke it. To claim that reporters simply and successfully mirror a real world, however, does contradict everything these essays suggest.

That the essays share a great deal does not mean they do not have different emphases and even some disagreements. James Carey argues, for instance, that you can't realistically expect to find meaning in daily news stories, in the "tissue-thin slices of reality" that individual stories so often provide. He advises attention to the whole "curriculum" of journalism, not just its first course, and argues that the story our journalism tells us is completed not in the news story alone but in the editorial and the column, the weekly newsmagazine, the monthly news essay, and even the books journalists write months or years after an event to flesh out its meaning.

This is a worthy caution to the efforts of other essays to find meaning in or behind the single, even the singular, news story. Carey draws attention to the problem of what unit of analysis an examination of journalism should engage. Is the story a coherent unit? Or is there some meaning to the page? (Several of the essays focus especially on page one as a unit of special significance.) Or is it the "coverage" rather than the "account," the set of stories over a period of days and weeks, that gives some meaning to reporting?

Other essays share with Carey's the view that the daily newspaper is far from transparent and that a reader has to bring a lot of equipment to it to understand it. There is no small amount of decoding to be done with this homely bit of literature. Leon Sigal shows that a knowledge of journalistic routines and bureaucratic intrigue is often required to sort out both what a story says and why it made its way into the paper in the first place—what source leaked it and why. Michael Schudson demonstrates how much cultural understanding is taken for granted in news stories—some of it universally shared (like the normal length of a lifetime) but some of it dependent on familiarity with historical experiences specific to or interpreted in specific ways by our culture or certain groups within it. Daniel Hallin intimates that a given news framework (the cold war) will come to seem natural (rather than ideological) to readers unfamiliar with alternatives to it, and only rarely will journalism itself apprise readers of what alternatives might exist. (Only occasionally do journalists themselves know.)

The essays here do not attribute a single voice or a coherent ideological structure to American journalism. For one thing, they take note of important differences among news institutions. Daniel Hallin's essay, for instance, makes a point of the difference between the *New York Times*'s "journalism of policy" and the *New York Daily News*'s "journalism of experience" in its coverage of the same events. For another, they argue for some degree of open structure in the fabric of the news. Carlin Romano, for example, holds the journalistic definition of facts and news to be "anarchistic."

But the essays nonetheless identify pervasive and powerful uniformities in American journalism. Indeed, Robert Manoff takes the remarkable similarities among news stories from different news institutions—and our common failure to find this truly remarkable—as a central issue to be addressed. What is unusual about this collection of essays is that working journalists, journalism educators, and media critics provide such constructively overlapping visions of how to understand the news. It is rare, in any event, to bring together such relatively diverse people without their talking past one another. This collection is all the more rare, we believe, in asking seriously of journalists the questions they themselves ask the world each day. Who? What? When? Where? Why? How? And, most of all, what do journalists mean by those questions?

One conclusion to draw from these essays is that news is more important and journalists less important than is popularly recognized. Journalists are less important not because they simply transmit, mirrorlike, the real world to readers—far from it—but because they refract the views of reality held by powerful news sources. News, as Leon Sigal writes, is "not what journalists think, but what their sources say." And, as he continues, it is mediated by "news organizations, journalistic routines and conventions, which screen out many of the personal predilections of individual journalists." Indeed, some of the essays argue that journalists consciously deny themselves power. Daniel Hallin holds, for instance, that reporters only rarely paint in a full setting for straight news stories in an intentional effort to make the news story a kind of minimalist art, stripped bare of the dramatic power a stage set can provide.

But if individual reporters are less important than we often imagine, the product they create is of greater importance than we often acknowledge. The news strengthens common understandings that hold a heterogeneous and sometimes explosive society together. The news tells us "where" we are in the world. The news reinforces and teaches us central understandings of "when" we are—how to understand a life, how to understand the lifetime of modern society. The news reinforces certain understandings of what authorities to defer to, what events to treat respectfully, what groups and topics to regard as trivial, what kinds of explanations to seek out. In a world where the news media provide so much of our information about what lies beyond our immediate ken, and at the same time offer unspoken guidelines about how to read that information, how to absorb it, how to take it into our lives, it is important to know how to read not only the news, but journalists and journalism itself. The essays that follow take this as their task.

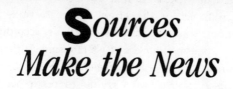

Sources
Make the News

LEON V. SIGAL

Police Kill Woman Being Evicted; Officers Say She Wielded a Knife

A 67-year old Bronx woman being evicted from a city housing project for nonpayment of rent was fatally shot by a police officer yesterday after she slashed at another officer with a butcher knife, the police said.

Authorities said the woman, Eleanor Bumpurs, who was described as "violent and uncontrollable," was shot in the chest when an officer assigned to the police Emergency Service Unit fired his shotgun. Members of the unit are specially trained to deal with emotionally disturbed people.

Deputy Inspector Thomas Coyne said the officer fired after efforts to restrain the woman failed, because he "feared for the safety" of the other officers.

"It appears that the shooting was within department guidelines," he said, but he added that a department inquiry into the incident had not been completed. All shootings by police officers are also investigated by a district attorney's office and presented to a grand jury.

Mrs. Bumpurs lived alone in a three-and-a-half-room apart-
ment at the Sedgwick Houses, at 1551 University Avenue and
West 174th Street in the High Bridge section. She paid
$89.45 a month and owed five months' rent, according to Val
Coleman, a spokesman for the city's Housing Authority.

"For months both the Department of Social Services and
the Housing Authority were trying to reach her to see if
something could be done to help her, but no one could get
through to her," Mr. Coleman said.

This story appeared on page 3 of the "Metropolitan Report"
section of the *New York Times* on Tuesday, October 30, 1984. Its
subject, the "who" in the news, was Eleanor Bumpurs, a person not
likely to make the news except as the perpetrator or the victim of a
crime, and if she did, not likely to be displayed as prominently in
the *Times* as in the city's two tabloids, the *Daily News* or the *Post*.
The only other "who" in the story, Officer Stephen Sullivan, does
not appear in person until the tenth paragraph, where he is identified by a police spokesman as the officer who shot Mrs. Bumpurs
while an attempt was being made to pin her with a U-shaped
restraining bar.

He said the officers tried using the bar to restrain Mrs. Bumpurs, who was described as about 5 feet 8 inches tall and
weighing 300 pounds, but Officer Stephen Sullivan fired
his shotgun when she lunged with the knife at one of the
officers.

The other people who appear in the fourteen-paragraph story are
its sources, Deputy Inspector Thomas Coyne, the police spokesman,
and Val Coleman, a Housing Authority spokesman. Apart from the
somewhat unusual circumstances of the case, the story's disclosure
—at a Police Department press briefing—was routine. So was the
story's appearance on an inside page of the *Times,* the day after the
incident. So, too, was the announcement of two official investigations.

Two days later, the *Times* carried a very different story, this time
on page 4 of its "Metropolitan Report" section. It began this way:

Police and Victim's Daughter Clash on Shooting

A police official yesterday defended his department's tactics in the fatal shooting Monday of a 66-year-old woman in her Bronx apartment and said there were no plans to revise procedures for restraining emotionally disturbed people.

Also yesterday, a daughter of the woman questioned aspects of the police account and asserted her mother was physically unable to attack the officers.

The police official, Deputy Chief John P. Lowe, said the police had decided against using tear gas or Chemical Mace to disable the woman, because "the theory was that she was elderly and we would be able to handle her without too much trouble."

Four more paragraphs followed detailing the circumstances of the encounter and quoting Deputy Chief Lowe's description of the events as a "tragedy." Two other sources then made their appearance:

In an interview yesterday, Mrs. Bumpurs's daughter Mary questioned aspects of the police account, saying her mother "suffered from high blood pressure and arthritis."

"And she had trouble moving quickly," Miss Bumpurs said. "Shotguns are for elephant hunting, not for an old woman who was terrified by people breaking into her apartment. They were there to kill her, not to subdue her."

Miss Bumpurs said she and other relatives had advised Mrs. Bumpurs, who lived alone, not to allow strangers into her apartment. "We had told her, 'Mom, don't open the door for nobody,' " Miss Bumpurs said. "When they busted the door open, of course, she got terrified and picked up a butcher knife. What would any old woman have done?"

George Kramer, manager of the Sedgwick Houses, where Mrs. Bumpurs lived, said Miss Bumpurs and other family members had been told of the eviction. However, Miss Bumpurs disputed his statement. She said if the family had known about the problem, it would have paid the back rent.

The story's remaining seven paragraphs rehearse more details of the first story. In this second story the subject is no longer Mrs. Bumpurs but the police officers who burst into her apartment. The origin of the story is not routine. Unlike the first story, based primarily on a Police Department press briefing, this story draws on interviews initiated by the reporter with three new sources. One source not in an official position, the dead woman's daughter, provides details which focus attention on police behavior.

Who is news seems to depend on who the sources for news are, which in turn depends on how reporters gather news.

Who Is News?

That Mrs. Bumpurs or her daughter made news at all is unusual. Ordinary people appear in the news relatively infrequently, though the frequency rises as they are caught up in official proceedings— arrests, trials, congressional hearings, even unemployment lines. Herbert Gans has studied who is news. He distinguishes between Knowns (political, economic, social, or cultural elites) and Unknowns (ordinary people) and finds that the Knowns make the news —in the newsweeklies and television news he studied—roughly four times as often as Unknowns. Four sorts of Knowns, incumbent presidents, presidential candidates, House and Senate members, and other federal officials, were the subjects of over half the domestic news stories on the network news and in newsweeklies Gans studied. The people in the news are most often the sources of news. Presidents and those around them are the most prominent examples, but it is not at all unusual for other people in official positions, like Deputy Inspector Coyne and Deputy Chief Lowe, to be in the news.

News, Gans found, is primarily about people, what they say and do. Fewer than 10 percent of all the stories he studied were about abstractions, objects, and animals. That "whos" are news is a matter of journalistic convention.

The human interest story is news personified. Long a staple of the tabloids and the tube, human interest stories find their way into today's elite newspapers, too. Early newspapers, like the newsletters of today, catered to a narrow segment of elites, providing them with recent commercial, financial, or political tidings. The penny press, first appearing on the streets of London and New York in the 1830s, substituted newsstand sales for subscriptions, used the human interest story to attract a mass rather than an elite audience, and used its mass appeal to raise revenues from advertising as a substitute for political and mercantile subsidies. The commercialization of the press spawned new patterns of news coverage, and journalists began reaching beyond political and shipping news to sample the rich variety of everyday social life in the city—crimes, accidents, the occasions of high and low society. The commercialization of news led to novel forms of presentation: the journalist was quick to borrow techniques from fiction writing to convey how events in the news felt to those who experienced them—the human interest story. Even in elite newspapers, the human interest story still survives as a genre side by side with the news story as a legitimate convention of journalism.

The peopling of the press goes far beyond such occasional human interest stories. The so-called in-depth interview, "up close and personal," in which the story is the interview, has become a recurrent feature of all newspapers. So is the "Man in the News," which provides details, sometimes intimate details, of the private lives of people caught up in public events—an obituary of the living, often with all its reverence. And sometimes news coverage extends to ordinary people, putting a human face on the raw statistics of social currents—interviews with farmers facing bankruptcy, families on welfare, troops in the trenches, perpetrators and victims of crime— in which the individual stands for a social aggregate.

Politics personified is also a staple of the news diet. The press typically reduces politics to a clash of personalities, pitting Ronald Reagan against Tip O'Neill, Caspar Weinberger against George Shultz, or Lyndon Johnson against Ho Chi Minh. Summit meetings of heads of government seem to exacerbate the journalistic inclination to personalize politics, as if the fate of the earth hung on a meeting of minds between Ronald Reagan and Mikhail Gorbachev. Television, with its compulsion to provide visual embodiment to abstraction, carries the pretense of personification beyond mere name recognition: needing celebrities to stand for political values and programs, it creates celebrities where there were none by re-presenting the same people again and again to represent social and political groups—Ted Kennedy to stand for liberals and Jesse Helms, the radical right; Gloria Steinem for and Phyllis Schlafly against the women's rights movement. Newspapers, too, feature the same few names repeatedly reacting to events of the day. As a matter of journalistic convention, identifiable individuals stand for groups, institutions, and values in the polity. Persons symbolize the impersonal in the news.

Personification can shade over into anthropomorphism. At times, for instance, the press portrays the president as if he were the embodiment of the government, if not of the whole country. It has written of "Reaganomics" as if President Reagan had repealed the laws of supply and demand, personally tamed inflation, and set the economy on an upward course. While such coverage is no doubt partly inspired by a White House eager to take credit for good tidings, the press often willingly plays along. It now lays responsibility for the seizure of American hostages by Iranian militants at Jimmy Carter's door, anthropomorphizing historical forces in a way the Carter White House encouraged it to do when it wanted to generate an air of crisis in order to get the electorate to rally round the president in anticipation of a tough challenge from Ted Kennedy in the 1980 presidential primaries. As a result, the press treated Carter as a symbol of the nation's ineffectuality, Reagan of its resurgent confidence.

As people become surrogates for institutions in the minds of journalists, it is reflected in news-gathering practices and press coverage. The press often treats Tip O'Neill and Robert Dole as if they were the Congress, its committees and subcommittees, and its byzantine procedures—at least to judge from the time the press spends interviewing congressional leaders and covering their press conferences, not to mention the space it devotes to what they say as opposed to what Congress does. The pattern of coverage is reminiscent of Liebling's Law, formulated by press critic A. J. Liebling, who posited that the importance of a news event is inversely related to the number of reporters assigned to cover it.

Personification even informs journalists' conventions of explanation. They tend to ask who was responsible rather than what was the cause. In attributing agency to personal, not impersonal causes, journalists ask "who" rather than "why." The penchant for pinning responsibility on people is a legacy of the muckraking tradition, which assigned blame for economic conditions to economic royalists and trusts more than to the workings of capitalism. The tradition lives on in the conventions of contemporary journalism, indeed, in the worldviews of journalists themselves. Asked to account for the way a particular event was covered, journalists talk about the predispositions of reporters, editors, or publishers more readily than about journalistic practices.

Yet more than journalistic convention accounts for the who of news. Understanding who is news and who is not begs a prior question: who provides the news?

Who Is a News Source?

News is not what happens, but what someone says has happened or will happen.

Reporters are seldom in a position to witness events firsthand. They have to rely on the accounts of others. Some developments—socioeconomic trends, swings in public opinion, shifts in official thinking—may not manifest themselves in events. Reporters tend to draw on the observations of others to describe these occurrences. And even when reporters are in a position to cover an event directly, they feel bound by convention to record what sources say has occurred rather than to venture, at least explicitly, their own version of the event.

The operative convention is objective reporting. Objectivity in journalism denotes a set of rhetorical devices and procedures used in composing a news story. Objectivity, in this sense, has no bearing whatsoever on the truthfulness or validity of a story. Nor does it mean that the story is free of interpretation or bias. No procedure can assure truth or validity or avoid interpretation and bias. Objective reporting means avoiding as much as possible the overt intrusion of the reporter's personal values into a news story and minimizing explicit interpretation in writing up the story. Reporters do this by eschewing value-laden vocabulary and by writing in the third-person impersonal, not the first-person personal. Above all, they try to attribute the story, and especially any interpretation of what it means, to sources. In matters of controversy, they attempt to balance sources with conflicting perspectives, if not within a single story, then from one story to the next as coverage continues over time. Keeping the reporter out of the news means relying on sources. Who reporters talk to thus tells a lot about news.

Social location restricts reporters' sampling of news sources. Reporters are not free-floating atoms in a mass of humanity. They occupy fixed places, geographically and socially, that bound their search for sources of news. They work out of the newsroom or a few bureaus in major cities around the country and the world. In those places, they are often assigned to beats in fixed locations. That puts them in a position to come into frequent contact with some sources and not with others.

Organizational routine further restricts how wide journalists cast their nets for news. Putting out a daily newspaper imposes a very strict regimen: every day, editors have another news hole to fill; every day, reporters need new stories to file. Their daily routine is all the more compelling because of limitations on money and staff.

Coordinating the activities of everyone involved in producing and distributing a daily newspaper imposes a routine on news gathering —the deadline. Stories must be written and edited, pages composed, several editions printed and delivered. Since each stage of production and distribution depends upon completion of a prior stage, it is essential to set and meet deadlines. Technological innovation in the form of computers has eliminated some steps in the production process, lengthening the time that reporters have to file their stories and revise them, but deadlines still impose an arbitrary cutoff to news gathering, enjoining reporters to write up the information they have in the hope of filling in the blanks another day. To satisfy the requirements of turning out a daily newspaper on deadline with a limited budget and staff, editors have to assign reporters to places where newsworthy information is made public every day. Reporters need sources who can provide information on a regular and timely basis; they are not free to roam or probe at will.

Social location and reportorial routine have a lot to do with who gets caught in the news net. Reporters are assigned to police head-quarters because they know reports of crimes and arrests will flow in from precincts around the city which are too numerous to cover individually. Thus, the first version of stories such as that about Mrs. Bumpurs's death will be the official police version, and other versions will emerge only as reporters follow up the story with other sources—if they try. They may not have the time to locate addi-tional sources and still file the story before that day's deadline. Follow-up will have to wait another day, if editors can spare a reporter to do it.

Because of the need for new stories every day, the scarcity of money and staff, and the readiness of government agencies to put out information in a form ready for transcription, newspapers and wire services allocate more of their national staffs to covering Wash-ington than any other place. By contrast, most news organizations do not have a large enough staff to cover business and finance. Business and financial coverage consumes significant staff resources because most industries are decentralized and there are few places to locate reporters where they will be in a position to gather business news quickly and efficiently. The obvious exceptions, the financial community in New York, the automobile industry in Detroit, and the entertainment business in Los Angeles and New York, are the ones most likely to receive routine coverage. Consequently, corpo-rate executives are unlikely to make the news apart from business or trade journals unless they go out of their way to attract attention or become the object of government scrutiny—in a criminal or anti-trust investigation or a congressional hearing. It is not surprising that many attentive readers of the press can recall the names of their governor, senators, and member of Congress, but have trouble nam-ing the heads of ten major American corporations.

In relying on sources, reporters follow other routines of news gathering. Legwork, in journalistic parlance, denotes a set of stan-dard operating procedures, a program, for news gathering: inter-viewing people either in person or by telephone rather than gathering and analyzing statistical data or poring over books and documents in a library. Mostly, reporters confine their research to newspapers and periodicals, as well as old clippings culled from the morgue, or these days, from computer storage. Legwork does not proceed at random. Reporters, whatever their assignment, have a network of contacts, potential sources of information developed over the years with whom they check periodically—"touching base," they call it.

A beat is little more than the formal routinizing of periodic checks with a network of contacts. Beats are locations where news-worthy information is likely to be dispensed routinely in a form readily transcribed into a story. Routine channels used for dissemi-nating information and hence for news gathering include press re-leases, daily briefings, press conferences, and background briefings —press conferences where the identity of the source is cloaked.

Coverage of the American government, in particular, is struc-tured along beat lines. The White House, Capitol Hill, the State Department, the Pentagon, the Supreme Court, and the Justice Department each have a group of reporters on more or less perma-nent assignment there. Organizing reporters by beat limits the range of their activity and also identifies them as convenient targets for potential sources wishing to disseminate information to the press, and through it, to other audiences.

Reporters assigned to a beat make the rounds of officials. Above all, they are held responsible for maintaining access to senior offi-cials on their beat and to official spokesmen, variously designated press secretary, public information officer, or assistant secretary for public affairs. Yet not all reporters cover a beat the same way. Michael Grossman and Martha Kumar have discerned four patterns of news gathering on the White House beat:

Routine Coverage. Newspapers everywhere rely on the wire services for coverage of spot news. Correspondents for the press and radio services of the Associated Press, for instance, are responsible for following the president's every movement—"covering the body," they call it—as well as all press briefings. Consequently, they rely very much on formal channels in the White House press office for their information.

Horizontal Coverage. News organizations that have abandoned spot news coverage to the wire services, typically the major regional dailies with small Washington bureaus, free their reporters to roam from beat to beat following up stories that emanate from the White House daily briefing. Newspapers with more than one reporter assigned to the White House beat also encourage such coverage.

Protective Coverage. Reporters who work for news organizations with arch rivals—the *New York Times* and the *Washington Post,* or ABC, CBS, and NBC—try to protect against being scooped by their competitors. For network correspondents, this often means tailing the president without filing a story, just to make sure he does not make news in their absence—and in their competitor's presence. For *Times* and *Post* correspondents, protective coverage means digging for details, background information, and analysis to fend off editors' queries about angles to be found in a rival's story.

Anthropological Coverage. Not as bound by daily deadlines or space constraints, some reporters, typically those who work for weekly magazines such as the *New Republic,* and the *National Journal,* or for the *Wall Street Journal,* avoid spot news coverage altogether and concentrate on filing longer, in-depth reports on the operation of the White House as an institution, the character and relationships of the people who work there, or longer-term developments in politics and policy.

Variations in coverage thus reflect differences in the staffing, routines, and competitive environment of news organizations.

Regardless of these differences in patterns of coverage, all reporters assigned to the White House do have one responsibility in common: they are supposed to gain and maintain access to the most senior officials on their beat, above all the president, on an exclusive basis if they can. Again, this is a matter of convention. By convention, reporters choose authoritative sources over other potential sources. But what makes a source authoritative? With the rise of the beat system, authoritativeness came to be identified with the ability to exercise authority in important political and social institutions. Presidents and governors, the heads of corporations and other private bodies, and those designated to speak in their behalf were all judged to be authoritative sources. In the 1920s and 1930s, celebrities such as Charles Lindbergh, Charlie Chaplin, Albert Einstein, or Babe Ruth still qualified as authoritative sources; their opinions on any subject were deemed worth reporting, and by implication, worth accepting. Even today, the appearance of celebrities at congressional hearings merits press coverage, but celebrity is less and less synonymous with authorititativeness. Indeed, by 1920 Walter Lippmann was able to write:

> The established leaders of any organization have great natural advantages. They are believed to have better sources of information. The books and papers are in their offices. They took part in the important conferences. They met the important people. They have responsibility. It is, therefore, easier for them to secure attention and speak in a convincing tone.

Whether or not this is so, journalists came to believe it, and once they did so, relying on authoritative sources became for them a habit of mind, a convention.

The convention of authoritative sources gave journalists a criterion for deciding whom to seek out in covering governmental institutions. As the press increasingly organized its news gathering around government, and especially the federal government, authoritativeness began to vary with formal responsibility for public policy: the higher up an official's position in government, the more authoritative a source he or she was presumed to be, and the better his or her prospects for making the news. The convention of authoritativeness has so strong a hold on journalists that they will take the word of a senior official over that of subordinates who may be in a better position to know what the government is doing from day to day. In the absence of any foolproof criterion for choosing sources who are likely to provide valid information, journalists are uncertain about whom to believe. They cope with uncertainty by continuing to rely on authoritative sources. The presumption of hierarchy—that those at the top of any organization are the people in charge and that those in subordinate positions do what their superiors tell them to—underlies the journalists' criterion for selecting sources even though journalists themselves recognize that this presumption is often of doubtful validity.

The presumption of hierarchy enables those at the top who know of misfeasance or malfeasance by subordinates to cover it up and inhibits journalists from uncovering cover-ups. During Watergate, when Bob Woodward and Carl Bernstein of the *Washington Post* filed a story that Howard Hunt, as a paid consultant to the Nixon White House, had been conducting an investigation of Senator Edward Kennedy, the *Post*'s metropolitan desk pushed to have it featured on page one. But executive editor Benjamin Bradlee was uneasy about relying on sources whose authoritativeness he questioned and whose identity he did not—and under claim of reporter's privilege, could not—know. "You haven't got it," he insisted. "A librarian and a secretary say this fellow Hunt looked at a book. That's all." Woodward protested that a "responsible White House source" had explicitly said Hunt was conducting an investigation of Kennedy. Bradlee tried to satisfy himself by asking Woodward and Bernstein about their sources' rank in government. Woodward, "a little unsure about the rules on disclosing sources to the executive editor," asked if Bradlee wanted the source's name. "Just tell me if he's at the level of Assistant to the President," the editor replied. Woodward described the official's position. Learning that the information had come from a junior White House aide and a former administration official, among others, Bradlee was unimpressed. He rewrote the lead and relegated the story to an inside page. "Get some harder information next time," he said as he walked off. "Hardness" of information, in the journalist's creed, seems to depend on the authoritativeness of its sources.

The president, by convention, is *the* authoritative source in the United States. He has no peer. Even when it is apparent that he is out of touch, or lying, whatever he says is still presumed to warrant publication and to reflect accurately what the government is doing. When it does not, that, too, is news, but reporters' practices are not always well suited to discover it. There are some memorable exceptions, of course, and Watergate is one. For the *Washington Post,* unlike newspapers based outside the capital, the Watergate break-in was a local news story, not a national one, and it covered the story that way, assigning two young metropolitan desk reporters who followed the standard operating procedures of crime reportage. The routines and conventions of White House reporting were ill designed to uncover the Watergate story, but the routines and conventions of police reporting were better suited to that task. They put Woodward and Bernstein in contact with law enforcement officials, including a key source in the FBI, who enabled them to unravel the cover-up. Yet even after their initial exposés, other newspapers continued to run versions of the events supplied by the White House press secretary and other senior officials. Indeed, so compelling was the convention of authoritative sources that the *Post*'s own White House correspondents continued to doubt the accounts of Woodward and Bernstein. The *Post* itself routinely printed White House denials of its own stories, although that did not keep the facts of Watergate from eventually emerging. The convention of authoritativeness may assure a hearing in the news for those in authority, but it is no guarantee of a "good press" so long as other sources are willing and able to talk to reporters.

Reporters will go a long way for authoritative sources, not only more readily accepting their versions of reality, but also acceding to the rules of disclosure they may set, embargoing stories until a release time they find convenient, cloaking their identities, at times even killing a story outright at their request. Tacit alliances form between reporters and officials on the beat, as each uses the other to advantage within his own organization. Reporters exploit their contacts in government to get the stories, especially the exclusives, they need to get ahead in their news organization. Officials exploit reporters' need for news to deliver messages to target audiences in an effort to muster and maintain support, both in and out of government, for themselves and their preferred courses of action. Similar alliances form between columnists and political groups, sometimes based on ideological affinity: Joseph Kraft had close ties to Henry Kissinger; Rowland Evans and Robert Novak are known for their network of contacts among the radical right in Congress and among neoconservatives and the AFL-CIO. News making thus affects who gets ahead—both in the press and in the government.

A case in point is an April 30, 1985, page-one account in the *Washington Post* of a dispute over a speech President Ronald Reagan was scheduled to deliver to the European Parliament in Strasbourg.

Both the lead paragraphs and the headlines, "Reagan Aides Clash Over Trip Speech" on page one and "McFarlane, Buchanan Clash Over Trip" over the jump, or continuation of the story, play up the personal aspects of differences over the rhetorical tone of the draft. But subsequent paragraphs elaborate the story line to suggest that the dispute was more than a clash of personalities between national security adviser Robert C. McFarlane and White House communications director Patrick J. Buchanan. It involved a struggle between factions within the administration over alliance relations and policy toward the Soviet Union and Nicaragua.

"In recent weeks," it reads, "McFarlane reportedly has become steadily more critical of Buchanan and the speech writers who report to the communications director for positioning Reagan in ways the security adviser considers unnecessarily combative and ideological." The dispute began over speeches on Central America, "where McFarlane privately has contended that the more combative tone has undermined efforts" to gain congressional approval and allied support for aid to the Contras fighting the Nicaraguan government. "But yesterday's clash," the story continues, "shows that the dispute extends to issues beyond Central America," presumably to relations with the allies and the Soviet Union. That interpretation is denied by a source at the end: "One senior official said that the problem was one of tone as much as of ideology. 'The speech writers want a game-buster every time,' he said." The implication was that at issue was not so much the substance of policy as the desire of speech writers to win "applause back home" and the contrary concern of foreign policy specialists that words calculated to appeal to "the American Legion in Philadelphia" might only deepen Western European disaffection with American policies. Even after the speech was supposedly toned down, it occasioned a walkout by left-of-center deputies in Strasbourg. The article also prompted a demand by ten radical-right House members that White House chief of staff Donald T. Regan "find and fire" those responsible for such leaks attacking Buchanan. That demand was itself later leaked to columnists Evans and Novak.

Who talked to the *Post* reporter and why? One clue comes from the byline: Lou Cannon. Cannon has covered Reagan administrations ever since the president was governor of California, and he has numerous contacts among senior officials in the White House and elsewhere, especially among the more moderate and long-standing of the president's aides. Other clues come from Cannon's own characterization of his sources: "a senior official," "an administration official often critical of Buchanan," "one official," and "one senior official." Cannon also expressly rules out Buchanan as a source. Obvious candidates include McFarlane or one of his senior aides on the National Security Council staff, Michael K. Deaver, who worked on advance arrangements for the trip to Europe, including the much criticized visit to the Bitburg cemetery, and Richard R. Burt, assistant secretary of state for European and Canadian affairs. All three were experienced in the ways of Washington. The initiative for the story came from a White House official prepared to vent his unhappiness with Buchanan, possibly Deaver, who was reacting to sniping from White House aides over Bitburg. Cannon then followed up the lead by contacting two or three other officials prepared to speak on a not-for-attribution basis. The target for the leak seems to have been not the public, but the president himself in the interest of prodding him to intervene and rein in Buchanan, since the dispute over the speech had already been resolved in favor of McFarlane's draft. If so, it backfired. Not only did it fail to bring Reagan in on McFarlane's side, but it also seems to have alienated chief of staff Regan, unhappy over what he took as indiscipline. It was the friction between Regan and McFarlane that culminated in McFarlane's resignation within the year.

The question of "who" is critical to both the content and the origin of Cannon's story. Although the dispute involved officials with different organizational interests as well as personal stakes in policy, the story highlights the clash of personalities in the White House, the who rather than the what or why of the controversy. Ascertaining who Cannon's sources were is essential to assessing just how personal or impersonal the dispute was.

As this example suggests, knowing how news is made is the key to understanding what it means. That requires, first, remembering that governments seldom speak with one voice. While the air may resound with the administration line, it also carries contrapuntal themes, which vary in pitch and intensity but are usually audible to the discerning listener. Since news tends to emerge from the government as the by-product of policy disputes or policy changes, interpreting the news requires that readers determine what is at issue in the dispute or change. It also requires readers to make inferences about the sources of information, the positions they hold in public life, the stands they are taking on the issues in dispute, potential targets for their words, and their possible motives in uttering them to reporters. Knowledge of the organization and politics of news making may enable readers to reconstruct the origins of a story—to infer from what it says or implies who its sources may have been, what channels reporters used in gathering its contents, and why the sources spoke to them. Often the story makes this explicit. Sometimes, in the case of background briefings, the fact that a backgrounder has taken place is evident from the simultaneous appearance of similar stories in more than one newspaper, all without attribution. Careful comparison of the various accounts and knowledge of the political context of the moment will enable the reader to make an educated guess about the story's origin. Other times, in the case of leaks to individual reporters, the source may be harder to pin down, but even then, the story may contain clues about the source's department or agency or policy orientation, if not to his precise identity.

Who the sources are bears a close relationship to who is news. One study found that as a consequence of reporters' social location, news-gathering routines, and journalistic conventions, nearly half of the sources for all national and foreign news stories on page one of the *New York Times* and the *Washington Post* were officials of the United States government. Most transmitted information through routine news-gathering channels—press releases, press conferences, or official proceedings. People not in a position to be covered routinely by reporters on a beat are much less likely to make the news. Ordinary people get into the news in two ways: when their paths cross that of a reporter on a beat, typically when they are caught up in official proceedings, or when reporters are set loose from routine journalism to do investigative reports. Mrs. Bumpurs is an example of the first; her daughter, of the second.

Who Is Not in the News?

Ordinary people are not the only ones who seldom appear in the news; journalists themselves are usually absent. That is not to say that the press itself is not news. It is. Indeed, the press can be obsessively self-absorbed with its own workings, especially when it sees its freedom being infringed. But the convention of objectivity dictates that in writing a story the reporter leave himself out of his account—that neither his person nor his point of view intrude conspicuously. Writing in the third person allows others to speak their parts, but allows the reporter as author to remain immanent.

In the 1960s, what Pete Hamill christened "the new journalism" came into vogue. By putting himself as well as his personal impressions and conclusions into his stories and saying so in his own words, the new journalist called attention to himself as author and to the news story as a genre. Television has forms for accommodating the journalist's persona; indeed, the journalist finds it hard to stay out of a television news story. At a minimum, he provides the voice-over, narrating what the film or videotape is trying to show the audience. Often he appears on camera to introduce the story and reappears at the end to deliver a short summation, "the closer." And the anchorman has no place to hide. The newspaper reporter, by contrast, can remain behind the story without manifesting himself in it. New journalism thus posed a deliberate and self-conscious challenge to the rhetorical pose of objectivity adopted by news journalism. As such, it drew immediate fire from traditionalists. A columnist like Hamill could get away with asserting his presence in a story, but news reporters could not. New journalism was nowhere to be found in the news columns; it has been relegated to the magazine and style sections of the newspaper.

Exceptions to the rule are therefore all the more startling. On Friday, December 18, 1981, five days after the military crackdown in Poland, the *New York Times* ran a letter on page one from its bureau chief in Warsaw, John Darnton, to foreign editor Robert B. Semple, Jr., under a brief italicized preface inserted by editors. "Dear Bob," the story began,

At least twice in the past 24 hours the official Polish press agency has used the word "normalization" to apply to events here. For Poles and other East Europeans this is a dreaded code word.

"Normalization" is what happened to Czechoslovakia after a Warsaw Pact invasion crushed the "Prague Spring" of 1968. In the peculiar jargon of Communist officials, in which words can mean their opposite, it is the restoration of orthodox authority. To people it is the almost unbearably painful process of watching the dismantlement, piece by piece, of freedom and liberties painstakingly won.

As if the epistolary form were not itself an unprecedented breach of the news tradition, the assessment was a personal one, without the customary attribution to sources or the designation "News Analysis." And the reporter managed to insert himself into his story by the device of the third person:

For someone who has lived here for almost three years, it is as if a door that was gradually opened has been suddenly shut.

"I can't see you now," whispers a Polish friend, as he answers his door and steps into the hallway, closing it behind him. "Didn't you hear? I was detained. I just got out. I'm sure you're being observed."

"We can't talk here," says another Polish friend standing in a stairwell, with a glance at a man nearby, who said he was a taxi driver waiting for a customer. He may, or may not, have been listening.

Shortly thereafter, Darnton was forced to leave Poland. His unusual story not only received a place of prominence in that bastion of news journalism, page one in the *Times*, but also helped his coverage of Poland win a Pulitzer Prize for international reporting. But the story of Poland was an exceptional one; the controversy between new and traditional journalism has subsided, resolved in favor of the latter. Journalists remain an unseen presence in the news columns.

Who Makes News and Who Governs?

Readers, whether they are attentive citizens or interested public officials, tend to lose sight of the fact that news is not reality, but a sampling of sources' portrayals of reality, mediated by news orga-nizations. To coordinate the activities of their staffs with a modicum of efficiency, newspapers can do little more than establish some standard operating procedures for sampling potential sources. Whatever procedure they adopt unavoidably biases their selection of content. While no procedure can assure a sampling to satisfy all readers, some procedures affect the likelihood that some points of view and some people will be systematically excluded from press coverage. While no procedure can exclude outright lies, stories that sample only one source or one group of like-minded sources are almost certain to be partial.

People who are routine sources for the press are also more likely to be favorably portrayed in the news. Partly, this is due to the skill they have in news management, in controlling the face they display in public. Partly, too, it is due to the relationship that develops over time between reporters and sources on the beat. News sources whom a reporter contacts regularly are, along with the reporter's own colleagues in journalism, an important audience for news. Re-porters are more likely to hear from them than from anyone else. While most readers remain faceless, reporters must confront their sources again and again, some every day and face-to-face. The feed-back that reporters get from sources—corrections, compliments, complaints, outrage, denial of access—probably has greater imme-diacy than the occasional reactions they get from the rest of their readership—letters to the editor passed along, telephone tips or criticism, comments from friends and neighbors. Feedback has im-pact in proportion to social distance. James McCartney, who cov-ered Washington for many years, has written of reporters' "vested interests in their beats." "A reporter," he says, "may hesitate to take a critical view of regularly tapped sources for the very human reason that he prefers to be greeted pleasantly when he walks into an office, rather than to be treated as though he were poison. His vested interest is in maintaining a pleasant atmosphere."

The causes of uncritical reporting go deeper than that. A report-er's performance on the job requires that he remain close enough to his sources to infer what their often elliptical comments mean and to understand their implications. That requires trying to figure out why he is being told something. Without putting himself in his sources' shoes, without role taking, reporters may misconstrue their sources' motive or miss it entirely, and with it, the nuances of what is being said. Yet repeated role taking may lead a reporter to embrace his sources' perspectives and to portray them sympathetically in print. The line between empathy and sympathy, between role taking and loss of perspective, is easily crossed.

Other reporters, assigned to different beats, hear from different sources. So do general-assignment reporters and those freed from their beats to undertake investigations. To the extent that their sources have different perspectives and preferences, the news will contain a range of political views. To the extent that reporters rely routinely on authoritative sources, their voices will predominate, but not necessarily to the exclusion of opposition voices. So even if journalistic practice predisposes reporters to rely primarily on people in positions of authority for news, it does not follow that the press consistently legitimates or delegitimates those in authority.

Those who argue, as Daniel Patrick Moynihan was among the first to do, that the press is part of an "adversary culture," recruiting to its ranks people "more and more influenced by attitudes genuinely hostile to American society and American government" and consequently inclined to delegitimate those in authority by emphasizing controversy and "bad news," have not made a convincing case. There is scant evidence that recent recruits to journalism are more questioning of social norms than their predecessors were. Moreover, the relationship between news content and journalists' personal political beliefs is a tenuous one, not yet demonstrated by systematic studies. Nor should that be surprising. News is, after all, not what journalists think, but what their sources say, and is mediated by news organizations, journalistic routines and conventions, which screen out many of the personal predilections of individual journalists. The convention of objectivity constrains journalists from being overtly adversarial in their stories. If they are to be adversarial, they must seek out opposing voices willing to go on the record. In so doing, they are constrained by their social location, news-gathering routines, and the convention of authoritativeness in their choice of sources. These constraints confine the selection of opposition voices largely, though not wholly, to those who themselves hold positions of authority in government or respectable groups outside. The quantity and quality of divergent opinion contained in the news thus depends on the presence of well-organized and well-positioned oppositions in and out of government, accessible to the press and articulate in stating their views.

In contrast, those who argue that the press consistently legitimates those in authority assume a relationship between the weight that the press gives to authoritative sources and the public respect accorded them that has yet to be demonstrated conclusively. Again, this is not surprising. First, readers bring their attitudes toward authority with them when they pick up a newspaper. These attitudes tend to be formed in childhood and primary schooling, and hence are deeply rooted and resistant to change. Second, public opinion surveys show that the respect Americans accord to holders of authority in society, be they presidents, members of Congress, corporate executives, labor leaders, or government bureaucrats, varies considerably over time. Yet journalists' reliance on them as sources of news has remained fairly constant. Third, although those in authority do get to shape much of the information and interpretation that make the news, readers do not always believe them or agree with them.

Overall, the effects of news content on the process of social legitimation seem difficult to measure, tend to vary with the times, and will be marginal at most. Those who see news content as crucial to legitimation or delegitimation may only exemplify the phenomenon of selective perception of news by readers—social theorists included.

Reporters' reliance on official sources for news and the press's inclination to anthropomorphize politics may affect relations among the institutions of government more than the standing of the government as a whole. The White House, with its capacity to centralize dissemination of information and control access to dissident views within its walls, can present itself as a relatively unified, purposive institution personified by a single person, the president. The White House, reporters say, treats the press like a mushroom, keeping it in the dark and feeding it a lot of crap. It also has the most prominent "who" in the news and in news making to exploit in trying to shape perceptions. The rest of the executive branch is not nearly as disciplined, though at times it, too, can appear to be a unified arm of the president to all but the closest observers. The Congress, by contrast, seldom looks unified or purposive in the news. Reporters, searching for conflict and trying to balance opposing views, present a picture of an institution riven by partisan, sectional, ideological, and personal differences, discordant, diffuse, even chaotic.

To the apolitical and to those predisposed to look upon the contention and confusion of democratic politics with disfavor, the Congress may seem like "a bunch of self-serving politicians" unworthy of attention or support. The sometime low esteem of Congress may be promoted by the impression that the news leaves on those who have this predisposition. Yet the portrait of the presidency as a unified, purposive actor may have perverse effects on its power as well. It may arouse unrealistic expectations, a belief that once the president says he wants to do something, it is as good as done. Americans may be especially prone to this form of rationalist fallacy. It may account, in part, for the sudden shift in popular attitudes toward defense between 1980 and 1982, away from concern that "more has to be done" on defense to acceptance that "defense spending is about right," after an election campaign in which both Jimmy Carter and Ronald Reagan kept saying how much they were going to spend on defense.

The press's preoccupation with personality and style also leads it to confuse personal popularity with political power. The personal appeal of a president may not translate into political effectiveness if congressmen and bureaucrats of all political persuasions remain unconvinced of the popularity of the president's policies, however much the public may like him as a person. In his path-breaking analysis, *Presidential Power*, Richard Neustadt captures this distinction with his concept "public prestige." By public prestige, Neustadt means Washingtonians' expectations as to how the president's constituencies—and their own—will react to his proposals and programs. Washingtonians include elites in Washington and outside whose support or forbearance the president needs in order to do

what he wants done, such as members of Congress, bureaucrats,
interest-group leaders, and corporate executives. It is his public
prestige, not his approval rating in the polls, that is a resource a
president can parlay into power. Popular presidents are not necessarily effective in getting their way, as Dwight Eisenhower's experience suggests and Ronald Reagan's second term may reconfirm.
They may succeed in structuring the terms of public debate without
winning it.

Journalistic practice may also affect the quantity and quality of
opposition voices that reach readers. Politicians running for president have long complained about this. Yet estimations of the importance of the press at election time are often inflated. When press
coverage can make a difference is in the preprimary stage of the
campaign and during the early primaries. Then the press is, in
Russell Baker's phrase, the Great Mentioner, paying attention to
some candidates and not others, conferring name recognition on a
few and thereby boosting their standing in the polls, which in turn
helps them to raise money and garner additional press attention.
Press attention matters more in a closely bunched field of relative
unknowns than in a race between two well-known candidates. At
the start of the quadrennial season, most news organizations practice
zone coverage, assigning a reporter or two to cover the campaign.
By the early primaries they switch to man-to-man coverage. Yet
few news organizations have the money and manpower to cover all
the candidates. Scarcity forces them to choose whom to cover, and
this choice is critical for determining who gets attention, and with
it, the chance to amass votes, volunteers, and funding. Senior editors make that choice, but they are influenced by what they hear
from their political correspondents, read in the press, and gauge
from the polls. Journalists are not alone in determining the attention that the press pays to some candidates and the way it portrays
them, however. Until the first results are in, they rely on the
campaigners themselves and on other politicians for judgments
about electability. Within the press corps, moreover, some political
correspondents and some newspapers exercise opinion leadership.
After the first caucuses and primaries, the results determine who
gets covered and who gets ignored.

If too much is made of the press's role in elections, too little may be made of its importance in governance, and in particular, in the formation and preservation of oppositions. The routines of news gathering and the convention of authoritative sources, when strictly adhered to, do help insulate reporters from the charlatans and hucksters who vie for attention. But they may also silence or distort opposition voices. Anyone not holding office in established institutions or recognized groups has no claim to publicity, but in mass movements or in riots, there may be no one in authority. Those who presume to speak for the movement or the rioters are often self-styled or self-appointed spokesmen. Reporters covering mass movements and riots continue to follow journalistic practice and seek out people in authority. The result frequently is that they turn to authorities in other institutions for information—police officers, social scientists, and again, public officials—many of them spokesmen for the very institutions under challenge from mass movements.

The decentralization of such movements, their characteristic refusal to appoint a unique official spokesman, and their need to resort to symbolic gestures in order to mobilize members or grab headlines generate press coverage portraying them as less than respectable, programmatically inchoate, and unlikely to succeed. Such coverage can have pernicious effects on the movement's internal organization.

The history of the movement against the war in Vietnam provides the best sustained example of how this can happen. Once the antiwar movement became a continuing story in the late 1960s, one to which some newspapers assigned reporters full-time, it was hard for movement leaders to say or do anything newsworthy that was not more extreme than anything they had already said or done. As long as reporters were routinely looking for the exceptional, there was always someone in the movement prepared to give them what they wanted, whether it was rhetorical excess or telegenic theater. Todd Gitlin has documented the consequences of news coverage for the Students for a Democratic Society (SDS) in *The Whole World Is Watching*. Once the news media turned the spotlight on the SDS, it generated a surge of new members, many from the South and Great Plains, whose radicalism was as much cultural as it was political and whose alienation was so thoroughgoing that they rebelled

against disciplined political action and even against organization
itself. They took their cue fron Bob Dylan: "Don't follow leaders."
While the Old Guard of the SDS wanted to continue local grass-
roots organizing on a variety of issues and not turn the SDS into a
national single-issue group, the new recruits—"Prairie Power," Gitlin calls them—were drawn to the SDS by its image in the news
media as the most militant antiwar organization on campuses across
the nation. Needing spokesmen for a movement that refused to
choose them, the press, especially television news, focused on
whoever held the bullhorn at rallies—the more radical-sounding
and deviant-looking the better. As militancy intensified, only the
militant were attracted to the movement, increasingly isolating it
on the left. Having singled out one or two leaders, typically those
with few followers, and having certified them as spokesmen for the
movement, reporters kept coming back to record what they said.
As the few got more and more media attention, they became celebrities, the movement's voice and identity in the news. Other leaders, not among the chosen few, began to resent the few who were.
The more celebrated the few became, the more they themselves, not
the movement or its political message, became the story.

In choosing "who," journalists prefer knowns to unknowns, and
when they have no knowns, they create them. Through the news,
these spokesmen acquired a following, but not a political base—an
atomized, geographically dispersed audience whom they could mobilize occasionally by transmitting symbolic appeals through the
news, not by face-to-face give-and-take and agreement on goals and
strategy. They thereby gained not power but notoriety. "Fame is an
asset," Jerry Rubin later wrote. "I can call up practically anyone on
the phone and get through. People respect famous people—they are
automatically interested in what I have to say. Nobody knows what
I have done, but they know I'm famous." Celebrity may be an asset
to the object of news attention, but it is a rapidly depleted one, and
its acquisition helped shatter what little political organization the
antiwar movement had.

The Vietnam Moratorium Committee, organizers of the largest
one-day protest in American history on October 15, 1969, tried to
avoid the pitfalls of such press coverage, but in the end they could

not control those attracted to the moratorium—or its public face. The Moratorium Committee wanted to differentiate itself from other, more radical groups and establish itself as the voice of the antiwar movement. Yet press coverage tended to obscure the differences among antiwar organizations. It also wanted to broaden the antiwar appeal, reaching off campus and across the nation to attract recruits of moderate, even apolitical persuasion, among adults as well as students. It decentralized activities rather than concentrating them in Washington, New York, Boston, and San Francisco, and held them downtown, away from college campuses. Yet the press paid the most attention to the largest rallies, often those at or near campuses. To project an appropriate image, the moratorium sought out public officeholders to address the rallies, scheduling them and other moderates to speak at midday and holding off radical speakers until later in the day, after reporters had left to file their stories by deadlines. It tried to give prominence to American flags, lest supporters of the war wrap themselves and their cause in the flag and lay claim to the nation's patriotic impulses. Even in its choice of symbol and name, the blue dove of the moratorium, not the red fist of a "strike for peace," it sought to convey moderation. Above all, it wanted nonviolent protest.

Yet no coherent political message came through the cacophony of voices in news dispatches; Vietcong flags carried by students in various states of dishabille were featured along with American flags and adults in conventional attire, especially in accompanying photographs; and stories dwelt on the few violent incidents while noting the generally peaceful nature of the protest. The Moratorium Committee had greater difficulty trying to define its program and its policy alternative. It never did figure out how to follow up its October 15 demonstrations and sustain press attention. And it never could frame a policy objective simple enough to transmit through the news and radical enough to appeal to militant antiwarriors, yet sophisticated and moderate enough to sound good to everyone else. Negotiating an end to the war would not do; the Nixon administration could always preempt that aim by tabling new proposals. In the end, the moratorium settled on a slogan, "Out Now," programmatically simple, if politically unattainable, setting the stage for its followers' disillusionment when it was not attained. News reports were quick to note the moratorium's programmatic incoherence and question its sustainability.

Press coverage of the nuclear freeze movement has recently retraced this pattern, with similar consequences for the movement. Who spoke authoritatively for the freeze was never quite clear to the press. At least two national organizations, one based in St. Louis and the other in Boston, competed with a host of local freeze organizations to define the movement's message. Meanwhile, President Reagan was shifting his stance, moving to the negotiating table and couching his proposals in language designed to appeal to disarmers. While the freeze seemed to stand for a halt in the development, production, and deployment of more nuclear weapons, Reagan was calling for deep reductions culminating in their elimination. While the slogans used by each side were simple, the reasons why a freeze made more immediate sense for American security were complex. The message never got through: the press, ever alert to contradiction and conflict, focused on apparent inconsistencies among freeze proponents. In the end, freeze supporters in Congress, taking advantage of reportorial routines on the Capitol Hill beat, displaced the grass-roots organizations as the arbiters of what the movement stood for. Even they had trouble spelling out whether a freeze meant a ceiling on weapons, or reductions, and which weapons developments would be halted and which permitted. Moreover, freeze-movement activity manifested itself mostly in door-to-door campaigning and public opinion. It could not compete effectively with the administration's ability to take new action. In the journalists' creed, newsworthiness poses a key question, "So what's new?" It was a question the freeze movement was not an answer to for very long. The press, with its short attention span, was soon distracted. That made it harder for the freeze to sustain the activism of its followers.

The defining condition of American democracy is the existence of potentially effective oppositions that are capable of replacing the administration in an election or that can affect the course of government even when they do not control it. The opportunity to voice opposition through the press is critical in this process. Who makes the news affects who governs and who opposes. If the voices of government, by their ability to dominate the news, get to define the issues that are politically salient, opposition voices frame the lines of cleavage over which policy battles are fought and thereby help define which outcomes are politically practicable. The press, in amplifying some voices and muting others, in distorting some messages and letting others come through loud and clear, affects the nature of opposition and hence of governance. The press does not do so on its own: groups differ in their ability to make their voices heard and to direct and shape their messages for the public. Yet who makes news, and who therefore reaches their audiences, helps determine the direction of political life in the American republic.

The Grisly Truth about Bare Facts

CARLIN ROMANO

> **A**ll the reporters in the world
> working all the hours of the day could not
> witness all the happenings in the world.
> —WALTER LIPPMANN

What does the press cover? The off-the-cuff answers come quickly. What it feels like covering. What sells papers. What the competition is covering. What it can get into the paper by 10 P.M. What it has always covered.

A few more dignified answers also come to mind. The news. Facts. Government. What's important.

Each answer implies a philosophy about the nature of news that rarely gets fleshed out in the newsroom. Journalists don't have the time to get philosophical, and no self-respecting managing editor would hire Bertrand Russell if he could steal a sportswriter instead. Managing editors occasionally cave in on hiring an ombudsman, but that's about it.

Does this mean the question isn't capable of a rigorous answer?

Not at all. But the variety of responses should remind us that no authoritative public standard, no philosophical Supreme Court, can rule on right answers to the question. If we accept the philosopher Ludwig Wittgenstein's view that the meaning of a word depends upon its use, and upon the language game in which it operates, we have to recognize that the language games in which the words "news" and "facts" operate do not include rigorous investigations into the meanings of the words themselves—analogous to the way lawyers, for instance, dissect the word "negligence." Nor is journalism a legally recognized profession like psychiatry or medicine in which authorized official bodies may decide what "neurotic" means, or judge the status of homosexuality as an illness or a "sexual preference." The closest thing to such an authoritative body in the United States, the National News Council, received little support from the institutional press. It was, in the title of a postmortem published on its short life and death, "Spiked."

In the absence of authoritative standards for journalistic concepts, the old-fashioned view that "news" is simply a mirror placed before reality still lives. Many daily newspapers continue to place the word "analysis" or something similar across a story judged to involve opinion—as if all the unlabeled stories surrounding it didn't also arise from opinion and analysis. In an editorial complaining about the CBS docudrama *The Atlanta Child Murders,* the *New York Times* opined, "All storytelling involves some distortion. But the difference between news and fiction is the difference between a mirror and a painting."

Unfortunately, public attempts by newspaper people to explain how the mirror works frequently turn into embarrassing fiascos. In its August 10, 1985, issue, the industry magazine *Editor & Publisher* reported on a panel about privacy led by Harvard Law School professor Arthur Miller before the Arizona Bar Association. "The discussion," wrote *E&P*'s reporter, "also uncovered a surprising ignorance among lawyers and lay people about the definition of 'news,' and the journalists were unable to explain adequately how they judge an item newsworthy."

Before you sneer at their incompetence, however, consider the two types of entities that the press claims to report—"news" and "facts"—and try answering some of the conceptual questions your-self. Ask yourself, for instance, whether everything a newspaper reports is "news." Is the weather news? How about the sidebar detailing the best routes to the Bruce Springsteen concert? Or the filler telling you Hartford is the capital of Connecticut? If every-thing in the newspaper is news, why do newspaper people on the features staff, or in the sports department, commonly refer to the city, national, and foreign desks as "news-side," or just "news"?

If the safest definition of news is what a newspaper deems to be news, and everything in a newspaper is news, how can we explain the difference between newspapers on a given day? Why do any two newspapers run scores of different stories each day? Are they missing more news than they report? If the test for news is that *every* news-paper would print it, many of the stories available each day are not news. But if we're pushed to the principle that news is what *some* newspaper would print, the floodgates open to anything from wed-dings in Des Moines to bingo games in Alabama.

Easy answers, even off-the-cuff ones, don't jump to mind. Tom Brokaw may know how to sign off from the "news," and reporters may succeed in getting it, but "news," unlike "Maryland" or "pine-apple," is a vague word on the cusp between the undefined and the self-contradictory.

The questions about "facts" are no easier. Are facts, for instance, states of affairs? Events? Situations? Objects? You can't get off easy by choosing one. It is, unfortunately, a logical axiom that synonyms ought to be interchangeable in a declarative sentence without changing the sentence's truth or falsity. In other words, if "bache-lor" and "never-married single male" are synonymous, any state-ment that contains one ("President James Buchanan was a bachelor") should stay true if one synonym replaces the other ("Pres-ident James Buchanan was a never-married single male"). "Fact" and its supposed synonyms don't meet the test very well. The philosopher Alan White states the problem powerfully:

> Despite what some philosophers say, facts, unlike events, sit-
> uations, states of affairs, or objects, have no date or location.
> Facts, unlike objects, cannot be created or destroyed, pointed

to or avoided. We cannot be overtaken by, involved in, or predict facts as we can events. We can find ourselves in, transform, or be rescued from nasty, serious, or ticklish situations, but not facts. Facts, unlike states of affairs, do not begin, last, or end. Although there *are* innumerable facts, facts, unlike situations or states of affairs, don't *exist*. A distinction can be drawn between the occurrence of an event or the existence of a state of affairs and the fact that such an event occurred or that such a state of affairs exists. Contrariwise, facts, but not events, situations, or states of affairs, can be disputed, challenged, assumed, or proved. Facts can be stated, whereas events and situations are described. There may be facts about an event, situation, or state of affairs, but none of the latter about a fact.

Confused? Ponder some of the ways we talk about facts, and White starts to make sense. While you're at it, ask yourself whether every claim in a newspaper is a fact. Consider the following lead: "For the nation's pastime it is the best of times and the worst of times." *USA Today* reported that about baseball in September, 1985, after Pete Rose broke Ty Cobb's hit record and baseball players testified about cocaine use. A logician would label the sentence necessarily false—whatever Charles Dickens might think—and a false claim can't be a fact. Or consider another lead from *USA Today:* "Investors are nervously anticipating a sub-1300 market." If only one investor was not anticipating a sub-1300 market, or not anticipating it "nervously," the statement is false. Is it still a fact because, in newspaperese, it really means "some" investors? Who determines the relevant criteria for nervousness?

If you're not even mildly humbled by these questions, you're probably a newspaper journalist. Be that as it may, the conceptual obstacles facing "news" and "facts" are just some of the factors that complicate any explanation of what the press covers. Because the two concepts remain the twin props of mainstream American journalism, it is best to mention their frailty early and yet postpone close inspection until the enterprise they support—all that everyday coverage—comes into focus.

In the main, this essay makes five key claims:

1. "What does the press cover?", taken in its most concrete sense, is a straightforward empirical question with a straight-forward empirical answer: box scores, beauty pageants, press conferences, Richard Nixon, and so on.

2. The decisions that govern press coverage are rational, not simply habitual, haphazard, or ad hoc.

3. The principles that govern those decisions, while rational, aren't "scientific" or logically compelling. No one need accept them, or even deal with them, the way one must accept the rules of gravity.

4. What the press covers, therefore, isn't what the press must cover. Nothing in the nature or meaning of "news" or "facts" —both notions whose meanings, in particular circumstances, depend on accepted conventions—requires the press to cover what it currently does.

5. If journalists understood—as some philosophers and scientists increasingly do—that what they present to the reader is not a mirror image of truth, but a coherent narrative of the world that serves particular purposes, what the press covers could become more flexible and better suited to our needs as readers and writers.

To justify these claims, however, one must satisfy both the Lippmanns and the Stewarts, two types of press pundits definable by how they'd expect to see the main question answered. The Lippmanns take after their spiritual father, Walter. In *Public Opinion,* his classic work on the press, he distinguished grandly between truth and news: "The function of news is to signalize an event, the function of truth is to bring to light the hidden facts, to set them into relation with each other, and make a picture of reality on which men can act." The Lippmanns strive to think big thoughts about their trade. The Stewarts, on the contrary, reckon in the spirit of the late Supreme Court Justice Potter Stewart, who announced that he couldn't define pornography but knew it when he saw it. The Stewarts prefer to steer clear of large principles.

Refining their opposition to each other in this context requires weighing claim number one a bit. Suppose we submit that answering "What does the press cover?" can be done because, with agreement on which publications count as "the press," we could examine all their issues, organize the stories into categories, and produce an airtight inductive statement of press coverage—a "kitchen-sink" answer that included everything from temperatures to obituaries. What would this inductive, kitchen-sink answer look like? In the language of logicians, an enormously long conjunction ("The press covers the president *and* the Congress *and* the baseball teams *and* . . ."). To some, this kind of answer may seem obvious and irrelevant. To others, it may seem questionable but relevant. Enter our two groups of journalistic thinkers.

As noted, the Lippmanns tend to be press theorists with a philosophical agenda for their subject—they object to the kitchen-sink answer. They believe "What does the press cover?" requires not an inductive survey, but rather an abstract statement of principles. They'd like to see and discuss possible candidates, such as "issues important to public discourse," "news," "signalized events," "key trends," "important processes," or what have you.

The Stewarts, for their part, tend to be press critics who simply want more of A covered and less of B, or hard-boiled newspaper people for whom Stewartism is the only intellectual reflex available. They object to that course because they believe any such statement of principles must involve the arbitrary definition of abstractions and thus trigger the intrusion of subjective values. They'd prefer to keep close to what's on the page—Tass covers factories, the *Miami Herald* covers the Caribbean, and so on.

Both groups rightly seek answers that suit their purposes. Their rival interests determine the intellectual neighborhood in which an answer to "What does the press cover?" must set up shop. The Lippmanns must recognize that the more any answer sets forth abstract principles, the more it falls victim to the second group's complaint. Saying the press covers "matters that are politically important to the community" requires a definition of the community in question (does it include bag ladies and Rosicrucians?), the meaning of "political" (does it include religious controversies that have an upshot for civil elections?), and what is "important" (does it include news of formal electoral propositions, like bond issues, that, while officially important to all, actually bore many voters?). The Lippmanns need to accept that specific answers to the question at least provide the data on which to build the principles they seek.

The Stewarts, in turn, must recognize that the vagueness of "news" or "facts" is no argument against addressing that vagueness and perhaps tightening up the conceptual content of the words, whatever the stubborn exceptions. As Wittgenstein suggested, a blurred concept is still a concept.

Both the Lippmanns and the Stewarts deserve a piece of the action. We start in the newsroom, with a look at what the press actually covers. We then return to the seminar room—to the analysis of "news" and "facts." That leads to a concluding "pragmatist's sermon" on why *what* the press covers matters less than *how* the public reads.

What the Press Covers

Guest Drowns at Party for 100 Lifeguards

I first spotted that *Philadelphia Inquirer* headline while flipping through pages of the next day's early edition. With my own deadline at hand, reading stories wasn't on my shortlist. But I stopped and scanned the lead graph.

> NEW ORLEANS—Although 100 lifeguards were present, a fully dressed man drowned at a party being held to celebrate the first summer in memory without a drowning at a New Orleans city pool.

I reread it. "How," I asked myself, "could *that* happen?" I flew through the story. One question I didn't ask myself was, "What is this doing in the paper?"

Any American editor who saw that story come over the wire, and could fit it into the paper, would have done so. Reporters call it a "Holy shit!" story, the kind that freezes the reader's cup of coffee—

or at least the arm holding it—in midair. The genre keeps wire editors sane and sensation sheets healthy. Third World journalists see it as the "aberration fix" in American news judgment, the instinct that makes our African correspondents care more about whether Idi Amin ate the liver of one of his opponents than about Africa's agricultural dilemmas. Longtime Washington reporter Arnold Sawislak nicely exploited it in a book's title: *Dwarf Rapes Nun; Flees in U.F.O.*

If it's true that you can find some reason why any story appears in a newspaper, "Guest Drowns at Party for 100 Lifeguards" boasted several. It recounted an event too unusual, too unbelievable, to be true. It expressed the extreme and sometimes cruel irony of life, a matter American newspaper editors find difficult to ignore.

If you examine your daily paper story by story, you'll find its content completely rational in this narrow sense: principled reasons, not merely practical ones (e.g., it was the only story available on the wire) explain a story's appearance. We can loosely define "what" the press covers as those matters that fit the various principles we can articulate for particular stories. Consider some headlines and the stories with them.

"Governor Approves 3 Executions," another *Inquirer* headline, was accompanied by the smaller subhead "Would Be the First in Pa. Since 1962." Several principles come to mind.

First, routine American journalism calls for newspapers to report the actions of their chief local governmental figures. That alone, however, might not have gotten this story into the paper. If the governor had routinely hired three clerks for his staff, no story could be expected. A second principle involved, the quintessential one, is "The press covers changes from the norm." Yet this principle, taken alone, does not get everything new into the paper. Little Billy's new paper route does not make the paper.

Even these two principles together do not guarantee the above story any column inches. The governor's writing of a book review for a local newspaper would be a public act, and a departure from the norm (since governors don't usually review books), yet no one might report it. Writing a book review isn't controversial. So a third principle supporting this story's publication is "The press covers controversy"—because many groups still clash over the death penalty. Newspapers report issues on which people vocally contend and seek action. Strong feeling doesn't suffice. Most people probably feel more strongly about unfair parking rules than about capital punishment, but they generally fail to organize opposition to them. Opposition to parking rules, unless it builds to action, goes unreported.

Consider another story, headlined "Israeli Jets Retaliate, Hit Militia," which the *Los Angeles Times* syndicated. It recounted an attack on pro-Syrian militia in Lebanon's Bekaa Valley. Here several principles could be offered in diminishing level of abstraction. "News includes violent actions between states" would be too broad —not every Iran-Iraq battle gets reported, nor every Cambodian-Thai exchange, and some countries get completely ignored. A narrower principle tied to specific countries predicts news coverage better: "News includes violent action by Israel."

"Jetliner Crashes Near Dallas" might be broadly explained on the principle that "Events that cause a large number of unexpected deaths are news." But not always, or, in some cases, just barely. The public notices this. In the August 8, 1985, issue of the *Inquirer*, the following letter appeared, headlined "Less Is More":

To the Editor:
   A July 20 headline screamed: "Dam Bursts in Italy, Killing 220." We got a four-column photo on the front page, and on page 7 another photo and a map of the affected area.
   On the same day, buried at the bottom of page 10, was an inch and a half on floods and mud slides [in China] that killed 275 and affected 1.5 million others.
   Just what is it that determines news? Access? Availability of good photos? Skin color of the victims?
   Or is it simply that natural disasters occurring in the Third World are considered commonplace, expected and quietly accepted?

The letter writer knew his principles. In *Coups and Earthquakes,* the finest recent account of foreign correspondence, former *Interna-*

tional Herald Tribune editor Mort Rosenblum refers to this as the "well-understood sliding scale: a hundred Pakistanis going off a mountain in a bus make less of a story than 3 Englishmen drowning in the Thames." Cultural familiarity usually determines the scale. The more victims resemble Americans or mean something to them, the fewer have to die to justify news space. Rosenblum cites a memo from a British press lord that once hung in the newsroom of his London daily: "One Englishman is a story. Ten Frenchmen is a story. One hundred Germans is a story. And nothing ever happens in Chile."

That memo plainly needs a rewrite today. With closer communications among Europeans, the numbers would fall, and South America's greater prominence on the world and British scene—try replacing Chile with Argentina in that memo—undercuts the last sentence. So the sliding scale itself can't be absolutely counted on, at least as usually formulated. The more than five hundred deaths originally feared from a Puerto Rican landslide in October, 1985, should have drawn widespread front-page coverage—Puerto Rico, after all, is part of the United States. Instead, many newspapers played the story inside, provoking anger among Puerto Ricans that the mainland press, perhaps out of racism, had treated Puerto Ricans according to the sliding scale. Here again we find that events force one to narrow principles, and narrow principles predict coverage better.

Thus, "Newspapers cover jet crashes in the United States" edges out "Newspapers cover jet crashes," for some papers hardly cover those in South America and Asia. Even this principle can change, though, if a trend develops. The series of plane disasters of mid-1985, resulting in the most casualties of any year in aviation history, heightened the press's appetite for "malfunction news" to the extent that a few stories ran on valves being replaced on planes with 737 engines.

As the examples above indicate, fashioning principles of news coverage can be a pretty freewheeling and endless business, one requiring constant attention to breaking events. Getting some practice at it helps before drawing larger conclusions. Most of us know the principles covered in high school civics courses: "The Press

Covers Congress"; "The Press Covers Labor-Management Relations"
(though it didn't always); "The Press Covers Elections"; "The Press
Covers Disasters." Professionals know the ones that journalism lead-
ers stress: "The Press Covers Stories It Can Substantiate"; "The
Press Covers News Important to a Democracy"; "The Press Covers
Its Local Territory." Others also suggest themselves:

The Press Covers Symbolic Events. The press sometimes covers an ordinary event, or gives it greater prominence, because it purportedly
carries great symbolic importance. Despite the principle that the
president's ordinary activities are newsworthy, not every horseback
ride makes the paper. But after President Reagan's 1985 operation
for removal of a cancerous colon growth, a story ran announcing
that his return to the saddle would be a heavily reported symbolic
event. Sure enough, in late August, "Reagan Returns to the Saddle"
stories appeared.

The Press Covers the Formerly Famous. Andy Warhol claimed that
everyone is famous for fifteen minutes in America, but newspapers
work on the rule that once famous, always famous. The doings of
once prominent news figures, if they are in any way out of the
ordinary, or clash with the figure's public image, become news. The
writing of a cookbook is not ordinarily news, even in a food or book
section, but the press swarmed over former Black Panther leader
Bobby Seale when he announced plans for one. Here a separate
principle undoubtedly fanned interest—the "social trend" principle. It urges coverage of examples that support social trends in
which the press has invested, such as the yuppification of America,
student quiescence on campus, and the fading of sixties social consciousness. Newspapers gave that spin to the Seale story despite
Seale's repeated claims that he hadn't significantly changed his political ideology from his Panther days. The high level of coverage
accorded Seale and former yippie Jerry Rubin, now running net-
working parties, can be contrasted to that given former associates
like David Dellinger, who provides a picture of greater consistency.

The Press Covers Anniversaries. Anniversaries offer reporters the opportunity to be historians, and that invitation to social climb usu-

ally proves irresistible. So the fortieth anniversary of the ending of World War II and the tenth anniversary of the fall of Saigon both provoked much coverage in 1985. The anniversary principle extends far beyond the news sections and has a trickle-down effect in a newspaper. On April 28, 1985, the book sections of the *Los Angeles Times,* the *Philadelphia Inquirer,* and the *Chicago Tribune* all featured reviews of David Butler's *The Fall of Saigon.* It was just one of more than forty thousand books published in 1985, but it surprised few newspaper people to see it widely reviewed on that day.

The Press Covers the Possible. Sometimes reporters can't get access to an extremely newsworthy event—e.g., the final moments of Korean Air Lines Flight 007—for purely physical reasons. Political obstacles also interfere, as in the Reagan administration's decision to frustrate coverage of the Grenada invasion. Political reasons can mature into legal obstacles—examples are the World War I censorship that banned mention of American casualties and the present peacetime discouragement of reporting on millions of classified documents. Sometimes the possible story becomes the impossible story (on a given day) for a mundane, mechanical reason—advertising. In many newspapers, the news hole depends, at least initially, on what remains after compositors or machines lay in the advertising. Whether the girdle manufacturer decides to buy his space on a given day may determine whether a secondary story about labor unrest in Sweden gets in. And sometimes possibility is very much the result of principled decisions about manpower.

Press coverage of the Middle East reflects that. In his book *Double Vision: How the Press Distorts America's View of the Middle East,* Ze'ev Chafets, former head of Israel's government press office, repeatedly argues that Israel suffers in the American press because its problems, unlike those of the Arab world, are open to view by American reporters. He writes:

> The Middle East is an enormous region, roughly the size of Europe, which, except for Israel, is "covered" by a tiny handful of American journalists—fewer, in fact, than the number of sportswriters at the *New York Daily News.* Most of these reporters can't speak the local languages or even read the news-

papers, and they usually bring little or no background to the
complex events that they are expected to cover. Even under
ideal circumstances it would be physically impossible for such
a small band of journalists, most of whom concentrate on the
same stories, to simultaneously cover more than twenty countries in a region and milieu they do not fully understand; and
the conditions under which foreign journalists are forced to
work in the Arab world are far from ideal.

Chafets argues that the thirty or so American staff reporters in
the Moslem Middle East on a full-time basis "don't divide up the
region in order to provide thirty different news items each day;
rather, they tend to compete with each other in the same places for
the same daily story. . . . They share the same conventions of what
constitutes news and go after the same stories; they also live in
dread of being scooped by the competition, and in foreign situations
that means they tend to keep a close eye on each other. Often they
cooperate, share information and, in doing so, reduce the risk of
missing a story—but also the possibility of discovering one."
    Beyond this, Chafets adds that "a good part of the Arab world is
physically off-limits to Western journalists." Slice-of-life stories
from Saudi Arabia, the Sudan, or Yemen are few, and dictatorial
regimes control much of the information.

The Press Covers the Easy. In some areas, information flows so fully
that the "possible" segues into the "easy." Washington information, churned out by thousands of public relations specialists for
government officials, officeholders, lobbyists, and corporations,
constitutes the foremost example. Leaks and press conferences
abound. Because current journalistic practice demands that reporters not simply reproduce press releases, they don't just sit back in
their offices and retype the material into their VDTs. But they
could. When the *Columbia Journalism Review* accused the *Wall Street
Journal* of frequently reprinting company press releases with few
changes, the newspaper resented it. Decades ago, the practice occurred more frequently.
    Michael Schudson, tracing the rise of public relations and its

effect on newspapers in his book *Discovering the News,* wrote that journalists resented the new industry because "news appeared to become less the reporting of events in the world than the *reprinting* of those facts in the universe of facts which appealed to special interests who could afford to hire public relations counsel." Skepticism toward the slanting of facts by so-called "flacks," strengthened by the growth of wartime propaganda and the public relations industry, have served to balance Lippmann's observation that "the publicity man" often got to shape the facts of modern life by default in a world of busy, overworked reporters. But the percentage of the news that directly arises from press releases and public relations—estimated at more than 50 percent in 1930—is probably higher now.

This may be most true in cultural and entertainment "news." Whereas the ordinary political or local editor often establishes an agenda at odds with the government's—spotlighting a corruption story, for example, on a day that the government invites coverage of an inflation report—entertainment editors often adopt the entertainment industry's agenda in full. Tying their stories to cultural products imminently on the market, editors offer skimpy profiles of actresses, musicians, or writers instead of stories with an investigative or conceptual bent. I've heard a reporter defend the denial of coverage to a local performer with the remark, "He doesn't even have a PR person."

The Press Covers Tasteful Matters. Most American dailies see themselves as family newspapers. Like many journalistic notions, the "family newspaper" concept is just a pretense. Editors who cite the concept usually envision a model that reflects the families of a few God-fearing ministers and no one else. In this family, no one curses, no one discusses nonmedical aspects of sex, everyone who can be offended will be offended, and the immediate response to any offense is a letter to the editor and a canceled subscription.

As a result, newspapers excise news on taste grounds alone. Families offended by insipid celebrity chat, macho postgame analysis by football coaches, hunting and fishing columns, society coverage, genuflection to organized religion, and endless local neighborhood minutiae are not taken into account.

The Press Covers Its Ass for Lawyers. With investigative stories, a gaining maxim holds that 10 percent of the story is for readers and 90 percent for lawyers. A reader may wonder why in the midst of a critical story the paper devotes so much space to a dubious person's background or to some attractive character trait. In fact, the story is being written with the jury in mind, so the paper will be able to demonstrate during a libel trial how it bent over backward to be fair.

The Press Covers Stories That Can Win It Prizes. In the busy modern world, attention spans are short and life works by shorthand. Journalistic prizes win cachet for one's paper from people who may not read it but who know that it has received prizes. A look at the most prominent journalistic prizes, the Pulitzers, indicates how they affect coverage.

To award them, journalists from around the country come to the Columbia Journalism School for a few days each spring. During that short time, they're expected to assess the quality of hundreds of submissions and suggest a few possible winners to the Pulitzer Prize Board. Often the jurors have no special expertise for the kind of coverage they assess—frequently, they are prize-winning reporters who have since become managers within their papers. Thus, a fine city editor from Kansas and a couple of fine assistant national reporters from the Northeast and the Southwest may decide on the excellence of a series about the Everglades. Or a few editors who have specialized in ascending through newspaper management may judge critical writing about classical music or architecture.

The journalistic conceit holds that good newspaper people can recognize top-notch reporting whatever the subject. But if the grading of good reporting, logically speaking, requires evaluating what *was* reported against what *might have been* reported, nonexperts will be at a loss. As the Janet Cooke fiasco demonstrated—an award to the *Washington Post* reporter had to be revoked after the discovery that she had made up the main character in her story—neither the jurors nor the board members can always sniff out the quality of the reporting before them (whether the writer has piped quotes, omitted important elements, or misreported key facts). The jurors may get lucky, but they may not. For many of the judgments made, the equivalent in the academic world would be the English faculty determining tenure for the Asian studies faculty. In evaluative situations like these, where awards are made without true expertise on substantive criteria, formal factors play a greater role in determining excellence. That's where the effect on coverage comes in.

Editors know what kind of stories win prizes. Series, for instance, win prizes. One-part stories don't. Stories that provoke government reaction, or policy changes, permitting papers to cover the reaction and include it with their applications, win prizes. Stories that provoke little response do not. While the introduction of a Pulitzer Prize for "explanatory journalism" may change things, it has been true that investigative stories about government corruption, no matter how routine the scenario, win prizes, and explanatory stories about culture don't, no matter how fresh or difficult the reporting.

As a result, a story that fits the Pulitzer profile—say, the malfeasance of a corrupt local official—may turn into a five-part series. The prize game requires it, even though the public, if polled, might prefer that the paper just report the corruption and leave the background, history, and sideshows to the DA's office (presuming the official isn't the DA). Again, American newspaper journalists tend to be copycats, thinking more in terms of "What things are covered?" and "How are these things covered?" than "What should be covered?"

The Press Covers Political Friends Favorably and Enemies Unfavorably. Recall how many strictly upbeat stories you've read about the Soviet Union, Bulgaria, or South Africa. Even if we concede their sordid politics, is it possible that no positive news exists to be reported from these countries—no human interest angles of the sort that fill our feature pages and end our evening news shows? In other words, if they are tickled, don't they laugh? Can you remember the last time any quote out of these countries was followed by "he said happily"? Comparing coverage of the People's Republic of China during the worst period of the Cultural Revolution and during the Westernizing reign of Deng (*Time* "Man of the Year") Xiaoping shows how our newspapers report more positive stories about a culture once Western values are on the upswing.

    Principles that explain what the press *doesn't* cover are often just the flip side of those keyed to what it does cover—e.g., it doesn't cover the impossible. But articulating some factors fills out the picture of how reasons operate on news coverage.

The Press Doesn't Cover Events if Doing So May Cause the Death of Innocents. Just as reporters may cover a story out of moral obligation (bringing attention, say, to the plight of homeless street people), so morality may constrain the press to exclude or hold a story. Moral constraint can both overlap with and differ from political constraint. The latter is best exemplified by national security requests such as the one that led the *New York Times* to mute its reporting of the upcoming Bay of Pigs invasion. There the *Times* did not withhold coverage to save lives so much as to permit an operation to take place that would, inevitably, cost some lives. Moral constraint applies when the press does not report facts in its possession in order to preserve human life. It takes a moral stand that certain people should not die because it reports particular facts.

    A widely covered example of this was the news blackout on the Israeli airlift of Ethiopian Jews to Israel by way of the Sudan in 1985. A number of reporters knew of the operation for some time but did not report it for fear the airlift would be stopped by the Sudanese. Thomas L. Friedman explained in the *New York Times* that the self-imposed ban was lifted after a reporter for a Jewish newspaper broke the story: "Once the outlines of the story appeared in the Jewish press, major news organizations that knew of the rescue and had held back publication felt they should no longer sit on it."

    A more common case has been the reporting of kidnappings. At the request of police, newspapers withheld reports of the kidnappings of heiress Patricia Hearst and former *Atlanta Constitution* editor Reg Murphy in the 1970s. After the incidents, a poll of

newspaper editors showed that 260 of 328 approved of the cooperation.

*The Press Doesn't Report Matters That Reflect Badly on People in Its Good
Graces.* In his book *The News at Any Cost,* former *New York Times*
legal reporter Tom Goldstein explains at length the special treatment that the *Times* accorded to Federal Judge Irving Kaufman, a
strong advocate of freedom of the press who writes regularly for
the *Times:*

> At the *Times,* I was forbidden to write about probably the best
> story I knew—the close relationship between Irving Kauf-
> man, a Federal Appeals Court Judge, and the *Times.* . . . the
> *Times* flattered him in its news columns and frequently had
> him write for the paper. The tightness of the bond was well
> known to many leading lawyers, and the overwhelming praise
> and absence of criticism of the judge in the newspaper's pages
> gave evidence to these lawyers that the coverage by the *Times*
> was far from objective.

On the other hand, subjects dear to a paper's senior editors may
enjoy unusually regular attention. Careful readers of the *Times*'s
cultural news coverage know that scarcely any information relating
to the playwright Eugene O'Neill goes unmentioned by the paper
and that productions of O'Neill receive lavish and almost always
positive coverage. They also know that Arthur Gelb, the paper's
deputy managing editor and cultural czar, is the coauthor, with his
wife, of an O'Neill biography.

The Press Does Not, on the Whole, Cover the Press. These personal and
institutional predilections may affect whole subject areas and institutions. Although press coverage of the press has increased, it is
largely a phenomenon restricted to a few major dailies, such as the
New York Times, the *Los Angeles Times,* and, more recently, the
Washington Post. Many newspapers (including my own) do not assign
a regular reporter to the beat. This situation endures even though
papers routinely cover institutions with unquestionably less effect

on the general public. If one compares the number of Americans who read newspapers to the number who go fishing, or care about hockey, or fashion, the newspaper readers win out. But you'll find few papers without regular hockey, fishing, or fashion coverage.

One reason given is that newspapers can't cover other newspapers objectively. Here the objectivity argument sanctions the ultimate lack of objectivity—a journalistic institution that considers every institution fair game for examination but itself and its brethren. Every newspaper journalist can cite cases of a newspaper's coverage being affected by its own involvement. If I note instances from the *New York Times* here, it is not because the paper does any worse than others in that regard. *Times* editors sometimes feel that press critics envious of the paper's power gang up on them. The real reason for the close scrutiny lies in the paper's combination of greatness and sanctimony. On a day-to-day basis, the *Times*'s fact gathering surpasses that of all rivals. Perhaps because it so clearly aims at and achieves an illusion of pure objective reportage at a level above other American dailies, the paper hates to acknowledge anything that clouds the image. As a result, coverage of its own role in public life suffers.

Nineteen eighty-five alone offered several examples. The *Times,* for instance, gave no attention to its lengthy labor dispute with reporter Richard Severo. Severo had reported the case of Lisa H., a young woman afflicted with the so-called "Elephant Man" disease of neurofibromatosis, for the paper. The *Times* maintained that it had some rights to the intellectual fruits of his labor—the book in which he expanded upon his reporting. Severo disagreed. Other papers and magazines covered the dispute.

Later in the year, the *Times* publicly upbraided a reporter, Jane Perlez, in an editor's note. She had written an unflattering profile of real estate executive Mortimer Zuckerman that the *Times* criticized for containing "opinionated wording," "pejorative phrases," and other ills. That, in turn, produced stories elsewhere asking whether the *Times* was offering special treatment to Zuckerman. The *Times* did not acknowledge the controversy.

Then, after several columns in which its Pulitzer Prize–winning columnist Sydney Schanberg took the paper to task for inadequately covering New York City's Westway controversy (a longstanding dispute about a massive road project), the *Times* relieved Schanberg of his column. Other newspapers, such as the *Washington Post* and the *Village Voice,* speculated on the reasons, noting that a relative of the *Times*'s publisher was an active supporter of the project (which Schanberg opposed). Again, the *Times,* apart from announcing that Schanberg would no longer be writing his column, did not report the controversy. Schanberg eventually resigned and later joined *Newsday.*

The Press Does Not Critically Examine Privileged Cultural Beliefs. Consider coverage of religion. Although the foundational beliefs of the major traditional religions in the United States—Jewish, Protestant, and Catholic—all fly in the face of modern scientific knowledge, the American press avoids any critical examination of their doctrines. Newspapers cover the issue of religious freedom, but coverage of, or debate on, the actual tenets of a religion is rare, unless it concerns "cults" such as Scientology, the Rajneesh clan that alighted in Oregon, or the Reverend Moon's variant of Christianity. Papers barely mention the activities of organized atheists. Only when religious beliefs clash with civil law, as in Catholic opposition to abortion, do papers highlight religious tenets. But even then, little critical focus is brought to bear on religious foundations. All sorts of interest groups in American society undergo such scrutiny, but when was the last time you read a daily newspaper article or editorial that questioned the authority of Jesus, or —more to the point—reported the belief in Jesus as Christ to be, in the opinion of so-and-so, mere primitive superstition. Some topics are taboo for the daily press.

They're taboo, in part, because they're the religions of the editors and their readers. The same rules seldom apply to religions without strong representation in the American press. In his book *Covering Islam: How the Media and the Experts Determine How We See the Rest of the World,* Edward Said calls attention to the heavy Western coverage of the Iranian revolutionaries' attachment to Islam. "Ironically," he writes, "only a few commentators on 'Islamic' atavism and medieval modes of logic in the West noted that a few miles to the

West of Iran, in Begin's Israel, there was a regime fully willing to mandate its actions by religious authority and by a very backward-looking theological doctrine." Said adds: "Israel's avowedly religious character is rarely mentioned in the Western press."

Perhaps the only sweeping principle that subsumes the reasons why the press does or doesn't cover something is the cliché principle —coverage conforms to the reigning journalistic clichés. Thus, the press will cover a petty crime that affects few, but ignore a book addressed to millions. It will cover the polar bear club that goes swimming in the winter, but not the socialist labor club that gathers every week. It can't resist—and didn't in 1985—a real "man bites dog" story.

The string of reasons could go on and on, and suggests an objection. Can't reasons be articulated for covering any piece of information, any event, that would be both tailored for the occasion and yet also boast some precedent—namely, some earlier news story that covered information or events for roughly those reasons? The answer is yes, so long as we treat "roughly" roughly. While coverage rules lack the formal authority of legal rules, they resemble the "holdings" that lawyers are expected to extract from case decisions —they're adaptable, modifiable, and stretchable. Reasonable journalists can phrase them in different ways and (like reasonable lawyers about holdings) disagree on their scope. All of which raises the issue of whether stringing out reasons makes much analytical sense.

Perhaps the most wide-ranging modern attempt to map the reasons for which American news organizations cover the news is Herbert Gans's *Deciding What's News* (1979), which focused on the practices of CBS, NBC, *Time,* and *Newsweek.* Gans's reasons span the spectrum between abstract principles (Gans calls them values) that would satisfy the Lippmanns (ethnocentrism, individualism, responsible capitalism) and more specific reasons that would satisfy the Stewarts ("firsts and lasts" news about innovations and demises, or "Foreign news has a sentimental attachment to European royalty, particularly those who serve as figureheads in otherwise democratic countries.")

Gans ranges across the landscape, and his observations are often right on target:

The incomes of rich criminals may appear in the news; those of the poor do not.

While breakthroughs in the sciences are covered, those in plumbing or auto repair are not. Members of high-status professions, such as lawyers or doctors, are newsworthy, whereas members of less prestigious professions such as accountants and nurses are rarely mentioned.

[P]lane crashes are usually more newsworthy than the winter breakdowns of tenement furnaces, even if they result in the same number of deaths.

Anyone who is serious about pondering what the press covers must read Gans's book, which is especially sharp on how class distinctions affect the news, and the tilt toward events over processes. But *Deciding What's News,* published less than a decade ago, also demonstrates how events can overtake many reasons and examples stated as commonplaces. Gans writes that "while corporate mergers are often newsworthy, there is little news about corporations per se, with the notable exception of multinationals." Since Gans wrote his book, however, newspaper business sections have proliferated. Even taking his book's specific focus into account, his truism about business coverage, like the British owner's truism about Chile, no longer rings true. Similarly, Gans's observations of how news from China tends to be negative or how nonviolent conservatives get little coverage in the United States are both dated.

This is not to fault Gans—he pays the price of his specificity. The five traditional news values cited by journalism educator Curtis MacDougall and familiar to generations of journalism students— timeliness, proximity, prominence, consequence, and human interest—may have greater endurance, but at the price of airiness and vulnerability to counterexamples. Principles that satisfy the Stewarts succumb to rapid change faster than those that satisfy the Lippmanns. By mixing previously separate coverage principles, single events exert enormous influence on news. If Rock Hudson had not collapsed in public and acknowledged having AIDS—allowing the powerful principles of celebrity coverage and the weaker ones of medical and homosexual coverage to converge—the subsequent mass of AIDS stories would not have appeared.

The Stewarts' kind of answer, therefore, can't be learned by rote and then trusted without further attention. Like legal holdings, rules for press coverage must always be weighed in light of the circumstances of the instant case. The managing editor must decide whether he wants to distinguish the event he faces, which seems to fall under a principle applicable to an earlier event, or not. The difference between American law and American journalism, however, is that while the legal profession must accept the Supreme Court's decision that Case B falls within the principle of Case A, no managing editor has to accept the *New York Times* decision that the hijacking of the cruise ship *Achille Lauro* must be covered like the hijacking of the TWA airliner. Journalists enjoy greater freedom than lawyers in this regard, being wholly responsible for what they choose to cover. A list of what the press covers, and its reasons for doing so, thus provides at best a snapshot of current news practice —as reliable as information on the enemy's current position in a war. That snapshot can fade, which may be the most important lesson to be learned from it.

If the Stewarts' answer cannot be permanent, the Lippmanns' answer is even more frustrating. All these reasons and principles leave us in an unattractive theoretical bind. Granted, press coverage is rational in the sense that reasons exist for every story published ("Whatever the president does is news"; "People care about Cyndi Lauper's health"; "We always run his stuff from Pakistan") and every story spiked ("No one cares about Canadian politics"; "We couldn't substantiate it"; "Let's wait for the place to simmer down and send in Woodstein") even though journalists, unlike appellate judges, depend on implicitly understood reasons rather than regularly stated ones.

But we are also stuck with an anarchy of reasons, a potpourri of principles as unconnected as the passengers who board a random plane flight. These reasons, as we've seen, crisscross, or gang up, or clash, in the context of particular events, without having clearly weighted presumptions in their favor. So decisions or habits contrary to those we've described (for instance, "The press does not cover major disasters") could be supported with equally articulable reasons ("We just get in the way, and the government can report them better")—i.e., be equally rational. All of this remains true, it should be noted, even if one concedes to the Lippmanns that grand theories of the press—the social responsibility theory, the marketplace of ideas theory—are also at work in the American press. True enough. But it is precisely because rival theories roam the American market that a kind of rational anarchy rules.

Consequently, we come to a third conclusion mentioned at the outset—the rational principles that govern coverage decisions are not "scientific." Unlike scientific laws, they can't be assumed to apply uniformly or to permit accurate predictions of future cases. Far from having the same force for all decision-making members of the press, they operate as rules of thumb whose persuasive force varies among various editors. In editor Fleet's newsroom philosophy, novelty may pack a generally higher value than community service. Editor Fleet might fill a news hole with a wire story about policemen who yodel rather than with a stringer's piece about a perfunctory school board meeting. Editor Grub, with contrary values, might run the stringer's story.

Put more philosophically, no sufficient conditions exist that guarantee the running of a particular news story on any given day. There is no "nontrumpable" set of reasons. It is imaginable, though unlikely, that even the report of a president's assassination could be withheld on national security grounds. Because the press does not codify or rank coverage rules the way casinos rank poker hands, or courts rank legal rules, no clear-cut guidelines exist for which principle preempts another. While the Supreme Court's understanding of the law overrides a circuit court's inconsistent view as a matter of American legal theory, a story about an African coup pushes a soft feature story off the front page only as a matter of journalistic cliché. Our familiarity with the habits of American journalism, and little else, lends the field its air of objectivity.

If the Lippmanns find the answer disrespectful of American journalism's hard clarity and soundness, one can only reply—that's just the half of it. What are hardness and soundness, after all, but worn-away metaphors of touch, with little relevance to language's pitfalls? Those pitfalls extend especially deep in the case of American journalism's prize quarries—"facts" and "news." If we just imagine what an assigning editor would say to a reporter who inquired, "It's not news and it's not a fact, but do you want to use it?", their centrality to "what the press covers" becomes plain. That centrality demands separate attention.

What the Press Claims to Cover: "Facts" and "News"

> It is no longer enough to report the fact truthfully.
> It is now necessary to report the *truth about the fact.*
> —Commission on Freedom of the Press, 1947

Reporters have company in thinking that facts are like sea shells to be scooped up and taken home. Western medical students since the nineteenth century have learned that they had better master a core set of "facts" in their syllabi even if they ignore mushier theoretical materials. Wall Street speculators risk vast sums of money on what they take to be facts coming over the ticker. Copyright law advances a similar black and white view, holding that courts can draw a bright line between literary "expression," which is creative and copyrightable, and "facts," which rest out there in the public domain and are not.

That kind of clarity, however, is a tough obligation to hang on a word whose root (Latin, *factum,* the past participle of *facere,* to do or make) means "made by man." A few journalistic aphorisms capture the sense of human shaping involved. "A fact merely marks the point where we have agreed to let the investigation cease," wrote a Canadian journalist and poet. Rosemary Righter begins her fine book *Whose News?: Politics, the Press and the Third World* with an unusually sharp chestnut: "Facts are the shadows that statements cast on things." But most of the trade takes comfort in the "hardness" of facts.

Sloppy ontological language may be part of the problem. Ernest Gellner, the British anthropologist and philosopher, defines "fact" in one social science dictionary as "anything described by an assertion which is *true*." Assume, however, that the statement "The late President Lyndon Johnson came from Texas" is true. On Gellner's account, LBJ is somehow a "fact," even though we would never talk that way, and nothing in the world at present corresponds to LBJ. Although some of our metaphors regarding facts seem to support Gellner—"digging" or "searching" for facts, or "discovering" them —all those uses are compatible with facts as statements, the sort of things for which one must search (or research) in books.

As we've already seen in Alan White's observations above, the preliminary reports on fact's ontological status (that is, its place in the process by which language represents the world) indicate what journalists seldom acknowledge or even articulate to themselves— that in the crucial distinction between language and the world, "fact" is a word that describes language *about* the world, and not the world itself. Ludwig Wittgenstein called attention to this in the appendix to his *Philosophical Remarks,* where he examined the word "fact."

He recognized that you can't point at facts the way you can at trees or flowers. ("You can of course point at a constellation and say: this constellation is composed entirely of objects with which I am already acquainted; but you can't 'point at a fact' and say this.") In keeping with his general program of dissolving philosophical difficulties by focusing on language use, he identified the misleading ways we often use the word "fact."

He noted, for example, that while the phrases "to point out a fact" and "to point out a flower" seem grammatically similar, the appearance deceives. When we say "to point out a fact," we always mean "to point out the fact that . . ." But when we say "to point out a flower," we don't mean to point out *that* the flower is one thing or another. As twentieth-century philosophers have shown repeatedly, the surface grammar of our language can create unnecessary philosophical puzzles.

If "facts" are shaky sorts of objects in the world, referring at best to statements or sentences about the world, then the shakiness inevitably has to travel down the conceptual line to "news." There, we'll see, problems of selectivity among putative facts independently weaken the notion. But first, other points ought to be made about the softness of "fact" as a journalistic concept.

Perhaps the simplest involves the resolution of disputes when rival "facts" arise from multiple reports of single events. Many journalistic disputes come without clear-cut umpires, and a paradigm case is the eyewitness report. Curtis MacDougall has kept alive a legendary one: the reports in New York newspapers of a woman's assault on Russian statesman Aleksandr Kerensky at the Century Theater. According to the *News,* she struck him on the left cheek with her bouquet. According to the *Times,* she slapped his face three times with her gloves. According to the *Mirror,* she struck him a single blow.

It happens a fair amount, as do discrepancies in quotations. To the profession's lasting embarrassment, it can't seem to agree on who uttered the classic formulation of news, "When a dog bites a man, that is not news; but when a man bites a dog, that *is* news." Journalists sometimes admit to cleaning up quotes for grammar and syntax, thus softening their hard "factuality" even more. Eyewitness accounts notoriously clash in legal cases, but there a court and the law of evidence are present to help sort things out. In many journalistic cases, no official organization—a court, a government, a scientific society—ever clears up the matter.

The frailty of reportorial perception increases when confronted with foreign cultures, and information-processing studies indicate that it is a general condition. Back in 1932, an English researcher named Sir Frederick Bartlett found that English audiences, if asked to repeat Kwakiutl folk stories, altered details in ways that made the stories more British. Bartlett hypothesized that putting unfamiliar facts in familiar contexts aided their processing. So the possibility of built-in accuracy, at the most rudimentary level, impairs the notion of "facts" straight off.

A more profound flaw in the notion of "fact" concerns the principle of induction. In its broadest sense, inductive reasoning refers to inferences that make it *reasonable* to accept particular conclusions on the basis of particular premises. Reasonable—but not safe. Inductive inferences lack the certainty of valid deductive inferences of the form:

Premise 1:	All men are mortal.
Premise 2:	Socrates is a man.
Conclusion:	Socrates is mortal.

The most common form of journalistic inductive reasoning is what logicians sometimes call "induction by simple enumeration" —the idea that if all observed objects or people of one kind have some property, then all objects or people of that kind have the property:

Premise 1:	Crow A is black.
Premise 2:	Crow B is black.
Premise 3:	Crow C is black.
Conclusion:	All crows are black.

In its journalistic form, inductive reasoning often involves asserting a claim about a whole set of individuals on the basis of a handful of observed members of the set. It shouldn't be confused with speculative generalization—e.g., when a paper claims that "100,000 people descended upon Central Park" without counting them. Inductive judgment, especially in its journalistic form, involves assumptions about unobserved matters on the basis of observed matters. We're all familiar with these judgments—they can appear in straightforward language ("Filipinos are a democratic people") or journalistic shorthand that borders on absurdity ("It is understood in India that . . .").

The problem is fairly clear. Since inductive judgments can't, strictly speaking, be verified as true, how can they be reported as facts? One can object that scientists face the same *logical* problem of the justification of induction. In fact, the philosopher W. V. Quine once joked that all scientific research should be stopped until the problem of induction is solved. But philosophically oriented scientists have long recognized that scientists must assume the regularity of nature if they're to devise revisable laws, and the natural world —helpfully—has thus far played along. Unfortunately for reporters, the "human" world isn't always so cooperative—sources tend to be much more atypical than crows. So when we come to inductive judgments about human phenomena (e.g., voter mood), assuming regularity is quite a stretch and inductively arrived-at "facts" are even harder to justify.

Yet inductive judgment remains one of journalism's chief hand-maidens. The credibility of all polling rests on it. Whenever we are told that "55 percent of Americans believe" something on the basis of 1,000 people interviewed, we are getting the pseudofacts of social science induction. They are facts only if general judgments not strictly confined to examined individual cases, and outside the natural sciences, constitute facts. The most ludicrous journalistic case is the common reporting feat of anthropomorphizing the whole nation. The tactic is taken to extremes by USA Today, which is constantly telling us that "We Like Chocolate Shakes" or "We Are Going to Europe More Often." Strictly speaking, the claims embarrass American newspaper journalism, and no journalist, placed under the more rigorous fact-finding procedures of science or law, could bring these Hegelian consciousnesses to the witness stand. While the practice may be innocuous in the case of USA Today, it can be invidious and destructive elsewhere. Said scores the Western press for describing "Islam" as a monolithic culture or political entity in the world. He points out that "it is both wrong and foolish to regard 'Islam' as a block, just as I think it is bad political judgment to treat 'America' as if it were an injured person rather than a complex system."

Understanding the difference between an event and a fact also underscores the weakness of the latter as an unimpeachable part of independent reality. In his book Medical Thinking, which probes the role of "fact" in medicine, Lester King asks us to consider the famous historical fact that "Julius Caesar crossed the Rubicon in 49 B.C."

King argues that for anyone familiar with Roman history, the statement contains an enormous amount of historical meaning. By crossing the Rubicon, Caesar defied the Roman Senate's command and thus provoked the civil war that changed Rome's history. The statement thus elliptically conveys multiple facts about Roman history. Even if we leave out the general Roman history, the statement, like virtually all statements, is capable of as much ambiguity as we choose to seek. Does it mean that Caesar and his army crossed the

Rubicon—an event including many thousands of describable sub-actions? Suppose some of the soldiers didn't make it across. Is the statement a fact? Even if several soldiers died, and the statement is in some sense untrue (because some of his army did not cross the Rubicon)? How many men must drown in the Rubicon before the ones who make it across no longer constitute Caesar's army?

The possible falsifications of the statement grow when looked at from another angle. The contours of the Rubicon have changed over the centuries, so how do we know what movements Caesar really made? The date of Jesus' birth, given the inaccuracy of early time-keeping, is unclear, so how can the date 49 B.C. place an event for us on the scale of historical time?

While questions such as these can strike the working journalist as frivolous, they highlight a point White makes—that a "fact" of this sort is a statement based on inferences from traces of the events. Any self-critical reporter will recognize how that phrase, "inferences from traces of the events," fits many facts in his pieces. Unfortunately for English speakers, their language is not especially well suited for reporting by inference. The anthropologist Franz Boas enjoyed pointing out that English makes a rather weak language for journalism compared to Kwakiutl, a Northwest Coast Indian language. Kwakiutl grammar requires the speaker of an assertion to specify whether that assertion is based on direct observation, on hearsay, or on something that appeared to the speaker in a dream. Boas observed that we would read our newspapers with greater confidence if they were written in Kwakiutl.

Instead, our journalistic assertions, like the claim about Caesar, often amount to disguised inferences from present evidence—hardly an epistemological Rock of Gibraltar. Of all American newspapers, the *New York Times* best shows its appreciation of this, particularly in controversial descriptions of political events. The signal is such constructions as "So-and-so could not be independently confirmed." Even the *Times,* however, can't do this for the vast majority of its claims, and independent confirmation would be vulnerable to the same problem.

The conceptual enemies of "hard" facts—as you may suspect by now—are everywhere. Some facts that a reporter acquires can, in a technical sense, be considered made by him. This especially holds true for quotes. If Seymour Hersh had not questioned Colonel X on a particular day, and elicited from X the statement that Memorandum A did indeed discuss the assassination, then the fact that X claimed Memorandum A discussed assassination would not exist. No one but Hersh, presumably, and in this case X, could attest to that particular fact. In journalism, questions often create the news, and neither questions nor interviews mosey around the world, waiting to be reported. When Third World press critics complain about distorted Western reporting, they frequently toss in the corollary complaint that Western correspondents ask the wrong questions.

Journalists can also make facts in a different way by manipulating the vagueness of language and choosing one word rather than another, one construction over another. Noam Chomsky has been a particularly astute critic of this from the left. He has noted, for instance, how headlines such as "Are the Palestinians Ready to Seek Peace?" in the *New York Times* contribute to a vocabulary in which the phrase "peace process" comes to be identified with peace according to one side's terms. Yet linguistic manipulation serves the left as well as the right, and many shades of opinion in between.

Take the press's use of the phrase "Star Wars" to describe President Reagan's Strategic Defense Initiative program. The *New York Times,* in a brief September 25, 1985, article headlined " 'Star Wars Plan': How Term Arose," described its genesis. The *Times* reported that President Reagan first outlined his program during a televised speech on March 23, 1983, and then the paper gave this account of the aftermath:

> Democratic reaction to the speech was critical, with Senator Edward M. Kennedy, Democrat of Massachusetts, calling the program "reckless 'Star Wars' schemes."
>
> The term "Star Wars" has since gained currency as a nickname for the space-based defense program despite protests from President Reagan, who appears to think it denigrates the effort and has connotations associated with science fiction, perhaps because of the movie of that name.

Note the explanation's clever syntax. Every action described, with one exception, comes with an identification of the actor or actors responsible for it. The Democrats produced the critical reaction to the speech. Senator Kennedy initiated use of the movie-title tag. President Reagan protested. The only action that goes begging for an actor is the widespread adoption of the phrase. The phrase "gained currency," a passive construction, does not identify who gave it currency. Perhaps we're to believe that the phrase, like some ambitious Washington careerist, simply arranged to be seen in all the right places at the right time.

The missing actors, of course, are the institutional media, who specialize in taking fresh phrases and beating them into the ground (we have been, at least, spared "Star Wars-gate"). Always friendly to simpleminded tags that can represent complicated issues, the media jumped on it. Yet consider all the reasons why the press should not use the phrase. The administration does not officially describe the system that way. The description came from a political opponent of the administration and the program. The phrase itself begs the central question of the program—whether the system would produce war or peace amid the stars. No one has proven that the weaponry would lead to star wars, rather than star peace, though much remains to be said. The ambit of activity involved, even if the weapons were used, would have nothing to do with stars—it would be in the orbit of this planet. So not the slightest literal rationale exists for describing the program with the phrase.

The press has not been oblivious to its creation of a fact—that the program is a "Star Wars" program. Both the *Times* and the *Washington Post* now put "Star Wars" in scare quotes when they use it, with the meaning "so-called." The tricky part is that the media did the so-calling. The press has simply excised the press's participation. The *Times* account suggests other irregularities in reporting the matter, such as its reference to the phrase as a "nickname." It is unlikely the *Times* would use a nickname for a person who disavowed it, deemed it disparaging, and could show that the usage stemmed from political motives. Moreover, the remark that Reagan "appears to think it . . . has connotations associated with science fiction, perhaps because of the movie of that name" comes across as disingenuous. This is, after all, the unusual case of the press, rather than the president, calling upon the movies first. A clearer example of stacking the deck can scarcely be found.

The press's adoption and propagation of slanted or inaccurate descriptions, which are then charged off to common usage, is a regular occurrence. Another 1985 example involved the well-publicized case of Bernhard Goetz, a New York City man who shot four teenagers aboard a New York City subway train. Before Goetz was apprehended, some New York newspapers envisioned the gunman as a subway "vigilante" inspired by the Charles Bronson movie *Death Wish,* about such a character. After Goetz's arrest, when the facts indicated that the "vigilante" label didn't fit, the press once again resisted giving up its identification label, whatever the cost to accuracy. A typical story, from UPI, referred to Goetz as the "so-called subway vigilante."

But the practice surfaces most frequently in political news. In her book *Nicaragua: Revolution in the Family,* Shirley Christian notes how headline writers in Nicaragua insisted on labeling the insurgency against the Sandinistas "la Contra—short for counterrevolution in Spanish"—even though many of the anti-Sandinistas denied being counterrevolutionaries. Because political facts, such as the character of the anti-Sandinistas or the status of the PLO as a political entity, are a matter of much weaker consensus than, say, the name of the largest city in Japan, newspapers monitor usage there more carefully. Linguistic minefields are everywhere because governments and other political interest groups do not make matters easy. As Thomas L. Freidman of the *Times* has reported, "The Israeli Army refers to all individuals who forcibly oppose their occupation in Lebanon—be they Lebanese or Palestinians—as 'terrorists'. . . ."

In the Saturday, October 12, 1985, issue of the *New York Times,* for instance, in a story about the hijacking of the Italian cruise ship *Achille Lauro* by four Palestinians, Samuel Freedman, a *Times* reporter who at that time usually wrote about the arts, described the terrorists' "execution" of the wheelchair-bound hostage Leon Klinghoffer, who was shot in the head and thrown overboard. "Execution," of course, connotes a legal punishment imposed by a political authority holding legitimate power. It requires a victim who has been convicted of an act triggering such punishment. It is language that terrorists and freedom fighters alike employ in the hope that the media will adopt it. Every time that word is used in reference to such an event, instead of "murder" or "kill," a different fact is being stated.

Sometimes the creation of a fact depends not on a journalist's choice of words, or clear alternate meanings of a word, but on reaction to an ambiguous word. A widely publicized press incident during the 1982 Israeli bombing of Beirut was a cable sent by Thomas L. Friedman, then the *Times*'s Beirut correspondent, to his editors. Friedman objected to their elimination of the word "indiscriminate" from the lead of his previous day's story about the bombing. As published, that lead read as follows:

> BEIRUT, Lebanon, August 5—Israeli planes, gunboats and artillery rained [indiscriminate] shellfire all across west Beirut today, as Israeli armored units pushed toward Palestinian refugee camps and neighborhoods on the southern outskirts of the capital.

Further down in the published piece, Friedman wrote that "no place was safe in west Beirut yesterday" and detailed how the gunboats had blasted the hotel district and beachfront areas, and Israeli rocket and artillery fire had "poured onto buildings, homes and offices everywhere in west Beirut."

Friedman argued that the previous day's bombing had "the apparent aim of terrorizing" Beirut's civilian population, and was "fundamentally different from what has happened on the previous 63 days." He argued that "the newspaper of record should have told its readers and future historians" that fact.

The word "indiscriminate," however, is ambiguous. Friedman clearly used the word in its intentional sense, which would require knowledge of actual Israeli intentions during the bombing. Only if the Israelis (or the commander of the bombing) had no reasons for bombing one place rather than another could that strictly have been true. Strictly speaking, it couldn't have been true, unless Friedman believed the Israelis might have bombed Tel Aviv as well. Friedman should have argued that "indiscriminate" can be used nonintentionally, as the description of the effects of an action, and written that the effects were indiscriminate, taking in the innocent and guilty alike. Because Friedman chose a word with truth conditions that, on one interpretation, require knowledge of intentions, and acknowledged his uncertainty of the intentions by describing the aim of the bombing as "apparent," Friedman undermined his argument for the word. He'd have been better off choosing another. The result, in any case, was a "fact" in the paper that did not reflect the reporter's sense of the event at the scene.

Word choice thus creates facts. The new journalists accepted such responsibility, but mainstream journalists often resist the idea that there is a choice. John Hellmann, in his book *Fables of Fact: The New Journalism as New Fiction,* calls it the difference between "the disguised perspective versus an admitted one, and a corporate fiction versus a personal one."

Where does that put us? In some ways, back with one of our first off-the-cuff answers—that what the press covers is what it feels like covering. For if facts are made of words, and words are soft and vague, and journalists control their softness and vagueness, then the journalist's freedom of coverage expands. Regardless of the events he attends, his flexibility in characterizing them remains.

From the exercise of this freedom, and from such influences on his decisions as habit, ideology, and his understanding of what readers want, come the "facts" that we conventionally accept as such in the press. The standard organization of an American daily exerts its influence. Copy editors put the brakes on departures from truisms, clichés, and standard formulations. Managing editors rule on disputes between subeditors. Rebels against mainstream journalistic beliefs don't rise to managing editor and don't get to arbitrate these disputes.

"Settled" historical truths such as Caesar's Rubicon crossing, and standard statistics from official organizations, make it into the paper. So do the myriad facts that so-and-so said such-and-such—assuming the paper considers the reporter reliable (the speaker need not be reliable, as was demonstrated by Senator Joseph McCarthy's many baseless but objectively reported accusations). So do innumerable dubious generalizations and presumptions.

Those generalizations and presumptions, of course, needn't involve momentous world issues. You can find them embedded in the modest domestic dispatch as readily as in the politically charged "special." In a *New York Times* story headlined "Dispute in Denver Pits Pinstripes Against Jeans," Iver Peterson reported on a battle in that city over a proposed convention center. Deep in the story, he wrote, "Denver is already suffering from a severe oversupply of office space." From the point of view of the prospective Denver renter? Not likely. He might think the supply equaled just what a fair market ought to supply. As with many "facts," this one depends on background assumptions.

On the whole, the best definition of a journalistic fact may be that it's an assertion with visiting rights. If cogently challenged, the guest will probably be kicked out by any reputable paper. Newspaper facts tend to be unchallenged claims rather than unchallengeable ones. *We* characterize *them*—not vice versa. Facts are "incomplete" because we want more. "Bare" facts are bare because we refuse to describe their clothes. "Brute" facts aren't born brute— they have bruteness thrust upon them.

When we leave the conceptual problem of "facts" and come to that of "news," all the individual moments of factual creation multiply thousands of times, and the need to select among facts increases the problems.

In a much quoted 1980 essay, the journalist and novelist John Hershey wrote: "The minute a writer offers nine hundred ninety-nine out of one thousand facts, the worm of bias has begun to wiggle." Yet while perhaps logically unavoidable, bias presents a greater danger when it arises from fiendish exactitude. Reinhold Niebuhr, the noted Christian theologian, recalled a daunting example in his "The Role of the Newspapers in America's Function as a Great Power." It was a film by Dr. Joseph Goebbels's Propaganda Ministry, "intended to discredit us as a nation of morons." It consisted of shots of mud fights, pie-eating contests, beauty contests. "Every shot was taken from an authentic newsreel," Niebuhr noted, "but the total effect was a complete libel on our life in the mind of anyone who could not put these facts in their setting." Observed Niebuhr: "Facts consist of hardly more than names and dates. There are events in history, and these events cannot be understood except in relation to a whole stream of previous causes. Every record of events is therefore also an interpretation of this stream of causes. In the strict sense, there is therefore no unbiased account of either past or contemporary history."

In a media society where a single grand theory of the press reigns supreme, identification of the "news" becomes clearer. Communist states, in effect, have Supreme Court–like institutions to determine news—sometimes a Ministry of Information. As Paul Lendvai points out in his book *The Bureaucracy of Truth,* it is commonplace in Communist countries not to report, or to report very skimpily, domestic disasters such as earthquakes and plane crashes. He quotes N. G. Palgunov, former director general of Tass, the Soviet news agency: "News should not be merely concerned with reporting such and such a fact or event. News or information must pursue a definite goal: It must serve and support the decisions related to fundamental duties facing our Soviet society."

In American society, the threads of news judgment, as we have seen, are not so easily pulled together. Knowing that the dictionary calls news "a report of a recent event" will not help one make specific assignments. Traditions therefore rule, including minor ones such as not giving Canada much attention. "Even Canadians who move to the United States lose interest in Canadian news," the managing editor of Canadian Press once remarked.

What results is a hodgepodge in which individual news judgments can be traced back to elements of various overarching press theories. The social-responsibility theory that the press should act as a watchdog on government fuels both incisive and boring political coverage. The theory that the press should, or at least is entitled to, respond to the tastes of its audience drives coverage toward the spectacular and sensational.

American journalists may be inclined to dismiss Palgunov's words, but similar views have gained rapid adherence among some Third World governments. Western journalists possess arguments to defend their practices, but they err if they consider them knockdown arguments that only the foolish or malicious can resist. Theories of press activity ultimately depend on deep assumptions in

political theory about how the state and its subgroups should operate. The conventional Third World criticisms of the Western news
system—that it perpetrates colonial values, focuses on disasters
rather than achievements, favors the abnormal over the normal,
events over processes, violence and conflict over peace, and reports
the Third World *to* the Third World (because of the domination of
news distribution by the four major agencies) through the eyes of
poorly trained Western reporters—challenge the complacency of
Western news thinking. As Anthony Smith and Rosemary Righter
respectively argue in their fine books on international news distribution, legitimate criticisms of Western practices lie behind the
often transparent political objectives of the Third World leaders
who voice them.

The upshot, then, of our two inquiries—into what the press
covers, and into the core sense of both "facts" and "news"—can be
capsulized. As a matter of philosophical and intellectual principle,
the American journalist can pretty much cover what he wishes. As
a matter of tradition and convention, he currently performs like a
skater signed on for familiar routines. "Breaking" news breaks when
we let it break. "Spot" news implies that we've decided where the
spot is. A "scoop" takes place when enough people think that it
matters who runs a story first. As in the case of facts, *we* characterize
news—it does not arrive on some divine daily budget.

Can this quasi-existentialist denouement offer any hints about
what the press should cover? The question is politically provocative,
because America's democratic experiment hasn't been tried under
different models of news coverage. By the time large waves of im-
migrants started to enter the United States, the older European
model of partisan journalism no longer flourished. It may be that
our mixed society maintains relative internal peace only because so
many differences are masked behind a journalism that discourages
the vocabulary of class, race, and ideology. If every newspaper here
took an openly partisan position, closer to the model of Italian and
French journalism, we might face a far more conflict-ridden society.

Yet certainly there should be no fear of change. The belief that
the press covers what it "naturally" must cover, and operates as it
has to, rests on more than journalists' lack of interest in the kind of

analysis offered here. It is also based on a poor knowledge of journalistic practice elsewhere. In Italy, with few exceptions, no newspaper copy editors exist. Editors assign writers a length for stories, and much material goes straight into the paper. In France, the press law distinguishes between facts more than ten years old and those more recent. In Thailand, radio stations have been known to change their call letters and frequencies during the course of a broadcast day. Our ways are not the only ways.

So reporters who look at other styles or theories of journalism and think, "It can't or shouldn't happen here," ought to reconsider. Some recent changes in American newspapers bode well for open-mindedness, such as the growth of trend and background reporting, and the increase of specialists on beats like law, business, design, media, and science.

On the other hand, nothing dictates changing the habits of American journalism for the sake of change. Philosophy, which urges us to be skeptical about press objectivity, also suggests we not worry about it. In both philosophy and the sciences, the notion of a hardbound truth in the world that researchers "find" or report has fallen on hard times. Ever since Kant argued in the *Critique of Pure Reason* that the nature of human thought makes it impossible to perceive things in themselves without shaping by the mind's categories, the idea that language or thought can precisely mirror the world has been skeptically received. In the twentieth century, that doubt about "naive realism" seems to have gained the upper hand in every field except American journalism. There the American journalist's belief in the possibility of objectively representing reality seems as naive as thinking the whole world operates in English.

In the hard sciences and social sciences, the most influential theory of scientific procedure in the last two decades has been the notion of "revolutionary paradigm" put forth by historian of science Thomas Kuhn in his book *The Structure of Scientific Revolutions*. According to Kuhn, we've traditionally misunderstood how scientific knowledge progresses. In the traditional view, scientists gather discrete facts through unbiased observations. As they fall into patterns, scientists formulate generalizations with predictive power. Nothing is assumed at the outset except for a few basic laws of thought and nature. The view squares nicely with the notion of an objective reality, waiting to be conquered.

Kuhn, however, argued that this picture of scientific procedure fits only periods of "normal science," when no one challenges fundamental assumptions and scientists operate under the rules of a given "paradigm," or model. The history of science, he asserted, also includes revolutionary periods, such as the era in which Einstein's paradigm of the universe replaced Newton's. One's objective reality, in other words, may depend on one's paradigm. Another radical philosopher of science, Paul Feyerabend, has noted that normal science's ordinary process allows data that do not jibe with scientific theory to be ignored, or ascribed to faulty procedures. According to Feyerabend, who sees scientific method as a kind of anarchy, the description of every fact depends on *some* theory, and "no single theory ever agrees with all the known facts in its domain."

Similarly, in the humanities, a variety of philosophers and critics in recent years have focused on the difficulties of rendering reality in prose. In Germany, Hans-Georg Gadamer, the father of hermeneutics, the theory of interpretation, has argued that reason and truth are historically conditioned concepts, though understandable in their cultural contexts if we're willing to put in the intellectual spadework. In France, the late "archaeologist of ideas" Michel Foucault argued that various notions whose "natural" content we tend to take for granted, such as "sexuality," are conventional constructs that arise out of power relations in society. The American philosopher Richard Rorty, in *Philosophy and the Mirror of Nature* and other works, has emphasized that what we do at best is tell stories about the world that become the histories of ideas and theories.

Journalists should take a cue from all this. If even philosophers and scientists—the intellectuals among us charged with delivering full-fledged descriptions of reality—are coming to accept their work as a kind of useful storytelling, then no beat reporter should get upset at the thought that his ten-thousand-word takeout on toxic waste didn't capture the subject whole. When asked whether his exhaustive history of the Nixon-Kissinger years, *The Price of Power,* caught the whole story of what had happened, ace reporter Seymour Hersh replied, "Maybe 5 percent."

On the contrary, if what the press covers should change, it should

change for other reasons—to shake up our conventions, or to facil-
itate political, moral, and aesthetic progress—not because of some
felt need to come closer to objective truth. For all we know, such
change would bring greater happiness—a world of "good news"
newspapers might be a happier and more productive world.

Yet change itself could never be enough to make reading the
news a passive occupation. For *what* the press covers matters less in
the end than *how* the public reads. Effective reading of the news
requires not just a key—a Rosetta stone by which to decipher
current clichés—but an activity, a regimen. It requires a tough-
minded, pragmatic nose for both information and nuance that alerts
the reader to when a new key is needed. Instead, the very uniformity
of American journalism tends to lull its readers into complacency.

Awestruck readers abound everywhere. Even smug Ivy League
English graduates, trained to dissect the neuroses behind the prose
of Virginia Woolf, or the poetry of T. S. Eliot, often read the *New
York Times* or *Wall Street Journal* as if God himself (rather than some
fellow Ivy Leaguers) had dictated it from the press room on Sinai.
What these readers need is not change—not just flip-flopped conventions—but instructions of the sort that come on any decent
aspirin bottle. They need to stop, every once in a while, when
reading the news, and ask themselves, "If my life depended on
proving the claims I've just read, how could I or anyone else do it?"
They need to read stories that seem balanced and objective, with an
"on the one hand, on the other hand" approach, and ask themselves
whether there aren't more than two sides to the issue. They need to
identify their cultural and political beliefs, to read publications that
oppose them, so that the hidden assumptions they encounter across
the journalistic spectrum are exposed.

Occasionally observed, such admonitions can gradually persuade
even the most benighted newspaper acolyte that his favorite paper's
coverage differs only in scope—not in kind—from what he happens
to notice himself. The only answer we can't fairly expect to "What
does the press cover?"—or "What should the press cover?"—is
"Everything."

WHEN?

Deadlines, Datelines, and History

MICHAEL SCHUDSON

David Sarnoff just happened to be the twenty-one-year-old Marconi operator who picked up the dying radio signals from the *Titanic* and kept to his keys for seventy-two hours passing on news of survivors to relatives. At thirty, he was general manager of RCA. Walter Trohan, a longtime Washington correspondent for the *Chicago Tribune*, began his career as a lowly police reporter for the Chicago City News Bureau. He covered for the rewrite man during the lunch hour. On February 14, 1929, a report came in that the city editor would not believe. Trohan, the only employee available, raced to the scene of the St. Valentine's Day massacre, and was the first seasoned reporter there. A few days later, the *Tribune* hired him.

Just as the theater world tells stories of the understudy who gets the big break at the last minute when the star gets sick, so the media world lives on tales of the cub reporter who was on the night desk when "the big story" broke. It is the central myth in the folklore of journalism. Nothing matters more than being in the right place at the right time and filing the story before anyone else does. It is the path to fame and fortune, professional advancement, and Pulitzer Prizes. The reporter's ideal answer to the question "When?" is "Just an instant ago—so recently that no one else even knows it happened."

Getting the news fast and, ideally, getting it *first* is of passionate interest to journalists. On November 22, 1963, the UPI White House reporter, Merriman Smith, sat in the middle of the front seat of the pool car in the presidential motorcade in Dallas. When he heard gunshots, he jumped to the phone and started dictating. His Associated Press rival, Jack Bell, seated in the backseat, was helpless to get out a story. Bell demanded the phone, but Smith said he wanted the Dallas operator to read the story back to him because the connection was faulty. This was obviously a dodge to keep hold of the phone. "Bell started screaming and trying to wrestle with Smith for the receiver. Smith stuck it between his knees and hunched up into a ball, with Bell beating him wildly about the head and shoulders. UPI beat the AP by several crucial minutes on the story, and Smith won a Pulitzer for his coverage of the Kennedy assassination."

Daniel Schorr's on-the-scene radio reporting from disastrous floods in Holland in 1953 brought him to the attention of Edward R. Murrow, who then hired him at CBS News. Dan Rather began his rise to prominence at station KHOU Houston with live coverage of Hurricane Carla. "Live coverage," Rather writes in his autobiography, "is the mark of a really good local news station."

But why?

Why should this emphasis on getting the story minutes or seconds faster than a rival bulk so large in journalism? Once upon a time, when a dateline could be two or three or ten days past and when newspapers could differ by days or weeks, not hours or minutes, "when" mattered. Andrew Jackson fought the battle of New Orleans because news had not reached him from the East Coast that the war with Britain was already over. That is not something that could happen today. Now, when news is a constant commodity—the wire always ticking, the radio always talking, the TV cameras nearly always available—the question of "when" is a question journalists care about infinitely more than their readers. The pressure journalists are under to be first is generated internally in news organizations. No one in the audience gives a damn if ABC beats CBS by two seconds or not. The journalist's interest in immediacy hangs on as an anachronistic ritual of the media tribe. Getting the story first is a matter of journalistic pride, but one that has little to do with journalistic quality or public service. It is a fetishism of the present, an occupational perversion, and one peculiarly American. The American editor E. L. Godkin noted this as long ago as 1890: "The stories which Parisian journalists tell each other in their cafes are not of their prowess as reporters, but of the sensation they have made and the increase in circulation they have achieved by some sort of editorial comment or critique; the American passion for glory in beats—meaning superiority over rivals in getting hold of news —they do not understand, or thoroughly despise."

The American focus on the scoop serves, in part, to cover up the bureaucratic and prosaic reality of most news gathering. The news organization is, as Philip Schlesinger put it, a "time-machine." It lives by the clock. Events, if they are to be reported, must mesh with its temporal spokes and cogs. Journalists do not seek only timely news, if by "timely" one means "immediate" or as close to the present as possible. Journalists also seek coincident and convenient news, as close to the *deadline* as possible. News must happen at specified times in the journalists' "newsday." Politicians adept at "making news" are well aware of reporters' deadlines. They schedule press conferences and public appearances to coincide with reporters' filing times. The astute press secretary in government or in the private sector schedules events to accord with the weekly round of the press, knowing on which days there will be the least number of stories competing for front-page attention. Much of the news the press reports is given to it by public officials who can pass it out routinely or with fanfare, urgently or casually, all at once or in pieces, depending on what kind of effect they want to achieve. The more the media emphasize the immediacy of news, the more subject journalists are to manipulation by public officials who know how to prey on people with stopwatch mentalities.

This reality—that news gathering is normally a matter of the representatives of one bureaucracy picking up prefabricated news items from representatives of another bureaucracy—is at odds with all of the romantic self-conceptions of American journalism. The insistence on getting the latest news and getting it first, the headlong lunge, the competitive rush that comes with a breaking story, all this is an effort to deny and to escape the humdrum of daily journalism. Moreover, the race for news—a race whose winner can easily be determined by a clock—affords a cheap, convenient, democratic measure of journalistic "quality." American society is too diverse and American journalism too decentralized for news organizations to measure themselves by criteria of literary elegance or intellectual sophistication. No small circle of intellectuals can influence the culture of journalism in New York and Washington the way it might in Paris. American journalists are left with competition by the clock. Their understanding of their own business focuses on reporting up-to-the-minute news as fully and fairly as possible.

But this is a serious misunderstanding. "Timeliness" in news is defined in practice not only by the recency of a reported event but by its coincidence with the searchlight of the journalistic institution. "Timeliness" operates not by Greenwich mean time but by a cultural clock, a subtle and unspoken understanding among journalists about what is timely and what events are genuinely "new." In their own minds, journalists may still live by the fetishism of the present, but their actual behavior betrays a very different, more interesting, and more complex relationship to time.

The Past Tense: Depths of the Past on Page One

Even the front page, presumably replete with news of the most important and up-to-the-minute events, has an orientation to time more varied and more complicated than journalistic values would suggest. The front page of the *Los Angeles Times* for June 12, 1985, is a typical example. The lead story reported that the identification of a body Brazilian authorities had exhumed June 6 as that of the Nazi war criminal Josef Mengele was confirmed by Mengele's son. This confirmation happened in the preceding twenty-four hours, but little in the story is understandable without some knowledge of the Nazi death camps of forty years before and the long-term efforts of "Nazi hunters" to track down Mengele.

Another story on the same page reported on a trade of alleged Eastern bloc spies for alleged American agents and held that it was "one of the biggest prisoner exchanges since World War II." The whole story has a historic air to it, describing the exchange at the Glienicker Bridge connecting East and West Berlin: "Crossing from east to west on the bridge, which was the scene of the 1962 exchange of Soviet master spy Col. Rudolf Abel for American U-2 pilot Francis Gary Powers, were 23 prisoners released from East German and Polish jails." The *San Diego Union* story on the same event, compiled from news services, began, "In a scene that could have appeared in a Cold War spy novel, the United States and East Germany exchanged 27 prisoners yesterday on a bridge linking East and West at a Berlin checkpoint." This lead turns a hard-news event into a mythic reenactment, even to the point of suggesting that the Glienicker Bridge links not only two parts of a city but two world leviathans of power, "East" and "West." (There is in this an implicit political geography. See Daniel Hallin's chapter, "Where?" for full discussion.)

On the same *Los Angeles Times* front page, a story on the annual meeting of Southern Baptists in Dallas reported the reelection of fundamentalist pastor Charles Stanley as president, and noted that this signaled the failure of moderate Southern Baptists' "most organized effort thus far to halt what they call the fundamentalists' six-year campaign to take over the denomination's seminaries and institutions." Not every newspaper, however, offers this sense that a timely event participates in a larger trend of some significance. *USA Today*'s coverage of the Baptists' convention reported simply that "fundamentalists prevailed" in the election, but gave no information that would lend meaning to this event.

The June 12 *Los Angeles Times*'s front page also carried a story on the death of Karen Ann Quinlan, whose relevance to readers was that ten years earlier she had lapsed into a coma, and her parents' efforts to have her disconnected from mechanical life-support systems had prompted a "historic right-to-die court decision." On this story, *USA Today* actually offered a number of significant details that the *Los Angeles Times* (relying on the AP) and the *New York Times* (relying on UPI) did not—including information on the Quinlan family and a box highlighting the chronology of events in the Quinlan case.

There are a number of things to say about this collection of stories. All of them take off from a "news peg," some event of the previous twenty-four hours that legitimates the story as "hard news." A paper like the *Los Angeles Times* deserves credit for frequently providing a relevant historic context for what could be—and, in many papers, often are—fragmentary hard-news bulletins, lifted out of time and out of context. But there is a larger issue here: many news stories would not be stories at all if some degree of shared historic depth could not be assumed. A body is identified, spies are exchanged, a young woman dies—these are not *important* (front-page) stories, however up-to-the-minute, unless they have an historic context. To ask "Is this news?" is not to ask only "Did it just happen?" It is to ask "Does this *mean* something?" And that question cannot be answered without making some assumptions about history.

The depth of time a newspaper invokes varies not only from one story to another but sometimes within a single story. On July 24, 1985, the *Los Angeles Times* reported on the meeting in Washington between President Reagan and President Li Xiannian of China: "Reagan Meets Li, Backs China Nuclear Pact." Here five different temporal dimensions are juxtaposed. The first relates to President Reagan: he is described as "returning to high-level diplomacy 10 days after undergoing cancer surgery." This sets the news in biographical time and instantly gives a sense of drama, and not a little sense of heroism, to this official meeting of heads of state. Does the heroic glow this lead casts over the president suggest that reporter Norman Kempster or the *Times* backs Reagan's policies? Not in the least. What it shows is that the reporter and his newspaper know that, whatever they may feel about Reagan's politics, they feel and are culturally obligated to feel empathy for him as a mortal being. This biographical time sense, rooted in the shared mortality of reader, writer, and subject, is one of the fundamental time dimensions of the news.

There are several more senses of time in the Reagan-Li story.

Reagan's endorsement of a pact allowing U.S. companies to supply materials for China's nuclear power program is described as an episode in a fourteen-month effort to sign the pact, held up "because of congressional concern that China might help Pakistan develop a nuclear bomb." Here two political time contexts are added to the biographical. There is not only the direct reference to fourteen months of presidential relations with Congress, but an implicit reference to forty years of concern about how nuclear weapons and their proliferation endanger the world's survival. A fourth temporal context is introduced when President Li is described as a seventy-six-year-old "survivor of the Chinese Communist Party's Long March of the 1930s." Most readers probably have little idea what this means except perhaps that it ties Li to the moment of birth of modern China and to the heroes of the Chinese Revolution.

But reporter Norman Kempster did not stop here. He noted, on his own authority, that Li's visit to Washington "came four days short of the 32nd anniversary of the end of the Korean War, the last time U.S. and Chinese troops faced each other in combat." This last sentence is unusual: why is it there at all? Kempster's story continues: "Although the two countries remain far apart on issues ranging from human rights to economics, Reagan and Li stressed matters of agreement and glossed over differences." Reference to Korea is clearly meant to offer a commentary on the relatively rapid turnaround in American-Chinese relations. The odd thing is that the reporter knew the anniversary of the end of the Korean War was imminent. Newspapers, institutionally, are not well organized for remembering the past and typically invoke it only in conventional ways. The temporal contexts that come most naturally to editors and reporters are the lifetime of a person and the time horizon of a generation that dates its decisive formation of political judgment to the 1930s and especially to World War II. How, then, Korea? In this instance, the reporter happened to have a calendar that *Foreign Policy* magazine puts out on "this date in history." "I usually glance at it every day or so," Kempster told me, "although I almost never write anniversary stories as such."

The same day's *Los Angeles Times* included a story from Peking— on page one, I suspect, only because of Li's visit—that reported on the Chinese government's display of seventy thousand books to help

Peking residents locate and reclaim materials seized from their personal libraries during the Cultural Revolution. A thumbnail sketch
follows of how, at the beginning of the Cultural Revolution in
1966, Red Guards went from house to house confiscating vestiges
of "old ideas, old customs, old culture and old habits," including
books.

Curiously, this was the second time the Chinese government
tried this form of restitution. A year earlier, one hundred thousand
volumes were displayed and a third of them reclaimed. Did this
make the news? Not in the *Los Angeles Times*—recency is not a
sufficient guarantee of newsworthiness, nor is uniqueness. There is
always a need for context—in this instance provided by President
Li's visit to Washington.

The question "Is this new?" is answered in a variety of ways in
journalism. For hard news, there must be a news "peg." As with
the story on the Chinese books, the recency of the event may not be
"peg" enough—the news peg may be an entirely separate event.
Certain stories, like Li's visit to Washington, are prominent enough
to magnetize others. Airplane "near misses" happen all too frequently and are rarely reported. But in the days or weeks following
a major airline disaster, especially one that raises questions about
air traffic safety in general, newspapers print more stories of near
accidents. Eastern bloc sailors in American ports defect "all the
time" according to the Immigration and Naturalization Service, but
only when a Soviet sailor tried to jump ship on the eve of the
Reagan-Gorbachev summit did the story of a Rumanian sailor-
defector also make the news (November 17, 1985, *New York Times*).

As these instances suggest, there is no clearly defined way for a
journalist to determine what's new and what's important. How,
then, does a reporter decide what recent happening is novel enough
or important enough to report? How does an editor decide which,
among several recent and novel and potentially important events,
deserves inclusion in the paper or featuring on the front page? There
is no formula. Reporters on a campaign trail hear their candidate
make just about the same speech over and over again in different
states or cities. They become very sensitive to slight variations in
the speeches. But when is a variation a significant variation? A
reportable variation? Sometimes reporters will ask this question

directly to the source they are reporting on; they may ask a candidate or the candidate's press secretary, "Does that statement represent a departure from your earlier position?" In this instance, the reporters are asking the candidate to give them a lead. Reporters will ask this kind of question when they get briefings from government officials. If the official cannot answer them satisfactorily, they may check with one another: "Do you think this is news?" "Is this a change in policy?" Journalists may also go back to check their own newspaper's "clips," or library of previously printed stories. One translation of the question, "is this new?" is "has our newspaper covered this before?" Now, thanks to computerized information services like NEXIS, journalists can call up recent stories not only from their own newspapers but from other newspapers to get a fuller sense of how to place a new event in the context of other events.

The different time dimensions that enter into stories on page one will vary with the subject of the story, the intentions and intelligence of the officials who provide the news, the seriousness of the newspaper, the knowledgeability of the reporter, and the set of presuppositions journalists carry in their heads. This makes for enormous variation—but it is far from random. While a story on a development in science might reach several millennia back or a controversy over authenticating a poem by Shakespeare dig back four centuries, only two time dimensions—the human "lifetime" and the "postwar world"—are taken for granted and require no explanation in reporting on political affairs. (For other kinds of reporting, there are other taken-for-granted dimensions of time: the quarter and the year for economic reporting or "the season" for sports reporting.) "Lifetime" refers to the lifetime or expected lifetime of a human being. Reagan's age is newsworthy because he is very old relative to other American presidents and because people expect men his age to encounter serious health problems. Karen Ann Quinlan's case became especially newsworthy because fatal illness or death in a very young person is especially poignant. The obituary is, in some respects, a model for other news stories. Everyone dies, but whose death is worthy of coverage? Even all famous statesmen and celebrities die, but which of them will merit an obituary on page one?

The second taken-for-granted time horizon in the news is the period of time going back to 1945 which the newspaper can call,

without any hesitation or self-consciousness, the "postwar world."
When Olof Palme, prime minister of Sweden, was murdered on
February 28, 1986, the *New York Times* reported in a subhead that
this was the "First Slaying of a Sitting Head of Government in
Postwar Europe." The newspaper took it for granted that no one
would ask "post–*which* war?" In a sense, time and space merge here:
1939–1945 represents the birthdate of American consciousness of
the globe and so it becomes the Year Zero of our historical reckoning. This time horizon can stretch back a little further, to the
Depression, the New Deal, and the rise of Hitler in the 1930s.
These past fifty or sixty years represent the time in which the
modern world has been born, the modern balance of power created,
the modern sense of political expectations and ironies forged. There
is a history before 1929, obviously, but it is rarely a part of the
cultural equipment of today's reporters, editors, and publishers.
The formative political experience of the men, and the few women,
who are the senior leaders of the news media today dates to World
War II and the events that led up to it. They recall something of
the lessons of their fathers, but most of all they know the lessons of
their own coming to political consciousness and arrival on a world
stage. As this changes, as people become leading political reporters,
columnists, and powerful editors whose formative political experience was the hopefulness of the Kennedy administration, the civil
rights movement, combat in Vietnam, or the antiwar movement,
the taken-for-granted temporal context of reporting will change.
Reporting will become less coherent and ideological presuppositions
less commanding, because no consensus governs the understanding
of the sixties the way a common understanding of "the good war"
prevails. The way the press portrays the sixties today is a bellwether
of what underlying assumptions will frame journalistic understanding in the next two decades.

The Continuous Present: The News Story as an Event with Duration

Events drop into the newspaper like pebbles in a pool of time. The
first day, you see only the immediate "plunk" into the water. That

plunk is what journalists imagine all journalism to be: hard, fast, new, breaking, well defined, a story that any fool would recognize as news. But if the pebble sinks without a trace into the pool of discarded newspapers, no one will ever remember it. Stories that matter are stories that persist and take different turns over days or weeks or longer. With an important "plunk," as time passes, the story grows, the ripples spread out into past and future, the time span enlarges backward and forward, the reverberations to past and future become the new context for the story.

Newspaper headlines are almost always in the present tense, but newspaper stories are almost invariably written in the past tense. (Captions under photographs are often written, like headlines, in the present tense, as if even the print media employees believe what they want so determinedly to deny—that a photograph puts the audience "there," on the scene, in the present.) And yet, the "developing" story that unfolds over time offers a newspaper version of the "continuous present" tense.

In May 1985, John Walker and several members of his family were arrested on espionage charges. The news began unspectacularly. The *New York Times* reported the initial arrest on May 21— on page 19. Two days later, on page 22, a follow-up story quoted officials who said it was unclear if the Walker ring had endangered national security. But, a week later, the case had become a scandal of major proportion. On May 31, the *Times* reported that officials expected more arrests and that the case was already "one of the most serious spy cases in the Navy's history."

On Sunday, June 2, the front page dealt not with the single case but with a trend in spying: "Experts Tell of Spying Surge and Vulnerable U.S. Secrets." The center of the story shifted from what to why, and explanations of increased espionage arrests included increased enforcement of espionage laws, increased numbers of Soviet intelligence officers operating in the United States, and increased numbers of Americans with security clearances.

The next day the government arrested a fourth accused spy, and the *Times* signaled the gravity of the Walker case in a new way: "A retired Navy radioman was arrested today in San Francisco and accused of involvement in a spy ring that the authorities said had smuggled military secrets to the Soviet Union for as long as 20 years." Now it was no longer "one of the most serious" spy cases but one that "may be the most damaging" in Naval history.

On June 5, the story enlarged again: a fifth suspect was arrested and the story reported that this is "perhaps the largest American spy ring working for the Soviet Union in 30 years." The earlier figure—that this ring dated back twenty years—did not link the Walker group to anything but itself; this new date of thirty years ago takes people back to the Rosenberg case, an instance of espionage that until this point had not been mentioned (but is referred to explicitly later in the same story).

This opens a new phase of the story—not the extent of the spying but the reasons for it. The *Los Angeles Times* reported on June 6 that John Walker began spying in the late sixties "to get money to shore up a failing South Carolina restaurant in which he had invested." This story begins as a small new angle on the continuing story, but it quickly establishes ripples of its own. The next day, the *Los Angeles Times* reported in a front-page news analysis, "Money Seen as Motivating Today's Spies." The first four paragraphs concern William Holden Bell, a civilian spy sentenced to eight years in prison in 1981. The key paragraph connecting the obscure Bell case to the Walker spy trial reads: "Whereas past breaches of U.S. security often involved men and women with left-wing ideological leanings, today's spies seem to be motivated by a simpler craving—for money." The Defense Department's director of counterintelligence argues that this is because the Russians trust Americans who claim to be interested in money rather than in politics or principles.

What began as the arrest of an accused spy became very quickly a specific tragedy of American security endangered and then turned into an exemplar of a growing incidence of espionage and a new kind of espionage. The story moved from the dangers of espionage to the bureaucratic mismanagement that allowed espionage to take place. This is not an unusual direction for stories written in the continuous present. The longer the glare of publicity rests on someone or something, the harder it is for the makeup to stay fresh. Moreover, the journalist is under obligation to find a new angle each day. The tyrannical questions repeat themselves every day the reporter goes to the desk: What's new? What can be added? What can you say that you (or your rivals) did not say the day before? The journalistic instinct is that there is always a story *behind* the story, and that it is "behind" because someone is hiding it. So a story on espionage becomes a story on security clearance: on June 7, the *New York Times* reported, "Weinberger Says He'll Cut Back on People with Security Clearance." Stories followed this one into the fall and early winter, detailing the successes and, more often, the failures and foul-ups of efforts to tighten up security. It seems hard, human affairs being what they are and journalism being what it is, for tragedy not to keep curdling into farce.

No journalist imagined in May that the espionage story would stay alive not only through the Walkers' trials at the end of the summer but through several other arrests of other spies in what the *New York Times* dubbed on December 1 the "Year of the Spy" in a Sunday wrap-up analysis. Whether Reagan administration officials anticipated the spate of spy stories, or even planted some of them, is harder to say. Certainly, the stories embarrassed the administration less than they delighted it, offering a regular chorus of empirical evidence for the administration's effort to convince the nation of the need to tighten internal security. The spy story faucet, once turned on, soon afforded the administration a tubful of "I told you so" tales to legitimate its cold war preoccupations.

The press, meanwhile, began to treat every new arrest not as a small, fragmentary incident but as part of a megastory of espionage. The *Chicago Tribune,* for instance, in reporting on November 26 on the arrest of Ronald Pelton, a former National Security Agency employee, observed that only twice before—in the early 1960s— had NSA employees been charged with espionage. The *Los Angeles Times* (December 22), reporting the arrest of Randy Jeffries, a former FBI clerk, noted that Jeffries was the eleventh American held on espionage charges in 1985. Earlier in the year, this story would have been buried deep in the paper; now it was page one.

The Future Tense: Tomorrow on the Front Page

Officially, the newspaper does not comment on the future. Some newspapers print horoscopes but take no more responsibility for them than for the futures promised in the personals columns. News-papers print weather forecasts—you can find a five-day forecast in many papers—but the press delights when futurologists, including weather experts, are proved wrong. An AP story from Coral Gables, Florida, November 19, 1985, could barely contain its glee in re-porting that a convention of meteorologists to discuss the past sea-son's hurricanes was interrupted by a hurricane. "We certainly weren't expecting this," one hurricane forecaster said, and another added, "When we have picnics, it rains. When we get together to ski, we get snowed in."

Despite this jocular hostility toward people who claim to know something about the future, the newspaper regularly writes about the future and seeks to explain the present in terms of a consensually agreed-upon sense of the future.

Newspapers regularly write with respect to the future: turkey recipes appear in the food section in the weeks before Thanksgiving; the real estate pages preview the opening of a new condo develop-ment; sports columnists speculate about who will win the next "big game" and why. The press acts as conduit for public relations agents; as cheerleader for upcoming community events; as "use paper" for people who want to know the weather for the weekend, or what movie to see, or where to take the children, or what streets are under repair on the route to work. The press reports on the future both as a willing conspirator with commercial ventures and as a citizenly contributor to community affairs.

Of greater political importance are the instances when the news-paper gets out ahead of some issue or provides the public back-ground for a debate that will become a matter for public discourse later. The more a news institution seeks to be a journal of influence, the more attention it pays to what will happen, not just what did happen. This is most notable in the *New York Times*. A good exam-ple is a story by John Herbers that appeared on the front page on October 25, 1985, about police officers' new opposition to the National Rifle Association on important gun control issues, "Police Groups Reverse Stand and Back Controls on Pistols." The story begins in a typical "Sunday" sort of way, as a background story about a large social trend: "In a sharp departure from the past, the nation's major police associations are fighting for controls on pistols, adding a new element to the long, bitter struggle over regulation of firearms." This is the kind of story that the news media are so often criticized for failing to write—it reports on a process, not a single event, a trend and not an instance. But the patient reader learns in the fifteenth paragraph that this story is more precisely timed than it seems to be: the House Judiciary Subcommittee on Crime is going to hold hearings in New York the next morning and legislation to weaken the 1968 federal gun control law, already overwhelmingly approved by the Senate, would come before the House "in a few months." The Senate had already passed the bill, after which the police lobby became more active, and it would clearly play a role in the House vote.

A story like this anticipates public debate. It makes available to the general reading public a sense of the battle lines and lines of argument on a vital public issue that otherwise would become clear only a few days before congressional debate—if then. In this kind of story, the press does not set the public agenda—Congress has done that—but more than any other institution, including the Congress, it makes the work of Congress part of the public forum. It thus potentially enlarges the congressional debate and the number and kinds of people who might participate in it. It is a way of reporting about the future that can materially affect the future.

Is it intended to do so? In this instance, no policy directive came from on high—and this is typical. John Herbers, a longtime *Times* reporter who covers state and local government and "trend" stories out of the Washington bureau, had often covered gun control and police stories through the years. He learned from a friend he played tennis with that gun control groups were getting some help from police groups they had not had before. He followed this up, confirmed it, and thought it especially interesting in light of upcoming legislation in the Congress. The hearings in New York were incidental but helped add to the immediate interest of the story. "The only agenda, as far as I'm concerned," Herbers said, "is I like for my stories to have an impact, to be read and noticed and to accomplish what the *New York Times* does, as no other paper does, to draw other media into the story." By that standard, he felt this story a success, with the *CBS Evening News* and *MacNeil/Lehrer* quickly picking up his lead and doing pieces on the topic.

Stories like this depend on reporters being released from the grind of daily journalism. The typical reporter has little opportunity to attend to what journalists call the "news that oozes" rather than the "news that breaks." Herbers, in contrast, has no deadlines to meet and generally takes two or three weeks to research and write a story. He goes as quickly as he does, he says, because "I begin to feel guilty if I don't produce." He is in a position to take a longer look and see a bigger picture and perhaps have the kind of impact on the media menu and the national agenda that most reporters (and most newspapers) rarely achieve.

News stories frequently depend on some common understandings about the future while they report on some event of the past. The lead story on page one of the *Los Angeles Times* on July 31, 1984, was the unlikely "Commuters Find Traffic No Problem." What made this nonevent an event?

Expectation. Monday, July 30, was the first weekday of the 1984 Olympics, and Los Angeles had been planning for months ways to keep the freeways from becoming hopelessly clogged with traffic. Even so, most people feared the worst—and freeways that could be negotiated more easily than on a normal business day thereby merited big coverage.

Similarly, Hurricane Gloria was a big story for days in New York in September 1985 not because New York newspapers or their readers cared very much about storm damage on the coast of North Carolina and not because the damage was severe (it was not), but because the storm was heading right up the coast toward the city. This is a way of reporting about the future (what will happen to New York?) as if it were the past (what happened yesterday in North Carolina?).

Uncomfortable as the journalist is in speculating about the future, in fact reporters sometimes write about the past through the prism of the future. On January 18, 1985, the *Los Angeles Times* reported the testimony of New York Senator Alfonse D'Amato that he would testify on behalf of "subway vigilante" Bernhard Goetz because he, too, feared New York subways. D'Amato, the story indicates, was one of only two senators at the hearing of the advisory Congressional Crime Caucus. Reporter Paul Houston observed that both senators criticized sentencing and parole practices and lack of prison space. "At the same time, they contended that they had initiated many actions to solve some of those problems. Both men are running for reelection in 1986."

What is that last sentence doing? It is presumably a fact, but it is not an additional fact of relevance to the crime topic. It is an underlying fact the reporter appears to think the reader needs in order to understand all the other apsects of the story. It explains the other facts; it is a warning to the reader not to take anything Senator D'Amato says at face value. We do not know if it is a good explanation, though it is one reporters regularly fall back on—that politicians are to be distrusted because they have self-interested political motives for what they say and do. It seems easier for the reporter, in this instance, to cast some doubt on the politicians' claims than to check them.

Another kind of reporting describes the past as if it *were* the future. This is often found in stories on economic indicators. In the *Los Angeles Times* for July 24, a story headed "Prices Up Scant 0.2% in June" reported on Labor and Commerce department statements released the day before that provide a monthly progress report on the economy. This is one of those instances where the journalist's quest for the predictable meets comfortably with the bureaucrat's quest for printer's ink. We might think of it as the Ptolemaic influence on American journalism, this attention to cycles of activity, monthly reports, quarterly reports that revise the monthlies, annual reports that reconfigure the quarterlies. In this case, the Labor and Commerce statements comment on a thirty-day period that ended three weeks before, yet neither the federal officials nor the journalist take the reports as historical commentary on the past but as tea leaves auguring the future. The White House comments that the report gives hope of a strong economy for the remainder of the year. Economic forecasters get into the game, employing a phraseology we might term the hedging future tense: "We may be seeing the tide turn"; "We have to wait and see if . . ."; "The falling dollar, which could boost the price of imported goods . . .";

"For now, inflation's trend is downward"; "Foreign suppliers would most likely try to cut prices"; and so forth. The *New York Times,* using AP dispatches, did separate pieces on durable goods prices (the Commerce Department report) and consumer prices (the Labor Department), sticking closely to facts and figures in the first case but moving liberally into the hedging future tense in the second. *USA Today,* in contrast, did not report on the government documents at all but did a story the day before anticipating the reports: "Today's Index to Show New Bargains." Unlike the *Los Angeles Times* and *New York Times* stories, this story is genuinely about the past, not the future. It focuses on food prices, reports that they fell each month of 1985, and features interviews with individual consumers on how their shopping habits have changed.

Related to the hedging future, but more complex, is what we can call the *semiotic tense,* used with events whose present significance is unclear but whose debated meaning bears on some future event. This kind of story appears during election campaigns but is most regularly used in covering diplomatic negotiations. The lead story in the *New York Times* on November 12, 1985, began: "A high-ranking Reagan Administration official said today that Soviet negotiators continued to insist on barring research into space-based defense systems although Mikhail S. Gorbachev has hinted that such research might be allowed." This disarmingly conventional lead moves quickly to the semiotic tense: ". . . officials said Mr. Gorbachev might have been trying to signal flexibility without being able to muster support within the military. Others said the Russians might have been unsure on how to handle the issue." The news here is not the difference between Soviet public and private positions but American speculation about what the difference means.

This is a complicated kind of reporting, and it becomes a puzzle within a puzzle because the Reagan administration officials, by speaking to the reporter, are themselves trying "to signal" something—even though the rules of news etiquette enjoin the reporter from pointing this out. The semiotic tense does not report events but provides government officials a place to elaborate interpretive webs as part of a negotiating and signaling process. Perhaps no other kind of reporting illustrates as well the way in which the media are instruments of governing. Unintentionally, the semiotic tense in the newspaper is the one tense most truly a present tense because the story itself is an act in the drama it reports on. The news story itself will never acknowledge this, but a story about disputed meanings becomes an element in politics whose own meaning will enter into disputation.

The Rhythmic Quality of News

In a fascinating book on why the seven-day week developed as a major division of time reckoning, sociologist Eviatar Zerubavel writes that his research began when his five-year-old son asked him, "Daddy, what's Thursday?" It is an extremely good question. A reader of newspapers could well answer that Thursday is the one noun most likely to appear in the lead sentence of a news story on Friday.*

Nearly everything else may vary, but this is constant in hard news: an orientation to the past twenty-four hours. Time is the scaffolding on which stories are hung, and the day is the chief unit of time. The result, of course, is that events in the world that are or can be made to appear timely, that is, linked to some development of the preceding day, are more reportable than events that move by less discernible rhythms. These events are more easily justified for front-page attention by an editor who does not have room for all the stories he or she would like to include.

But it is clear that the fact that something happened yesterday is not sufficient to make it news. Sometimes newsworthiness has to do not only with timeliness but with the ease with which an event can be placed in a cycle or rhythm of time. Election stories are easy to

---

* This is not true of the *New York Times,* one of the few papers that still with some regularity uses a full dateline—the identification, before the first paragraph of the story, of the place and date of the story's writing, as in "Washington, January 11." The story will then be written from the temporal viewpoint of the reporter, not the reader. When the story says "today," it means January 11, even though the story appears in the January 12 edition of the paper and readers read it on January 12. The *Washington Post* is inconsistent about this, sometimes using a dateline, sometimes not. Most metropolitan dailies have dispensed with the dateline and write stories from the temporal vantage of the reader. The *Times*'s use of the old-fashioned dateline signals its professional and antipopulist stance.

report not so much because something newsworthy happens each day in an election campaign (although, of course, candidates do their best to see that this is so), but because journalist and reader alike know the election date and know when the story will *end*. Because everyone knows the story will end the first Tuesday after the first Monday in November, every speech, every poll, every alliance, every debate, every gaffe can be weighed and measured against a day of judgment. The reporter, the editor, and the reader all know *where they are* in the story—near the beginning, the middle, or the end. The election story has a cadence, a rhythm, and is easier to read and absorb because readers can tap out the beat.

The most notorious consequence of journalism's love for stories whose ending they can anticipate is the "horse race" style of covering elections. Sometimes, even in the best of newspapers, the result is a caricature of itself:

> Sen. Gary Hart of Colorado made it two in a row Sunday, with a come-from-behind victory that snatched away Walter F. Mondale's front-runner status.
> Hart's upset victory in Maine's Democratic caucuses gave him vital additional momentum just five days after his surprise triumph in the New Hampshire primary and nine days before the crucial Super Tuesday contests in nine states. (*Los Angeles Times*, March 5, 1984)

Election reporting can always count on an end point to give news a location in time that most reports do not have.

Reporting on legislative activity is correspondingly more difficult much of the time. This is well illustrated in a *Los Angeles Times* story of May 25, 1985, headlined, "Did Senate Vote Deal Fatal Blow to Future of MX?" The answer is: the reporters cannot be sure. They write, "The lopsided Senate vote to limit deployment of the MX missile to 50 unless the Reagan Administration can find another basing plan dealt a profound and perhaps fatal blow to the future growth of the MX program." *Perhaps* fatal? Well, the Pentagon portrayed the vote as a victory, since some senators had sought to limit deployment to forty missiles, not fifty. "But," the reporters tell us, "the Senate decision Thursday represents one of the extremely rare occasions in which Congress has made a clear—and possibly successful—effort to sharply curtail a major weapons program already under way." But defense appropriations have a way of returning to the floor of Congress. A bill once introduced and defeated may be introduced again. Compromises can be made. Adjustments can be arrived at. A story about failed or failing legislation, especially budgetary legislation where judgment is not "yes or no" but "more or less" is not a story with beginning, middle, and end. It is a P.D.Q. Bach spoof of a Beethoven symphony: how many endings are there? how many times will it roar to a climax only to return for one more reprise of the opening theme?

The sense of an ending that gives body and rhythm to a story need not be a date like the first Tuesday in November. It can be a clear-cut finish without a date. In hostage crises, the hostages will either be released safely or killed. The Iranian hostage crisis was mentioned every night on the evening news for fifteen months. It was not *timely* news—it was old hat. Most days it was not timely *news* because nothing new or different had happened. But the gravity of the opposition of the two outcomes—freedom or death, rescue or humiliation—provided a dramatic structure that kept the story a story.

This is what the press handles best: stories that are timely, that have anticipatable end points, and that have end points that figure in simple, binary possibilities—the election or the game will be won or lost, the Dow-Jones will go up or down, the defendant will be judged guilty or not guilty, the criminal is apprehended or at large, the patient survives or dies, the child is missing or has been found. Stories that are more complex than this—the budget, for instance—if they are to be covered well at all, are translated into a binary opposition of this sort: the president is going to get his way or he is going to lose to the Congress. The media found a comfortable way to report President Reagan's tax revision initiative when they discovered in Representative Dan Rostenkowski a skillful and attractive antagonist to set against the president.

The "sense of an ending" that gives shape to news stories works powerfully in reporting on the president. Presidents have two built-in historical contexts—their four-year term of office (or two four-year terms) and their place in relation to all past presidents back to George Washington. The weight of the latter context can be invoked in stories as somber as the State of the Union message or as lighthearted as "All the President's Popcorn," a May 23, 1985, *New York Times* story on what films President and Mrs. Reagan watch, and including a general history of presidents and their movies from the 1942 installation of a movie theater in the White House on.

The State of the Union message figures in both the president's career in office and in his historical place in a succession of presidents. Newspapers frequently locate the address in both contexts. The *San Diego Union* (George Condon, Jr., Copley News Service), on January 26, 1984, for example, stressed the presidential term of office in its lead:

> In his third State of the Union address to a joint session of Congress, the President cast aside the dire talk of economic woe that dominated his first two such speeches and delivered an upbeat talk that stressed traditional values, spiritual renewal, heroes and "the American dream."

But the story also positions the speech in relation to the president's next term of office:

> Speaking to the nation only four days before he is expected to use purchased television time to announce his candidacy for a second term, Mr. Reagan struck the themes that are expected to power that campaign, repeatedly sketching in bold strokes a self-portrait of a leader who tackled what he called "the worst crisis in our postwar history" and made "a new beginning."

An accompanying news analysis devoted itself exclusively to the theme that the address "was clearly designed to launch his reelection campaign on prime time television." The *Los Angeles Times* struck the same chord: "In a speech that could serve as a blueprint for his expected reelection campaign . . ." (This is another example of using the future as an explanation for the present.)

The two temporal contexts—the term of office and the position in the line of presidents—are sometimes joined in reporting, as in the *Washington Post* article "President in Pursuit of a Legacy" (David B. Ottaway, November 13, 1985), which begins:

> President Reagan heads for his summit meeting with Soviet leader Mikhail Gorbachev next week having revived public confidence in American foreign policy but without a towering achievement to leave as the centerpiece of his presidential legacy, according to a wide spectrum of admirers and critics alike.

The story puts Reagan in a line of presidents by noting that he has no foreign policy achievement comparable to Nixon's opening of relations with China or Carter's Camp David accords. (Presidents Ford and, of course, Johnson are conveniently forgotten.) The headline imputes to Reagan the desire to leave a "presidential legacy" as his second term moves on to its close, and so it ascribes to Reagan a sense of his *own* political ending as a motivation for his actions in Geneva. Whether or not Reagan felt such motivation, the story itself never says, but it would be convenient for journalism if he did because it provides an anchor point for taking the measure of the man and his career.

The rhythm of news is regulated not only by a sense of an ending but a sense of recurrence, most notably in the cycles of the week and the year. The newspaper not only uses time but keeps time for its readers, a kind of mass media wristwatch, close by for frequent consultation. On Wednesday or Thursday, we can expect the big food section of the paper with hints on menu planning and shopping for the weekend. On Thursday or Friday, the entertainment section will be big, preparing us for the weekend's change of pace. Saturday's paper is thin, an appetizer for the feast of print that will arrive Sunday morning. The *New York Times* and some other papers have created a kind of singsong cycle of the week: Monday sports, Tuesday science, Wednesday living, Thursday home, Friday weekend.

The Sunday paper is very special, a mass-media substitute for or supplement to the church service. It asks the reader to look backward and forward, to remember, to evaluate, to plan. Its time horizon, even on the front page, is much less closely connected to the previous twenty-four hours than the daily paper. On Sunday we get "The Week in Review" or equivalent expansions of essayistic writing on politics and the economy of the recent past, and also prognostications of things to come as complex as detailed "trend" stories or as straightforward as the television schedule for the next seven days.

The special character of the Sunday paper comes in part because readers have more time to read on Sundays, in part because Sunday is a day in our culture for reflection, relaxation, and entertainment, and in part because journalists are no more fond than anyone else of working Saturdays. The work life of the journalist in some measure dictates the time horizon and rhythms of the news story. That most White House correspondents are reporters who began following the president during a campaign helps create the four-year and eight-year time horizon that dominates presidential reporting—that is the limit of the journalists' own memories. An unusual instance is the practice of the *New York Times* of giving experienced foreign correspondents leave to write a long "think piece" at the end of their tour of duty in a country. On October 9, 1985, veteran correspondent R. W. Apple, Jr., completed more than eight years as London bureau chief and wrote a long front-page essay, "Britain Is Still a Land in Decline but Many Old Virtues Are Alive." Here, curiously, the newsworthiness of the story relates to stages in the career of the reporter rather than to the timeliness of the events he reports.

Generally speaking, however, journalists take their cues about rhythm from social institutions beyond the newsroom and from cultural calendars widely shared. There is always a New Year's story, a Halloween story, a set of Christmas season stories, and so forth. The anniversary—of a person, institution, or event—is regularly "news" in the media. Anniversaries, beginnings (debuts, openings), and closings (deaths of people or institutions) provide an opportunity to exercise some kind of self-conscious sense of history.

When the San Diego Symphony moved into an old theater newly refurbished, the *Los Angeles Times* (San Diego County edition) not only covered the opening but ran a piece on the *original* opening of the building as the Fox Theater more than fifty years before. When the anniversary, opening, or closing is significant enough, reporters wrap a sense of history around it throughout the coverage. This is true of presidential inaugurations. The January 21, 1985, issue of the *Los Angeles Times* was impressed at Ronald Reagan's taking "the historically rare step" at his second inaugural of canceling the parade because of bitter cold. This merited a second front-page story with the kicker "Breaks 1873 Record" and the headline "Cold? It Was Probably the Coldest Ever." Meanwhile, on the left-hand column, a seasonal feature story on how Russians deal with winter provided an ironic—one might say cold war—commentary on the inaugural report: "Muscovites Thriving on Bitter Cold."

When news reporters become self-conscious that they are writing a story with a past, as they are in doing anniversary stories, they are inclined to look for incongruity or irony. The *New York Times* did a long front-page story on December 1, 1985, a year after the Union Carbide poison gas leak at Bhopal, India, and noted in the lead that "misery and rehabilitation can be seen side by side" in Bhopal. A reader who gets through the full story is more likely to believe the story better summarized in the reporter's tenth paragraph: "Bhopal today is permanently scarred in many ways." But there is no incongruity there, and it does not fit the reporter's sense of what makes a strong lead. The *Times*'s interest in the Bhopal anniversary was much greater than its interest in a new event in Bhopal—an anti–Union Carbide demonstration involving three thousand people (although, in fairness to the *Times*, its page-eight coverage of this event was much more than most papers provided). As in this example, it is clear that the press is not dependent on a dramatic "event" to report as long as it can find some legitimate, culturally sensible peg—like an anniversary—from which to examine an issue in greater detail.

If not incongruity, then irony comes naturally to the journalist in a historic mood of nows and thens, same time last year, and so on. In a *Los Angeles Times* piece on July 31, 1984, Charles P.

Wallace opens the story "Last Combat Marines Leave Beirut Quietly" this way:

> When the U.S. Marines were sent here two years ago, they were accompanied by a blaze of favorable publicity and the high hopes of two nations. When the last combat Marines began their withdrawal from Lebanon on Monday, they left in at atmosphere of melancholy.
>
> In a touch of final irony, the job of guarding U.S. installations here was already being assumed by a force of Lebanese fighters recruited from private militias, including the same groups that dueled with the Marines in their foxholes last year.

The appeal of incongruity and irony is all too enticing for journalists when they self-consciously compare past and present. Journalists can do little with what is unchanging, continuous, because they are tied, sometimes straitjacketed, to the convention of the "news peg." What *changed*? What's *new*? What justifies writing this story *today* and not tomorrow? The *Times* missed the main Bhopal story, even from its own account, which was one of continuing tragedy and loss more than of incongruity, of rebuilding amidst misery. The press repeatedly has missed a sense of the continuity of political protest in the sixties generation by focusing on the more engagingly ironic tales of radicals turned yuppie as in the following *San Diego Union* (April 8, 1985) story:

> The year was 1968. The month late August. The city Chicago. Among those tear-gassed during the protests of the Democratic National Convention was a just-graduated Notre Dame English major, John J. Blake.
>
> Today, more than 16 years later, Blake lives the American affluent dream here.

The story describes how this thirty-eight-year-old former radical has become a "success-oriented conservative Yuppie." Available social research on the fate of sixties radicals indicates that they have retained strong liberal or radical views and stronger-than-average involvement in political activity. But there is no "news" in continuity, no easy answer to the question "when," and no tale as catchy as that of a protester turned accountant. (Continuity is a story only when journalists expect discontinuity: octogenarians who work forty-hour weeks or keep up their lifelong passion for skiing make the news because the culture expects them to be moving more gently toward their good night. These stories also greatly interest and perhaps comfort younger people who worry at forty or fifty or sixty-five if they are over the hill. Again, the lifetime is a shared biological and cultural experience of time that fundamentally structures news.) Irony is the attitude of the observer, the person who has seen it all, the person for whom *plus ça change, plus c'est la même chose,* the person whose sense of history is one of eternal recurrence rather than direction. Journalists are better historians, I think, when they are less aware that they are writing history.

The Subjunctive: The Language of Supposition in the Press

Every element of the news story—who, what, when, where, how, why—is an effort at explanation. "What's happening?" "What's up?" *"Qué pasa?"* "What gives?" These questions do not seek only the information that John Doe was born, died, won an election, lost a race at precisely 10:32 A.M. on Thursday or Friday. They want to know *what this portends.* Readers want not just to know but to understand.

To ask the journalist to help readers understand may be asking too much of someone in the midst of events and under the weight of deadlines. The journalist's minimal obligation is not to help the reader understand but to *get it right:* was it 10:32 or 10:31? Was it John Doe or Jon Doe? But the journalist's hopes and ambitions go well beyond this, even on a daily basis. If the reporter's assignment is to do the required stories and to get them right, his or her ambition is to get the stories on page one. That requires answering the apparently simple questions—like "when"—in a way that gives importance to events. Journalism—on television, radio, and in print—does not just tell readers what happened but identifies what is publicly important to them.

All the while, the ideology of American journalism is that news reporters report and do not interpret. The falsehood of the present-tense headline is symbolic of this—it suggests that the news report is a camera snapshot, a perfect image (although even a photograph is obviously not a perfect or unbiased image). The past tense of the news story, simultaneously, gives the reader the sense that anything he or she reads is history—it can be documented, it can be confirmed or proved false. It is not speculation. It is not opinion. It really *happened* and really *happens* at the same time.

Some forms of news reporting break away from this convention and operate by other self-conscious conventions. Feature reporting operates by different rules from hard news. The difference is not clear-cut; it's a case of "I know it when I see it." Sometimes it is said that hard news is important, while feature news is "interesting." Or it is said that hard news covers what is "timely" (but it should be clear by now how flexible a category "timely" is) and features cover what is timeless. Some feature stories do focus on what is considered eternal or universal in human affairs, but another common brand of features do not deal with what is but with what might be. I call this *subjunctive* reporting. The subjunctive is a grammatical form that people regularly use without being aware of it. According to the dictionary, the subjunctive is "that mood of a verb used to express supposition, desire, hypothesis, possibility, etc., rather than to state an actual fact, as the mood of *were*, in 'if I *were* you.' "

Feature stories are often written subjunctively. In features, a part often stands for a whole, an incident is meant to illuminate a larger meaning. The reporter accepts and hopes that meaning will not be rigidly confined but will lap over beyond the immediate events described. The daily front-page feature story in the *Los Angeles Times* is frequently subjunctive in mood. Take, for instance, the October 16, 1985, story on "Telecommuting: Computers Cut the Cord to the Office":

> Three mornings a week, Rick Higgins chugs vitamins and orange juice, puts on a suit and, like many other Southern Californians, hops into his car for a 40-minute commute to an office in downtown Los Angeles. On the other days, the San

Fernando Valley resident enjoys a leisurely breakfast and occasionally even a bike ride before work. Those are the days he telecommutes.

Who is Rick Higgins? The experienced newspaper reader understands at once that it does not matter. The story is not about Higgins. Higgins is simply a flesh-and-blood stand-in for a social trend, telecommuting. Telecommuting, not Higgins, is the story. But telecommuting is not yet a story. It is not yet newsworthy, but it is likely to become so. As reporter Martha Groves writes, "telecommuting has not yet become a major force in the corporate world," but she thinks it may be a major force one day. The orientation of the story, then, is not to tell the reader about people like Higgins and how they live, but to give the reader a sense of how he or she may live a few years down the road. This is "possibility" and "supposition," the subjunctive voice in the news.

Another case is even more striking. On June 22, 1985, the front-page *Times* feature, by Michael Wines, is headlined "Dayton's Toxic Waste–Water Peril: 'Nothing is Happening.' " The lead reports that a 1982 study of Dayton, Ohio, landfill found toxic wastes in the water supply for Dayton's suburbs. Several years later, nothing is happening, neither city, state, nor federal officials have acted on the study. How, then, can this be a news story when no "event" has taken place? And why should inaction in Dayton, Ohio, concern readers in Los Angeles, California?

Again, the experienced newspaper reader intuitively knows that this is not a story about Dayton; Dayton is standing in for other communities, probably including some in California. Sure enough, the fourth paragraph says that there are tens of thousands of toxic waste sites throughout the country threatening the nation's health and, despite efforts to clean them up, "the national record reads like a thousand Daytons." Somewhere specific becomes everywhere in general, and a story about what has failed to happen over the past several years is really a story about what may happen in the years to come if some action is not taken soon.

The stories on telecommuting and on toxic waste in Dayton are not like the story on the consumer price index—they do not report

the past as a direct index of the future. They are more like the story
the ghost of Christmas future tells Scrooge: they show what might
be if certain trends continue. The telecommuting story is one of
curiosity and interest in what the future might bring; the Dayton
story is much more like the tale Scrooge listens to, of what disasters
the future holds if he does not mend his ways.

Feature reporting takes a backseat to hard news in the journalistic
hierarchy of importance. The subjunctive is undervalued, if not
underemployed, as a journalistic form. News reporters place greatest emphasis on what may often be the least publicly vital feature of
media work—getting out the story on the most recent events.
There are many more varieties of journalism than this, however,
and rich possibilities in the different tenses that the language of the
newspaper can encompass. To take advantage of them, however,
requires an assertiveness on the part of journalists that is hard to
come by. As long as both reporters and officials play by the agreed-
upon rules, the officials continue to set the public agenda. *They* have
been elected—or appointed by elected officials. *They* are responsible
to the voters. Journalists have no such legitimation. When they
take the English language and its various possibilities into their own
hands, they challenge the everyday politics of the press that, on the
whole, keep the news media a fourth branch of government, the
unofficial outlet for official voices. When they seek a sense of time
independent of official clocks, they make a claim to professional
autonomy that rides up against a powerful politics of time.

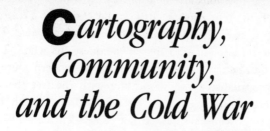

Cartography, Community, and the Cold War

DANIEL C. HALLIN

Most news stories begin by saying where:

SANTA BARBARA, Calif., Aug. 20—The White House announced today that, despite Soviet objections, the United States would proceed with the first American test of an anti-satellite weapon against an object in space.

But after the dateline, many stories drop the question "where" altogether, or give it the most perfunctory answer. A plane crashed. Where? Irving, Texas. Mrs. Winnie Mandela was arrested. Where? South Africa, of course; and she was taken to jail in Krugersdorp, which (if one cares) is "southwest of Johannesburg." Sometimes a brief word of explanation is required. Mrs. Mandela was arrested in Soweto, "which is home to more than 1.5 million blacks," the *New York Times* tells us, "and is viewed by the authorities as a tinderbox of political unrest." But this really tells us why more than where: why was Mrs. Mandela banned from Soweto? Where seems a simple fact, as straightforward as it is uninteresting.

Like most questions journalists answer—or choose not to answer —the question "where" is not as simple as it seems. Consider the story on the White House antisatellite announcement. A number of geographical locations are mentioned in this brief paragraph, for a number of different reasons. Just as the *New York Times* described Soweto to answer the question "why," the *Los Angeles Times* uses "the White House" here to answer the question "who." To refer to a place as an actor is a common device in modern journalism. It gives the journalist a way of dealing with the fact that so many "actors" are complex entities, often speaking through numerous representatives who have "asked not to be identified." When journalists mention places, they may be doing something more than just giving us a bare fact about the location of an event.

"Space" is also a where. Not much is said about it, and it is tempting to dismiss its appearance in this story as unimportant. But a story like this does, very subtly, tell us something about space, or present space to us in a certain way. Space, after all, can appear in the newspaper in many different guises. On the science page it appears as an object of a certain kind of knowledge. In coverage of Halley's comet it often appears as a source of entertainment, or, more profoundly but more rarely, as nature in the aesthetic and philosophical sense. In coverage of space exploration, it has generally appeared as an arena for technological adventure and accomplishment and a twentieth-century "frontier." Here it appears as an object of political struggle between the United States and the Soviet Union. And this raises the question of whether space will soon be appearing in the news primarily as a strategic resource and arena of global conflict.

Here we come to one of the major arguments of this essay. Journalists not only tell us where a particular event took place, they also tell us where we are in a more general and much more important sense. They communicate to us images of our neighborhoods and cities, of the nation and the world around it, and even of the universe, images which for many of us may constitute most of what we know about the world beyond our immediate circle of experience. Sometimes these larger "where" answers are given explicitly. In the early 1960s, for example, the *New York Times,* in its "Week in Review," provided its readers with a clear and simple geographic representation of the world political system, an image of the world divided into two concrete, mapable camps of Freedom and Totalitarianism. More often, however, since journalism focuses on the specific rather than the general, these grander images of the world emerge implicitly in the news, the product of many journalistic decisions made without any thought of answering the question "where" at this level. If space is beginning to appear as part of the cold war battlefield—a world image which is making a comeback after a period of decline—it is not because any journalist decided to describe space that way but, among other reasons, because news is what the White House says and does (wherever the White House may happen to be).

The narrow "where" in this story is of course Santa Barbara, California. Santa Barbara, however, has nothing to do with the story, which would be exactly the same if it were reported from Washington. So why is it mentioned? The dateline is a convention of the newspaper that serves to establish the *authority* of the news report. In the eighteenth and nineteenth centuries, when firsthand information from distant places was difficult to come by, newspaper stories were often entitled "Latest News from Europe," or accompanied by a proud boast that they came from "our own correspondent" in such and such a place. The dateline became institutionalized as coverage through wire services, large staffs of correspondents, and networks of stringers became a standard practice. Today we generally take it for granted that news stories will be reported from "the scene," and the dateline has become mainly a formality, though reference to place still, in some circumstances, plays an important role in establishing the authority of a news story. The dateline can be a useful piece of information for decoding a story—but also, at times, a misleading piece of information.

And so we come to the second major point of this essay. Answers to the question "where," both narrow and grand, perform many different functions in the news: there are many different reasons why journalists refer to geographical locations. I will deal with five such functions. They include:

Place as authority, which we have already encountered.

Place as actionable information, as when a community newspaper tells us where the Neighborhood Watch meeting will be held.

Place as social connection, as when the hometown of a person in the
news is mentioned, giving readers in that town a sense of participation in a distant event. This will lead us into a discussion of the
newspaper as a creator of community, and in particular into a case
study of *USA Today*'s effort to create a mass national "where" for a
mass national readership.

Place as setting. Setting is a basic component of narrative. But
most news "stories" do not really have settings. This is true in part
because so much journalism is policy journalism, reported from
Washington offices and briefing rooms, and in part because setting
is a powerful enough rhetorical device that it frequently runs afoul
of the norm of "objectivity." The use of setting in news reporting
is often problematic: physical descriptions of, for example, political
demonstrations can serve to stereotype them. But the absence of
setting can also be problematic, in that it drains the news of the
depth of lived experience.

Place as subject. Finally, places are sometimes the main subjects of
news stories. "The Phillippines: Another Iran?" is a typical headline
for such a story, as is "A Neighborhood Begins to Return from
Decay." Here the whole story answers the question "where." We
then need to ask when different kinds of places get in the news,
how they are presented, and what images of them emerge from the
totality of news coverage.

Place as Authority, and the
Uses of the Dateline

Although the dateline is basically a formality today, references to
place do still serve to establish the authority of news reports. This
is most common in television, where the reporter appears before a
setting that shows he or she was "really there"—the anchor appears
in Beirut or, more routinely, the Pentagon correspondent appears
next to a briefing-room podium with an official seal. Smaller newspapers will sometimes send their own reporters to the scene of a
major event, and similarly emphasize their presence; often the reporter in such a case will write more personally, referring to his or
her own experiences or feelings in the setting in question. Most of

the time, however, major newspapers establish their authority subtly, in phrases such as "officials here believe," or "according to
observers here"—"here" being the place listed in the dateline.

Authority aside, does the dateline provide the reader with information useful for interpreting a news story? Sometimes. What is
really important to a journalist, much more than being "on the
scene" in the sense of simply being present in the location of some
event, is sources—people to talk to. Datelines matter mainly because people in different places often say different things. It is
common, for instance, for reporters "in the field" to have a very
different view of a political crisis in some part of the world than
those in Washington. The view from the field is usually more nu-
anced than the one from Washington, since a Washington reporter
deals with U.S. policy toward many areas of the world, and, particularly when a crisis in some area suddenly becomes news in the
United States, will have few sources and little background information through which to filter official statements, which may themselves be based on rather fragmentary information. There is a
tendency, too, for Washington reporters to see things solely from
the point of view of United States interests, or at least to sound that
way, since it is considered their job to "reflect the thinking in
Washington"; while reporters in the field may come to identify
more with local perspectives—usually those of the Westernized
middle class in the country in question. One of the clearest cases of
this split between Washington and foreign reporting is legendary
among reporters who covered Vietnam in the early 1960s. The *New
York Times* one day printed two stories side by side on the front
page, one from Washington and one from Saigon, with a little note
apologizing to the reader for the fact that they gave diametrically
opposed versions of an important new development in the Buddhist
crisis of 1963.

But datelines can also be misleading. A reporter, for example,
can easily be in a foreign country and have few sources there outside
of the American embassy and perhaps a taxi driver or two. Sometimes being "on the scene" is a positive disadvantage to gathering
significant information. Kim Willenson, a *Newsweek* reporter who
was part of a press pool assembled to test the Pentagon's new pro-

cedures for taking journalists along on future Grenada-type military operations (it seems to be taken for granted that there will be more such operations), later wrote that he found his colleagues back at the Pentagon had better access to information than he. News stories, too, are always to some degree collaborative enterprises, and thus are not produced only in the place listed on the dateline. This is less true of newspapers than of television and newsmagazines; weekly magazine reporters, for instance, usually submit long "files" which are rewritten, bringing in other material, by writers in New York. But even a newspaper story is written by a person in one place, for editors and readers in another place, and often with an eye toward important audiences elsewhere—Washington bureau chiefs, if the reporter aspires to go to Washington someday, Pulitzer Prize committees, other prospective employers, and so on.

One interesting manifestation of the multiple points of view in newspaper reporting can be found in the relation between stories and heads. Reporters don't write their own heads; editors write them. And sometimes heads will either contradict or substantially change the emphasis of a story. In 1981, for example, Alex Drehsler of the *San Diego Union* traveled to guerrilla-controlled areas of El Salvador, where he produced some of the earliest firsthand reports on the guerrillas to appear in the U.S. press. The dateline was Chalatenango Province, El Salvador—in this case a very significant piece of information, since firsthand reporting from guerrilla zones could not be taken for granted. But it made a lot of difference where the stories were published, as well as where they were reported from. The stories were sold to many papers around the country, and were played very differently in different papers. In the liberal *San Francisco Chronicle,* for instance, one story bore the head, "With the Rebels in El Salvador—How They Win the People." In Drehsler's own paper, the conservative *Union,* the same story ran with the head "Salvador's Revolution: Just the Beginning; Marxists Court Peasants in Bid to 'Liberate' All of Central America." The story itself had both elements, and should probably be seen as a kind of compromise constructed out of the journalist's experiences in Chalatenango, his own roots in the United States, and the pressures of surviving as a journalist for a conservative paper. (Drehsler later resigned when the paper decided it couldn't afford to keep sending him on long trips into the mountains of Central America. A reporter traveling with guerrillas in the countryside, after all, can hardly be expected to file daily stories. Most datelines are capital cities, places where telex machines and regular sources of "hard news"—government ministries, embassies, and the like—are readily available.)

Place as Actionable Information

Late in August 1985, as a new school year approached, the *San Diego Union* sent four teenagers to a local shopping mall to buy clothes. The resulting story began this way:

> Parents, take comfort.
> Four teen-agers hit Fashion Valley Center a few days ago, each with a hypothetical $150 budget for a dynamite back-to-school outfit, and not one came back looking like a member of a rock group.
> From North, South and East County and San Diego, they converged to go shopping and wound up looking ready for a snapshot to send Grandma.

A story of this sort is meant to be useful for taking a particular kind of action—buying. In order to take action, people need various kinds of information. The most important kind of information provided by this story had to do with the fashion preferences of teenagers. It also provided geographical information: it reminded readers about the availability of a centrally located place of consumption where they could presumably reproduce the wonderful results achieved by the *Union's* test teenagers. Many newspaper stories provide information about where to do things the readers are likely to want to do; the Friday "Arts and Entertainment" or "Weekend" section is jammed with material of this sort.

Place as actionable information is generally found in certain sections of the paper. Besides "Weekend" sections, these include travel and real estate sections, and sections with titles like "Currents" or "Living." It also can be found throughout the paper in advertise-

ments. It is relatively rare in the news columns; and this says a good
deal about contemporary American journalism and culture. News is
mainly about politics, and most people are assumed to be spectators
to it; private, not public, life is the arena of action for ordinary
people. Occasionally, major newspapers will print actionable information about public affairs, usually when a community consensus
is assumed to exist. The *New York Times* has printed information
about where to donate money for Ethiopian relief. But it is very rare
for a newspaper to give, for instance, advance details about where
to assemble for a political demonstration—as it would for a Colum-
bus Day parade, which is seen as a leisure and "civic" rather than a
political activity. At times, actionable information is specifically
left out of news coverage: during the urban riots of the 1960s, news
organizations often cooperated with local authorities in keeping out
details that might tell potential participants where the "action"
was.

Place as Social Connection, and the
Newspaper as a Creator of Community

"One day . . . a wounded paratrooper captain walked into the aid
station. . . . He was Captain Francis Sheehan, of 22 North Grey
Street, Indianapolis. . . . We happened to get together because he
used to read my column in the Indianapolis *Times*." Why did Ernie
Pyle, the "GI's friend" of World War II, always give the hometown
and often the street address of the soldiers he wrote about? Because
it gave the reader a sense of participation. People in Indianapolis,
and above all on North Grey Street, would say, "Alright, a hometown boy!" They would enjoy the news more (and perhaps also like
the journalist more, since he had established a symbolic connection
with their community). And they, along with many others around
the country who might have relatives in Indianapolis, or simply
imagine North Grey Street as a typical American neighborhood,
would feel a vicarious sense of participation in the war effort. No
wonder journalists received the same kind of draft deferment in
World War II that was granted to defense workers and others
deemed to be performing essential service: they were essential to

establishing the sense of national community that made possible total mobilization for the war effort.

In today's more privacy-conscious world, it is rarer for newspapers to publish the street addresses of people in the news, outside of some fire and police reporting. It is still common in smaller local papers, however, and they are a good example of the role newspapers play in establishing a sense of community in a large and anonymous world. Consider, for example, the neighborhood paper in urban America. My own neighborhood in San Diego, Golden Hill, has such a paper, called simply *The Paper*. Here is the lead of a typical story:

> Monday morning, Sept. 9, electrical overloading caused a fire that destroyed the home of Sandra Benson at 1938 Bancroft St., and damaged two neighboring houses. Maria Kellenberger had just watered her yard when the fire began. Despite the efforts of her neighbor, Teddy Solorio, 15, to keep the blaze confined to the Benson home with a garden hose until the fire department arrived, the Kellenberger residence lost two front rooms to the fire.

The neighborhood is the closest thing to a face-to-face community that most of us have. But even the neighborhood is often abstract and anonymous, particularly in the mobile Sunbelt. We know people on our block, or at least some of them; we patronize certain local businesses. But two blocks away everyone is a stranger. Some people, mostly those who own local businesses or participate in organizations of one sort or another, have some firsthand knowledge of the neighborhood as a whole. For many, however, the newspaper is the main institution that provides a sense of belonging. It can do this in many ways. For some, the story of the Golden Hill fire will certify a personal experience as something more than merely personal, as a public event of interest to the wider community. Some might learn the name of a neighbor they had met but never spoken to. Others might simply think, "So that's where the smoke was coming from," reflect on the personal drama that transpired while they were going about their daily routine, and thus feel a sense of fellowship with a neighbor they had not met. Still others might be sparked to think about interests they had in common with the rest of the neighborhood: in this case, *The Paper* quoted a number of residents complaining about a slow response by the fire department, and raised the issue of the substation in the neighborhood that had been closed in the 1950s.

Creating a sense of belonging to a larger community is one of the basic social functions of the newspaper. But it is not always an unproblematic role: defining a community is a political act that can involve exclusion as well as inclusion, and the stressing of certain interests and ties over others that might define the community in a different way. Here it will be useful to consider the unusual case of *USA Today* and its effort to create a mass national readership—an effort that if successful will surely change the face of the American newspaper.

Creating a National Readership: *The Case of* USA Today

In most countries, the press is primarily a national institution. Not so the United States. The United States has only four major national dailies. Three of them—the *New York Times,* the *Christian Science Monitor,* and the nation's first national daily, the *Wall Street Journal* —reach specialized audiences interested in detailed information about politics and the economy. The other is new and experimental: *USA Today.* The vast majority of American newspapers are local.

Why should this be? Surely, federalism is an important reason, along with the sheer size of the country. Another reason may have to do with the fact that the press in America is a commercial rather than a political institution. Newspapers in Europe are traditionally vehicles of politcal discussion. In America, they are vehicles for advertising and at the same time, for their readers, tools for everyday living. And the practical community in which everyday life takes place is the city or suburb, not the nation. For the businessmen who read the *Wall Street Journal,* the nation is a real arena of action; the Dow-Jones average and the prime rate affect them in a practical way. For readers of the *New York Times,* similarly, national politics is something real, if only in the sense that they talk and think about it on a daily basis. For most of the public, however, the nation is more a symbolic than a practical community.

This is not to say that the American press doesn't cover national politics. On the contrary, national political coverage on the *New York Times* model is the most important category of "hard news," dominating the front section of most major metropolitan dailies. In the *Los Angeles Times*, for example, during the week of July 28 to August 3, 1985, front-page stories broke down like this: national, 53 percent; international, 33 percent; local, 9 percent (most local stories are in a zoned section of their own), and state of California, 5 percent. Like the *New York Times* and other major papers, the *Los Angeles Times* covers the nation in a particular way, easy to see if one looks at the datelines of national stories. During this week, twenty-one of thirty national stories appearing on the front page were reported from one city: Washington, D.C. There were as many stories from Africa—nine—as from the rest of the United States outside of California and Washington.

On the front page of a major American newspaper, the nation means official Washington. And focusing on the concerns of Washington narrows the national political agenda in important ways. If Congress, the White House, and other organized political forces happen to be debating tax reform or international terrorism, rather than poverty or the environment, the latter will be almost entirely absent from the news, however great their underlying importance to the community. For better or for worse, however, it is Washington news that people seriously interested in national politics are assumed to want.

But the *Los Angeles Times* doesn't have to rely exclusively on national news to build its audience; a large part of its readership may simply glance at the front page and then look inside for information about sales and movie schedules. *USA Today* is in a very different position. Launched by Gannett in 1982, the colorful, fast-reading paper is intended to compete with television and magazines for the national advertising dollar. All it can offer is some species of national news. But people who want to know the behind-the-scenes politics of "Star Wars" or the tax plan can read the *New York Times*.

USA Today had to come up with a new kind of national news for an audience—which Gannett had spent more than a million dollars on market surveys to identify—of people who wouldn't read jumps and didn't like the slow-paced, colorless political reporting that filled the front pages of most daily newspapers. No wonder the paper declares as its purpose, "to serve as a forum for better understanding and unity to help make the USA truly one nation." For USA Today, the creation of a broad national community—on some basis other than the traditional basis of national politics—is a commercial imperative. This imperative leads USA Today to give a distinctive answer to that larger "where" question, the question of where we live, what kind of community we belong to.

On Tuesday, October 29, 1985, the front page of USA Today included the following stories:

The right-hand lead: "Pay Hikes at Record Low; Productivity Up." Above the lead: "Bang-up July 4 Weekend for Miss Liberty." In the center of the page, the "Cover Story": "Innocent Girl Puts Charm to Work." Above this story was a large picture of "Princess Di," who was soon to visit the United States. The heading above the picture: "How Di Won Her Prince."

Next to the lead: "Fresh Hope for Families." This was a story about relatives of Americans held in Beirut, who were going to Washington to meet with President Reagan. The story also included two paragraphs about Marilyn Klinghoffer, whose husband Leon was killed by the hijackers of an Italian cruise ship. Her picture appeared with a head, "Leon Was 'Everyman.' " Also: "150 Rescued as Hurricane Sweeps Gulf."

Finally, in the lower left- and right-hand corners were two boxes. On the left was a regular feature, "USA Snapshots," subtitled "A Look at Statistics That Shape the Nation." And on the right, a box with the head "Wanted: '85 Achievers," announcing nominations for "people who have made a difference," who would be saluted by USA Today.

Aside from boxes, the front page contained six stories. Two were reported from Washington. One was from New York, but it was about the national ceremony surrounding the Statue of Liberty. The "Lady Di" story had an Australia dateline, but was again about an essentially placeless national event, the upcoming visit of the princess. (Inside, *USA Today* has a regular half page of international news, and on most days that is the extent of foreign reportage.) The Gulf hurricane story was the most regional of the bunch, though it had no dateline and stressed national trends ("the fifth Atlantic-spawned hurricane to hit the USA this year.") Inside, there is a regular page of local news entitled "Across the USA," with one feature story and a series of news briefs ("Iowa City—Authorities say man using propane torch to kill box elder bugs caused Sunday fire that razed 2-story barn.") But for the most part, *USA Today*, naturally enough, focuses heavily on news that in some sense concerns everyone, regardless of location. Like the front page of the *New York Times* or the *Los Angeles Times*, therefore, *USA Today* offers a highly centralized image of the nation.

But the focus of *USA Today*'s America is very different from that of the *New York Times*. There were, to be sure, two Washington stories on the front page of the issue we are considering. Neither, however, concerned national politics. The lead story was a business story. The other Washington story was about the hostage relatives. Aside from a special page devoted to the hurricane in the Gulf, and the standard "Newsmakers" page, the paper contained a page and a half of national news. Only three stories, however, were about Washington politics. Others included a story on the Walker spy case, one on a Soviet sailor who, it was thought, might want to defect (both more human interest than political stories), reports on heart transplants, the arrest of Bhagwan Shree Rajneesh, and a consumer tip from Ralph Nader.

The journalism of *USA Today* is not a journalism of issues and of politics, but of symbols and of everyday life—everyday life, however, understood not as a material struggle (as it seems in a paper like the *New York Daily News*), but as itself an "upbeat" symbol of "USA" unity, defined primarily by the mass culture of leisure and consumption. National political news on the *New York Times* model is concerned with the movers and shakers; their priorities and concerns define the nation. *USA Today* is concerned with "everyman" (in the words of the story on Leon Klinghoffer)—not with the particularity of individual lives, but with the ways in which ordinary people share, usually through mass culture, in some kind of national life. So in place of national politics, *USA Today* is concerned with: consumption ("Cherry Coke Blossoms into Cola Hit"), leisure ("USA's Barbeque Binge"), television and other forms of entertainment, celebrities and human interest stories, health ("Ham Jordan Fights Cancer; Celebrates Good News"), and consensus values and beliefs ("We Still Believe in American Dream").

Sports are also frequently on the front page, and *USA Today* has devoted considerable resources to making its sports section superior. Sport is one area of life in which different regions of the country, and, vicariously, the fans in them, can participate actively in the life of the nation; one of the few ways most cities make news on a regular basis is through their professional sports franchises. The enormous colored weather map that covers the back page of *USA Today*'s front section is another of its most successful features, now being copied by many papers around the country. Weather, of course, is the classic subject for conversation among strangers, and thus a natural for the quick production of "community" in a mass audience. Finally, *USA Today* is obsessed with statistics, which, as Warren I. Susman has observed, have been used since the 1930s to submerge the bewildering diversity of American society in the notion of the "average man." Statistics appear in *USA Today* both in the regular "USA Snapshots" box and in frequent front-page stories. The story headed "We Still Believe in American Dream" was based on a poll commissioned by *USA Today* on the birthday of Horatio Alger.

When it deals with politics, *USA Today* tends to focus on the president, who appears as a kind of elevated everyman and symbol of the nation rather than as an advocate of policies which people might disagree about—as a monarch rather than a prime minister. (Ronald Reagan appeared at *USA Today*'s coming-out party in 1982, perhaps sensing that it was an excellent vehicle for his style of politics.) The Reagan-Gorbachev summit in November 1985 brought out this tendency particularly strongly. A few headlines from political stories in 1985:

February 6: "Reagan Tells His Vision for All USA"
May 29: "Tax Revolution: 'Go For It' "
November 7: " 'Stop This Futzing Around': Reagan to
Gorbachev"
November 14: "Bring Us Together; Reagan's TV Pitch
Tonight at 8 EST"
November 15–17: "Reagan Off on 'Mission of Peace' "

USA Today is generally upbeat, full of achievers and smiling faces. There is a regular feature entitled "Upbeat USA." But the upbeat spirit pervades the paper. A good example can be found on November 1, 1985, a day when most of the press was full of gloomy economic news. "The country's foreign trade deficit soared to an all-time high of $15.5 billion in September," the Associated Press reported, "while the government's main gauge of future economic activity posted a scant 0.1 percent increase. . . ." Here is how *USA Today* handled the story: "Although a flurry of news was released Thursday that painted a poor picture of the USA's economic health, some experts say the economy will continue to grow modestly throughout 1986." The head: "Economy's 'Bottom Line Points Up.' " Rarely does one find anger in the breezy pages of *USA Today* —except under one condition, which is seen as a unifying factor in *USA Today*'s America—anger at foreign enemies, above all terrorists. One lead story during the *Achille Lauro* hijacking bore the head, "Ship Killing: 'Get Those SOBs.' "

USA Today's issue the Friday before the "Super Weekend" of Super Bowl XIX and Ronald Reagan's second inauguration represents particularly well the paper's view of the nation (which is in many ways closely parallel to Reagan's own appeal). Reagan had granted *USA Today* an exclusive interview, which naturally was the subject of the lead story. Near the bottom of this story, there were a few brief paragraphs on policy issues, but most of it dealt with personal matters. The head was "Reagan: I'm the Boss; Decisions Are His, He Says." In boxes on either side of the banner were the usual guides to what was inside the paper, but they were bigger than usual, and were headed: "Super Game Guide" and "Super Inaugural Guide." Under the banner were three boxes in the form

of television sets, one for Saturday, one for Sunday, and one for
Monday, with a red, white, and blue title under them: "What
You'll See—Day By Day." The "Cover Story," under a large color
picture of Reagan, was titled "To D.C. or Not . . . That's the
Question," and talked about who, among "the USA's movers and
shakers," was going to the inauguration and who to the Super Bowl.
What *USA Today* hopes to do is to position itself alongside the
television networks as a leading daily guide to and celebrator of
American mass culture. And what happens to politics, the usual
meat of journalism and center of national concern, is that it becomes
simply one more branch of mass culture, something to read about
or watch on television when the Super Bowl is over.

Notice the similarity between *USA Today*'s image of America
and the image of the city that appears in the "Currents" section of
the *San Diego Union,* as represented in the back-to-school shopping
story discussed above. The four areas of San Diego from which the
Union chose its four young shoppers are very diverse. The North
County area, for example, is generally wealthy, the South County
area, near the Mexican border and the Navy shipyards, is mainly a
working-class area with a large minority population. The economics
of advertising are such that newspapers have a special interest in
attracting "upscale" readers. So one generally finds heavier coverage
of places and issues that are of interest to these desirable members
of the advertising audience. Still, journalistic principles compete
with the demographic imperative to a degree, and the diversity of
the city pushes its way into the paper, particularly when controversies erupt involving poorer neighborhoods. This occurs, however,
mainly in the news sections of the paper. Feature sections like the
Union's "Currents" are much more likely to portray the city as major
advertisers like to see it. The diversity of San Diego is obliterated
by the $150 outfits the *Union* sent its four students (three white and
one black) to purchase. In *USA Today,* the difference between the
news sections, with their journalistic ethic, and feature sections,
which are more clearly vehicles for advertising, tends to disappear.
USA Today gives the answer to "where" that national advertisers
want to hear. Its America is their America—happy, homogeneous,
prosperous, and overwhelmingly concerned with the affairs of private life.

Place as Setting

Setting is a basic element of narrative and a rhetorical device of considerable power—so much power, in fact, that journalists generally refrain from using it when reporting hard news about political events. Here is an exception, from the *Los Angeles Times,* July 28, 1985:

> KWATHEMA, South Africa—Rutherford Ndlovu woke up last Sunday to the rumble of armored cars rolling down his street, the loading of rifles and shotguns outside his bedroom window, and then the shouts of policemen and soldiers shooting off the locks of three neighboring houses and breaking down the doors.
>
> "It was like one of those war movies when the Gestapo comes and arrests everyone, but this wasn't on television—it was right next door," Ndlovu said.

"Feature" leads like this either introduce a central character, draw the setting for the story that is to follow, or both; and in doing so they generally push the story off the dead center of "objective reporting," suggesting a stand of some sort toward the events in question. To give an event a setting is to make it concrete, like "real life" or a dramatic representation of real life. The reader is thus invited to "experience" the event rather than merely to be informed about it, and as a consequence, the emotions of real life are invoked in a way they seldom are by a report that remains on the level of information and analysis. Here a person touched by the event invokes a scene from popular drama to convey his own feelings, and the journalist structures his story around that powerful visual image. We naturally feel empathy for Ndlovu and disgust at the action of the South African government, far more strongly than if we had simply been told in the more traditional lexicon of objective reporting that South African "security forces" forcibly searched so-and-so many houses in a black township.

For a number of reasons, the use of setting is relatively rare in political reporting. Most political reporting, first of all, is about the policies and statements of governments and other organized political actors. Journalists learn about these policies by attending briefings and calling sources, mostly in Washington offices. These settings might, in fact, be interesting to the readers, who have not seen them. But to journalists, they are part of the everyday routine of reporting, and have no news value. Because the use of setting (the same applies to character, and the two usually go together) so often puts the reporter and the newspaper in the position of taking a stand, moreover, journalists tend to stay away from it when covering events about which people disagree, sticking instead to the dispassionate style that is considered appropriate to hard news. South Africa is an exception. Events in the streets have been so dramatic and unpredictable that they have stolen the spotlight from policy coverage; official sources in South Africa, and to some degree in Washington, have not been considered credible; and a powerful consensus in the United States has freed journalists of the need to appear neutral on the subject of apartheid.

By making the news concrete, by giving an event the detail of lived experience, setting and character can lend the news human depth, countering the tendency for hard-news coverage to treat politics as a chess game, ignoring its human consequences, simplifying its human complexities, and in the process probably rendering it incomprehensible to a large part of the reading public. But the feature treatment also has considerable potential for mischief. It can stereotype as well as humanize. It can also personalize so much that instead of promoting a deeper understanding of large historical forces, it makes them disappear.

Stereotyping, for example, is what happens in the following description of the scene of an arms control demonstration, reported in the *San Diego Union* on May 12, 1982:

> The chill air had thinned out the crowd of about 2,000 last night at the "Peace Rally" at Balboa Park's Starlight Bowl when Daniel Ellsberg walked to the podium with his 5-year-old son and started talking about miracles. . . .
>
> The rally brought out many groups favoring an end to nuclear technology and war—and the sidewalk outside the rally was lined with people espousing different philosophies.
>
> Shaved-headed and Saffron-robed Krishnas offered carob

candy; "Bread Not Bombs" T-shirts were being sold from tables; Sierra Club members wanted petitions signed for the resignation of Interior Secretary James Watt; a Free Speech Radio station offered programs; and a group of Moslem students asked for support in overthrowing Iranian leader Ayatollah Ruhollah Khomeini.

Here setting serves the purpose of ridicule. The image the reporter draws on is a common one in coverage of protest activity: the proliferation of causes, all appearing as equally without depth. The *Los Angeles Times,* by contrast, covered the peace rally (a term it used without quotation marks) as hard news, more or less as it might cover a Washington press conference. Most of the story was filled with quotations from the speeches, and the setting was described only in the last paragraph: "The rally, complete with a rock band and posters that proclaimed, "Bread not Bombs," was sponsored by . . ."

Then consider the following story on Cinquera, a village which William Montalbano of the *Los Angeles Times* calls a "dusty, red-tiled, nowhere microcosm of the violence that wracks El Salvador." The story was heavy with physical description, including this conclusion:

Numbers never tell the story . . . and are almost never right. A more accurate reflection of the Salvadoran reality Wednesday was the pathetic emptiness of Cinquera and its survivors; open doors to empty houses, a skinless bass drum rocking on cobblestones, a schoolgirl's essay entitled "Art in the Middle Ages," forgotten under fleeing feet.

Unlike South Africa, Central America is intensely controversial in the United States. So it might seem like the kind of story journalists would hesitate to report in a soft-news style. But here the use of setting implies a different kind of political stance, one that by personalizing the story takes it out of the realm of political controversy. Cinquera had been attacked by guerrillas, who overwhelmed the army garrison there, and then, according to residents,

killed those who had cooperated with the government. Why was
this terrible violence taking place? The story gave a three-paragraph
summary of the political background to the conflict: Sometime in
the 1970s, "a priest whose name is not remembered politicized the
poor. . . . Landowners and the town establishment . . . struck
back," killing peasants who had joined the priest, and the priest
and some of his followers went into the hills to join the guerrillas.
It was these peasants who came back to Cinquera, according to the
story, to settle an old score.

But for the most part, the story is not concerned with politics.
In fact, in the particular way it portrays the setting of Cinquera, its
basic message seems to be that politics is not important: all one
really has to grasp is the disruption of people's lives, which an
outside observer with little knowledge of the history or context of
the conflict could easily see in the disruption of the environment of
everyday life.

This is a common "subtext" in reports on political conflict that
are given a feature treatment. It has its advantages and disadvan-
tages as journalism. On the one hand, an exclusive concentration on
questions of policy and ideology can certainly obscure what politics
means to ordinary people. In the spring of 1985, for instance, the
press was full of reports on Central America like the following from
the *Washington Post*: "A hesitant consensus appears to be growing in
the Reagan administration that the effort to preserve a democratic
state in El Salvador is succeeding." The head was "Glimmers of
Success; El Salvador Is Looking Better in War and Politics." Quite
apart from the issue of whether the assessments of the military
situation or the character of the Salvadoran government in the article
are accurate, reporting of this sort pushes the human dimension of
war out of the picture. (One can of course imagine versions of the
same approach from the opposite political perspective, sympathetic
to the left; though this would never be found in the "establishment"
press.) On the other hand, politics does matter. The violence that
destroyed Cinquera has causes worth understanding, and whatever
becomes of that "dusty, nowhere microcosm," it will have consequences for future Salvadorans, albeit in ways that may be hard to
predict.

It is, incidentally, common in feature reports to take a particular setting, that is, a particular place at a particular time, as a "microcosm" of a larger and more complex reality. But unless the reporter puts the microcosm carefully into context, this is usually misleading. Rarely are the same forces at work in the same way everywhere at once. In the case of El Salvador, for instance, the degree to which the guerrillas or the government use violence against civilians clearly varies from one part of the country to another, and from one period of the war to the next.

Consider, finally, the following pair of stories on rent control, one from the *New York Times* and one from the *Daily News*. From the *Times*, June 3, 1985:

Rent Curbs Are Said to Foster New York Tenant Inequities

As the State Legislature prepares to renew New York City's rent regulation system, housing analysts are debating whether the system—begun in 1943 to cure a wartime housing emergency—has become part of the disease.

A system meant to protect tenants at the expense of landlords has evolved, many experts on both sides of the debate say, into a set of rules that serve some tenants at the expense of others.

The system protects incumbent tenants, experts say, while penalizing newcomers and those who wish to move within the city. They say it serves many middle-class tenants while providing little help for the poorest residents.

From the *Daily News*, June 30, 1985:

Biz Rents Are Out of Control

A 71-year-old dress shop owner on Flatbush Ave., Brooklyn, will go out of business after not being offered a lease renewal—even though she has rented the store for more than 50 years.

A 73-year-old gallery owner on Madison Ave. is about to retire because he cannot afford to pay his increased rent, which is going from $2,500 to $7,500 a month.

A Queens couple will close their children's shoe store in south Richmond Hill after 26 years of business. The landlord did not offer lease renewal because a national hamburger chain is interested in opening a restaurant there.

The lack of a commercial rent-control law in New York City has left its casualties. . . .

The cases that get the biggest headlines . . . occur in gentrifying Manhattan neighborhoods, but the lack of control affects stores all over the city. Most often hurt are small neighborhood shops that cannot compete with large chain stores or new restaurants that can afford to pay high rents.

There are obviously many differences between these two stories. The one that interests us here is that the *New York Times* story has no setting, while the *Daily News* story has several—specific businesses in specific locations. This is typical. Most city news in the *Daily News* can be located somewhere on the map of New York. *Times* stories typically cannot be located anywhere; they transcend, or claim to transcend, all particular locations. This is because the *Times* and the *Daily News* operate on very different models of journalism: the journalism of the *Times* is a journalism of *policy*, that of the *Daily News*, a journalism of *experience*. Each has its limitations. The *Daily News* reports the experiences of particular individuals or neighborhoods, but provides little analysis of how these experiences are related to larger social processes. The *Times* provides exactly this kind of analysis, often at great length; the story quoted here was part of an extensively researched two-part series on the effects of rent control. It may have had its flaws as an analysis of the political economy of New York housing; it focused on the failings of rent control, for example, and seemed just to scratch the surface of the deeper causes of New York's housing crisis. It also wound up offering little hint of what alternatives there might be to rent control. Still, it was clearly a serious effort at a general analysis of the rent control issue.

But the *Times* articles left another question hanging. On balance, the series left a strong impression that rent control was irrational, bad not just for landlords but for most tenants (a view consistent with the *Times* editorial position on rent control). Yet throughout its coverage, the *Times* had to acknowledge that most New Yorkers were passionately in favor of rent control. A number of rent control advocates were interviewed, and statistics were provided which gave some hint of why support for rent control might be so strong, statistics, in particular, showing what percentage of their incomes New Yorkers devoted to rent. Still, one left the stories with the feeling that some piece of the puzzle was missing. The missing piece was the kind of concrete housing horror story from this or that neighborhood in Brooklyn or Queens that appears regularly in the *Daily News*. Without this kind of reporting, the *Times* not only couldn't fully explain why, in the words of the head of the second article of the series, rent curbs were "Politically Entrenched," but also missed the human tragedy that lay in the failures of policy outlined by the experts it had interviewed.

The best journalism combines narrative and analysis, using particular settings to give human depth to analysis, and analysis to put those settings in their wider context. But this is not an easy kind of journalism to do, requiring more time and space and often more knowledge about the country or issue in question than a journalist producing for a daily newspaper or wire service normally will have. It also tends to be pushed aside by the hardheaded "Is the policy working?" perspective that has come to be accepted as the "objective" way to report political news.

The *New York Times*, incidentally, not only covers rent control from a different point of view than the *Daily News*—from the perspective of the housing expert in an office high above Manhattan, rather than from Flatbush Avenue—but covers it much less. Rent control is an everyday concern of the *Daily News*, a relatively rare one for the *New York Times*, appearing mainly when there is a special "peg" like a vote in the legislature. That, of course, is related to the demographics of the two papers' readerships, the readers of the *Times* being to a large extent outside of the central city. And the differences in journalistic style and priorities that result, in part, from the demographics of the two papers naturally lead them to answer the larger "where" question very differently: New York appears a far different city in the *Daily News* than in the *Times*. The differences are too numerous to outline here, but one or two are worth mentioning. The New York of the *Daily News* is a struggle for existence; that of the *Times* is a paradise of consumption and culture, and at the same time a social problem—the city is something to be *enjoyed* and *managed* rather than something to *survive*. The New York of the *Times* is also a national capital; that of the *Daily News* is a (very large and diverse) small town, highly suspicious of outsiders (note the hostility to the unnamed national hamburger chain in the story above).

Because of their symbolic potency, settings are often deliberately created by political actors hoping to affect news coverage. One manifestation of this is the "photo opportunity." In 1981, for example, after U.S. jets had shot down two Libyan planes which had attacked them during U.S. maneuvers off the Libyan coast, President Reagan posed for photographers on the bridge of an aircraft carrier, wearing a cap with "Commander in Chief" written across the back and looking out over the flight deck as fighters were launched. The picture appeared across the front of the *Daily News* ("New York's Photo Newspaper," as it bills itself) under the head "Ron on Libya Incident—We've Got the Muscle."

There are other ways to handle photo opportunities. The *San Francisco Chronicle* reported one set up by California Governor George Deukmejian like this:

> Governor Deukmejian talked of Lake Tahoe's scenic beauty yesterday and posed for pictures on a precipice overlooking magnificent Emerald Bay.
>
> Area environmentalists, however, charged that something was wrong with this stunning picture.

The story then went on to discuss controversies over Deukmejian's environmental policies. It was not accompanied by a photograph.

At times, efforts may also be made to limit coverage of particular settings, as when Reagan's visit to the German military cemetery at Bitburg was shortened. According to press reports, camera angles were set up so that it would be difficult for the media to get a clear shot of the president in that controversial setting.

Place as Subject

Finally, places often appear as subjects of news. This happens for a number of different reasons. Often, for example, journalists covering some major national event will fill their extra time reporting on their surroundings, usually in a feature/human-interest mode. The towns along I-70 in Missouri became newsworthy when journalists had to travel that superhighway to cover the 1985 World Series. Places are also covered as potential sites of leisure-time activity. The travel section is an obvious example: there places appear as commodities which can be purchased and enjoyed. The articles include practical information about how to consume these places: "The first time you visit Rio de Janeiro, fly," says the *Los Angeles Times Magazine.* "The second time, I suggest you go by ship." This is combined with the familiar sensuous imagery and what might be called "idealist materialism" of the culture of consumption. Politics and economics are excluded, and the pleasures of consumption are elevated to a spiritual plane. The *Los Angeles Times Magazine* continues:

> On the noonday of my initial arrival in Rio, I lunched with a Brazilian newspaperman at a gracious restaurant called Ouro Verde, overlooking Copacabana beach. We drank a *caipirinha* cocktail, a tasty concoction of raw rum laced with lime, and ate, of course, Brazil's national dish, *feijoada completa,* a sovereign masterpiece of culinary art—black beans, rice, sausages, pork and more . . . much more.
>
> My host talked winningly. "To discuss this city as a *place,*" he said, "is misleading. Rather you should understand that Rio is a spirit, constructed of emotion. . . ."
>
> "I should hate," he continued, "to know Rio's per capita income, because such mundane matters actually impede understanding. Would you seek to comprehend a lovely woman by memorizing her blood pressure and her pulse count? Never!"

Finally, and most importantly, places appear in the news when they become objects of political controversy, as when a part of a city is slated for redevelopment, or a particular country becomes an object of superpower confrontation. As this last statement suggests, most places are not covered on their own terms—from the point of view (or points of view), for example, of their own residents. This is true at all levels of news coverage: a particular problem in a city neighborhood, for instance, is not likely to receive much coverage in a citywide newspaper until it becomes a problem at city hall; and when it is covered, the point of view of city hall or its various factions is likely to dominate the coverage. But at no level is this more true than at the level of international politics, where the "geopolitical" perspective that has dominated foreign policy thinking in Washington since World War II has similarly dominated most news reporting.

Geopolitics: The American Image of the World from the 1960s to the 1980s

Let's begin by jumping back a bit more than two decades, to an era when the American image of the world was much simpler than it is today. On December 20, 1962, the following story appeared in the New York Times, reported by David Halberstam:

> DAK PEK, Vietnam, Dec. 18. Dak Pek is a far outpost of the non-Communist world, a small, knobby patch cut out of rugged mountains better suited for a tourist showplace than a military stronghold.
>
> Today it stands as a small island in the midst of the major Communist infiltration route along the Ho Chi Minh Trail from North to South Vietnam.
>
> Here a handful of tough United States Special Forces men day after day live a precarious existence training several hundred Montagnards, or mountain tribesmen, and continually probing the area for Communist moves, for this is South Vietnam, but it is far from friendly territory.

The New York Times in the early 1960s was full of outposts of the non-Communist world, near and far. It was very unusual, in fact, for any foreign location, least of all a mountain village in a "back-water" like Vietnam, to make the *Times* if it could not be described as an outpost in the great struggle between the free world and communism. Much of the rhetoric of the cold war, as it appeared in the press in this period, was so strident that it appears absolutely lunatic to us today. But, at the time, it defined the limits of "responsible" political discussion, and pervaded the reporting of virtually every event that took place outside the borders of the United States. As we shall see in a moment, the power of this worldview, though it has been eroded, remains very great.

The cold war view of the world is a "geopolitical" view. One way to see what this means is to look at the role played by maps in the foreign reporting of the early 1960s, particularly in the *New York Times*'s "Week in Review." The use of maps in foreign reporting might seem an obvious technique, since most Americans have limited knowledge of geography. But maps like the ones that dominated "The Week in Review" during the 1960s, often spreading across eight columns when major events were taking place, were not there simply to show people where Berlin or Vietnam was located. Their function was to explain the meaning of the conflicts in question, and to impress upon the public their importance. The use of maps for this purpose goes back at least to World War II. Frank Capra's *War Comes to America,* for instance, used animated maps to explain to soldiers being sent to risk their lives around the world why Americans could not be indifferent to events far from their shores.

Maps are better, of course, at representing some things than others. They are good for representing nations as geographical entities or "strategic" locations, not so good at representing them as political, social, cultural, or historical ones. But it made sense during World War II to look at the world as though it were a giant game of Risk, in which nations were distinguished from one another only by the color of the armies that happened to be occupying them at any given moment. In a world war, great armies marching across borders rendered local politics irrelevant.

Twenty years later, for a complex set of domestic and international reasons, Americans were still looking at the world in more or

less the same terms. The article that accompanied one *Times* map
from 1964, written by Neil Sheehan, explained the "stakes" in
Southeast Asia like this:

> The American position in Asia is preserved by powerful naval
> and air forces that function through a system of interlocking
> bases on the islands of the Pacific and along the periphery of
> the Asian continent from Hawaii to Japan, Taiwan, the Phil-
> ippines and Thailand to Pakistan. These forces form a shield
> which protects friendly Asian countries and a sword which can
> strike at any time along thousands of miles of exposed Chinese
> coastline.
>
> Southeast Asia is crucial to this strategy because it lies
> directly athwart the American line of sea and air communica-
> tions between the Indian and Pacific oceans. The islands of
> Indonesia form a wall with narrow openings between the two
> bodies of water. The Strait of Malacca between Singapore and
> Sumatra is the third most important waterway in the world
> and its loss would be comparable to the loss of the Suez or
> Panama canals.

The story then went on to outline the Rube Goldberg process of
the "domino theory," represented in the map, that was assumed to
be the inevitable outcome of the "loss" of Vietnam—and which of
course we now know was nonsense.

What was excluded by the geopolitical worldview was any serious
attention to the internal politics or history of countries like Vietnam, Thailand, or Indonesia. The conflict in Vietnam, for example,
besides being a front in the "global struggle" between the United
States and the Communist powers, was also two other things: a
peasant rebellion against a semifeudal social order, and a part of the
continuing national struggle against foreign domination. Neither of
these aspects of the conflict received much attention in the American
press, preoccupied as it was with shields, swords, and strategic
waterways. The entire corpus of *New York Times* coverage from 1960
through 1963 contained two references, both very brief, to the
problem of land tenure. And as for the history of Vietnamese na-

tionalism, it disappeared in the cold war; one *Times* story described the French Indochina War as "a seven-and-a-half-year struggle between the French army and foreign inspired and supplied Communists."

What is the media's image of the world today? Let's consider two more recent maps. On October 25, 1985, following a Reagan speech at the United Nations, the *New York Times* ran a map titled "Reagan's Five Trouble Spots." It looked a lot like the old maps of the early 1960s. There was an important difference, though, which could be seen in the title: the view of the world contained in this map was *attributed* to Reagan. The *Times* stopped short of accepting Reagan's geopolitical view as its own.

Newsweek, on the other hand, ran a map titled "Pacific Power," which appeared as part of a cover story on the Philippines in November 1985, not long before the fall of Marcos. Here was a traditional geopolitical view of the "stakes" in the Philippines presented without attribution. The emphasis in the story itself was the same:

> Immediately at stake is the future of the two largest American military installations outside the United States. Sitting at the southwest edge of the Pacific Ocean, Clark Air Base and the Subic Bay Naval Station are ideally situated for projecting American strength into the South China Sea and the vital sea lanes that channel oil from the Persian Gulf to Japan. They also provide an effective counterweight to the rapid Soviet naval buildup at Camh Ranh Bay in Vietnam. The loss of the bases could alter the balance of power in the Pacific, jeopardize billions of dollars of American trade, shake the confidence of China and Japan—and possibly loosen their ties to the West. If the United States were forced out of the Philippines, says Rear Adm. Lewis Chatham . . . it would be tantamount to "abdicating the South China Sea to the Soviets."

Like its predecessors of the early 1960s, the *Newsweek* story said little about how Filipinos saw the "stakes" in their own political struggle.

In the early 1960s, a single world image dominated the international coverage of the American press. But Vietnam, détente, and the Sino-Soviet split weakened the iron grip of the cold war mindset. The 1980s are, therefore, a period of confusion: a number of different perspectives on the world coexist, often awkwardly, in the news columns. The cold war view surely remains the most powerful, particularly today, in the wake of Reagan's reelection and many years of effort to restore its dominance in American politics, carried out by political forces ranging from the far right of the Republican party to neoconservative Democrats. The Philippines, after all, would never have made it on the news agenda simply because its people were rebelling against a repressive government backed by the United States; only when it became a threat to the security of "the West" did it become newsworthy. The struggle of East against West remains the basic organizing principle in foreign affairs coverage.

There are, however, two other perspectives on world politics that have considerable influence on news coverage. The first I call the human rights perspective, since it rose to prominence during the period of the Carter administration when "human rights" became a major slogan of U.S. foreign policy. The second I call the Fortress America perspective. The two have sharply different political implications.

Here, for example, is an excerpt from another story on the Philippines, this one from the *New York Times Magazine,* November 3, 1985, reported by Steve Lohr:

> The shootout and chase in Southeastern Luzon was but one minor skirmish in the escalating warfare between Communist insurgents and the government of Ferdinand E. Marcos. . . . [C]omplacency has been replaced by alarm as the Communist rebellion has grown rapidly in the last couple of years, aided immeasurably by political and economic developments that have amplified the appeal of the radical alternative the guerrillas espouse. . . .
>
> The National Democratic Front advocates an anti-American foreign policy, demanding the removal of two large United States military facilities. . . . [M]ost analysts agree that their

loss would be a major setback to American security interests. . . .

Still, the leftist revolution gaining ground in the Philippines seems to be a home-grown phenomenon. It is a third-
world nationalist movement preaching non-alignment,
although critics point out that, as with the Sandinistas in
Nicaragua and other rebel movements elsewhere in the third
world, the N.P.A.'s true orientation may not be revealed until
it has succeeded in gaining power. Its revolutionary ideology
is borrowed from Marx, Lenin and Mao, but its leaders say
they are adamantly opposed to falling under the sway of any
superpower. Moving into the Soviet orbit, they insist, can
never be a part of their program.

The cold war worldview is front and center here. As the dominant
theme in America's post–World War II view of the world, reporters
rarely fail to pay obeisance to it. Still, Lohr's story is very different
from the *Newsweek* story. The writers of the *Newsweek* article did not
feel compelled to add even a brief reference to "critics" who might,
for example, argue that the ability of the United States to "project
its power" in the South China Sea was not the most important thing
at stake in the Philippines. Lohr, in contrast, presents the cold war
view of the Philippines as a particular interpretation which might
be open to question; most of the article, moreover, was concerned
with the way Filipinos of many different political perspectives saw
the causes of the conflict and the prospects for the future. (Here,
incidentally, is an example of journalism that combines narrative
and analysis. The story begins with a feature lead, reported from a
guerrilla camp on the island of Luzon, and is relatively rich in
particular people and settings.)

The human rights perspective is not so much a comprehensive
worldview, comparable to that of the cold war, as an insistence on
looking at each country to some degree on its own terms. This may
give it a disadvantage in competition with the cold war view, which
has the power of simplicity, making it easy for journalists to explain
local crises they may know little about to an audience they assume
will care little about those crises. "We assume that most of the

people we are reaching have 'zero knowledge and zero interest in the subjects we intend to cover,' " wrote ABC producer Av Westin, explaining why a 20/20 segment on Nicaragua began by telling the audience, "The Cubans are there and the Russians are coming."

> There has to be something that will relate the story to the basic concerns of the television viewer. . . . The simplest way is to tie it to American interests. . . . Central America is just south of our borders; Cuban interests and other dangerous forces are at work there. An understanding of that locale in terms of American national security makes it all the more important for the distracted viewer to pay attention.

For the most part, it is in prestige papers, usually in reports from correspondents in the field, that one finds reporting from the human rights perspective. In Washington reporting and in reporting in smaller papers and on television and radio, the cold war view dominates more strongly, though it jostles for space with another very simple world image that has developed since Vietnam, that of Fortress America.

Consider the recent surge in reports on terrorism. Often, of course, terrorist incidents are connected with cold war politics, as when the Reagan administration speaks of the Soviet Union "exporting terrorism." But, typically, this is not the case. In the *USA Today* story, mentioned above, that ran under the head "Ship Killing: 'Get Those SOBs,' " there was no mention of Communist countries or cold war themes. In television reports on the Beirut hijacking earlier in 1985, similarly, cold war themes were for the most part absent. On CBS, for instance, while the hijacking crisis continued and four American Marines were killed in El Salvador, the news was full of phrases like "prelude written in blood to a volume of terrorist violence against the United States." There was no mention, however, of East-West conflict.

There was also no mention, in either the *USA Today* or CBS reports, of the fact that in both the Middle East and El Salvador, the United States had intervened militarily, taking sides in civil or national conflicts. "Anti-USA terrorist acts" appear in this kind of reporting as essentially without any political context. And the world appears not as a great global struggle between West and East, nor (as in the human rights perspective) as a decentered set of nations, each with its own particular problems, but as a hostile sea in which America struggles for survival against waves of irrational hatred.

This worldview is never really articulated explicitly as a framework for understanding the world. But it is implicit in a great deal of news coverage. In a sense, it has been around for a long time. Third World critics of the Western media have long noted, correctly, that the Third World rarely appears in the news unless a political or natural disaster of some sort is taking place. But it was in the 1970s, with the Arab oil embargo and above all the Iran hostage crisis, that the Fortress America view began to gain prominence. (Even before the hostage crisis, a *Time* cover story on the Iranian revolution bore the title "Iran: Anarchy and Exodus," over a picture of a man with a gun trampling the American flag.)

The Fortress America view is most prominent in media directed at a mass audience assumed to be uninterested in politics, whether it is a downscale mass audience ("Ron Raps Misfit Outlaw Nations" was a recent *Daily News* head) or an upscale mass audience of the sort *USA Today* hopes to build. In part, this is because these media, including television, personalize most news, and the Fortress America perspective is more personal than geopolitical, focusing, for example, less on global politics than on the injustice done to particular victims of terrorism and the menacing persona of the masked terrorist or fanatical revolutionary. The *Chicago Tribune*—which like most metropolitan papers falls somewhere between the "mass" press and the "prestige" press, led one story on the December 1985 terrorist attack at the Rome airport like this:

> ROME—Four Palestinian terrorists who staged a massacre at Rome's Leonardo DaVinci Airport on Friday drugged themselves before they set out on their mission, authorities said Friday night.

The group that carried out this particular attack is indeed considered fanatical, motivated more by a desire for revenge than by any coherent political strategy. But its rise to prominence has political causes, closely related to the policies of "civilized" countries. By putting the emphasis on drugs rather than politics, however, the *Tribune* story merges the Rome attack into a general stereotype of "senseless violence" that appears to surround the United States.

A sensational lead like the *Tribune*'s is not going to appear in the *New York Times* or *Los Angeles Times*. But in more subtle ways, the Fortress America image is present at this level of the press as well. The sheer volume of high-emphasis coverage of terrorist attacks against Americans is perhaps its most important manifestation in recent years. These attacks can produce multicolumn heads for days on end, while the deaths of many other civilian victims of political violence, often in wars in which the United States is deeply involved, in Central America, for instance, or Angola or Kampuchea, go unreported. This kind of ethnocentrism is neither new nor unique to the U.S. press. But in America after Vietnam and the Iran hostage crisis, it seems particularly significant, as a contributor to a growing national persecution complex.

Consider, finally, the following, from a March 1984 series on Central America in the *Los Angeles Times* ("a look at the turmoil in America's backyard"):

> Now, the United States finds itself immersed in Central American wars without winners, elections without mandates and misery without end. It laments a revolution gone astray in Nicaragua and struggles to head off another in El Salvador. And it recoils from abuses of human rights by allies for whom repression and killing are time-honored tools of authority.
>
> With huge infusions of arms, money and ideas, the United States now seeks to redress Central America's historical imbalances, because it is right, they say in Washington, and because it is important.

Like much coverage of Central America, this story, by William Montalbano (whose Central America coverage we encountered above), has elements of all three American worldviews. "The roots of Central American tumult are home grown if, indeed, Soviets and Cubans try to manipulate them to their own advantage," Montalbano wrote in the same piece, invoking both the cold war and human rights perspectives (he also reported on Central American memories of the history of American intervention). But the dominant image was of the United States "caught up" in the violence of the Third World, trying to help other people straighten out the mess they had made of their own countries, but risking, to quote Montalbano's last line, being "cruelly manipulated by [the] aftermath." This same view is reflected more subtly in a great many reports on political crises in the Third World, as when a story on the Philippines (again from the *Los Angeles Times*), under the head "Decline of Marcos Poses Ticklish Dilemma for U.S.," centered around the American efforts to head off "chaos" (a euphemism for "revolution"?) by encouraging the Marcos government to institute reforms.

Montalbano's story had a Central America dateline, the other a Washington dateline. but each reported its respective political crisis primarily from the point of view of U.S. officials, as a "ticklish dilemma" for the United States; and each implicitly portrayed a world teetering on the brink of chaos which only the wise and benevolent United States could hold at bay.

The Role of Journalism in a Very Large World

One of the basic conditions of modern life is that we live in worlds too large to be known directly. The evolution of the newspaper is intimately connected with this fact. Newspapers arose in the trading cities of Europe at the dawn of the age of capitalism and imperialism, as a source of information for merchants whose interests extended far beyond the communities in which they lived their daily lives. And the press rose to prominence as a social institution as the development of the city, the nation-state, and a highly interdependent world political and economic system thrust individuals into a world they could know only indirectly.

How well does the modern American newspaper put people in touch with the larger world around them? In a way, very well indeed. A typical edition of the *New York Times* will contain, in the front section alone, news from about thirty cities in fifteen to twenty countries around the world, tens of thousands of words of information gathered by professional correspondents with high standards of accuracy and impressive access to whomever they might wish to question, from the meek to the mighty. A major metropolitan newspaper contains, in fact, far more information about the world around it than most people can possibly consume.

But at another level, the newspaper is a very inadequate means of contact with a complex world. Two problems seem to me most important. First, places, whether they are neighborhoods or nations, generally appear in the news in highly abstract terms. Iran was "spinning out of control"; now the Philippines are a "ticklish dilemma" for Washington; this neighborhood is "gentrifying" and that one is "decaying." But what it means to live in these places, what they are like as settings for human action, we do not usually learn. American journalism would benefit a good deal from a little more human depth, and one way to achieve that is to pay attention to the settings in which things happen—though as we have seen, particular settings must be seen in their larger context, or "feature" reporting can become simply a vehicle for stereotyping or reducing events to narrow personal terms.

Second, journalists need to take greater responsibility for the general images of the world they convey along with news of specific events. Most news stories answer the question "where"—or any of the five W's, at many levels. In the typical Washington story on foreign affairs, for instance—like the "ticklish dilemma" story on the Philippines—"where" is Washington, "who" is various government officials, "what" is that those officials said something, and so on. But a story like this also tells us, among other things, "who" we are as Americans, and "where" we are in the sense of what kind of world surrounds us. How these larger questions are answered is probably much more important than the who-what-when-where-why of particular events, which will after all be quickly forgotten. But it is not something journalists think much about. To a large extent, it comes about as an unforeseen consequence of other things journalists and the news organizations that employ them are doing: *USA Today* is trying to build a particular kind of audience to sell to national advertisers; the Pentagon correspondent is trying to cover his assigned beat; the editor of the series on Central America is looking for a catchy formulation that will "sell" it to the average reader—"turmoil in America's backyard." But whether they like it or not, journalists are not simply reporters—that is, people who convey information. They are teachers, preachers, and ideologists: they tell us how to see and understand the world. It is a role that both they and we, the readers, should keep in mind more often.

*T*he Dark Continent
of
American Journalism

JAMES W. CAREY

> **M**en can do nothing without
> the make-believe of a beginning. Even Sci-
> ence, the strict measurer, is obliged to start
> with a make-believe unit, and must fix on a
> point in the stars' unceasing journey when
> his sideral clock shall pretend that time is at
> Nought. . . . No retrospect will take us to
> the true beginning: and whether our pro-
> logue be in heaven or on earth, it is but a
> fraction of that all-presupposing fact with
> which our story sets out.
> —GEORGE ELIOT, *Daniel Deronda*

Journalists are writers of stories and, after hours, tellers of stories as
well. The stories they tell are of stories they missed, stories they
got, stories they scooped, and cautionary little tales that educate
the apprentice to the glories, dangers, mysteries, and desires of the
craft. One such story—one that might be called the "quest for

146

the perfect lead"—features Edwin A. Lahey, a legendary reporter of the *Chicago Daily News*. Like most stories invoking legends, it is perhaps apocryphal, but its significance is less in its truth than in the point it attempts to make.

The story begins with a celebrated murder case of 1924, the Leopold-Loeb case. Nathan Leopold and Richard Loeb were teenage graduate students at the University of Chicago when they killed fourteen-year-old Bobby Franks in an attempt to commit the perfect crime. They made one mistake—a pair of Leopold's eyeglasses was found at the scene of the crime. They were arrested, brought to trial, and defended by the famous barrister Clarence Darrow. He had them plead guilty but successfully argued against the death penalty. Both were sentenced to life terms for the murder plus ninety-nine years for the kidnapping.

Nathan Leopold was paroled in 1958 and finished his life in Puerto Rico doing volunteer medical work. Richard Loeb was killed in Stateville Penitentiary in 1936 after making a homosexual advance toward another prisoner. Eddie Lahey, who covered the story for the *Daily News*, began his report with this lead:

Richard Loeb, the well-known student of English, yesterday ended a sentence with a proposition.

Even if invented, the well-knownness of the story tells us something of the imagination and desires of American journalists. What makes the lead so gorgeous is not only the way in which it encapsulates most of the elements of the news story—the five W's and the H—but does so through a delightful play on words—journalistic prose brushing up against poetry, if only in the ambiguity it celebrates. The lead also illustrates a necessary condition of all good journalism: a profound collaboration between the writer and his audience.

Lahey marks this collaboration by the assumptions he makes about the knowledge his audience brings to the story: that they were constant readers who would remember Richard Loeb as an actor in a twelve-year-old drama; that they would remember who Loeb was at the time of the 1924 crime and therefore catch the irony of the "well-known student of English"; that they could appreciate from the drills of schoolmasters the play on preposition and proposition; and, finally, they would grasp the dual meaning of "sentence" in the sentence.

If the assumptions Lahey makes about his audience and the cleverness of his language set this lead apart, the desire it expresses and the elements contained within it make it emblematic of all journalism. All writing, all narrative art depends upon dramatic unity, bringing together plot, character, scene, method, and purpose. The distinctive and tyrannical aspect of daily journalism is the injunction that the elements be assembled, arrayed, and accounted for in the lead, the topic sentence, or at best—here is where the inverted pyramid comes in—the first paragraph. The balance of the story merely elaborates what is announced at the outset. (The long, often interminable stories of the *Wall Street Journal,* and many similar feature stories, are the exception; they, as T. S. Eliot said of Swinburne, diffuse their "meaning very thinly throughout an immense verbal spate.")

In Lahey's lead, the character, as is usual with American journalism, has pride of place: Richard Loeb is both the subject of the story and the sentence. The scene, when and where, is given in the Stateville dateline (conveniently both a place *and* a prison) and in the commonest word in any lead, "yesterday." The plot, the what, is cleverly implied, though left undeveloped, by the action and reaction—"ended a sentence with a proposition." Only the how is omitted from the lead (he was killed with a razor) and awaits another sentence.

And where is the why, the explanation of the act, the elucidation of the purposes, however misaligned, of the actors? Why did Richard Loeb make an advance, if indeed he did? Why did James Day, for that was his name, murder Richard Loeb, if that is what he did? No one, certainly not Eddie Lahey, knew. The why was merely an insinuation. It would be established, if at all, only by the courts. James Day, in fact, was acquitted on grounds of self-defense. Was it all an elaborate mistake, a behavioral ballet of misunderstood intentions? Lahey merely insinuates a why—he appeals to his readers' commonsense knowledge of what goes in in prisons, of what men are like in captivity. We must read the why into the story rather than out of it: Richard Loeb as a prisoner of sexual desire as well as of the prison itself.

The omission of the how and the insinuation of the why is absolutely unremarkable: indeed, it is the standard practice of daily journalism. How could it be otherwise? At one level, how merely answers the question of technique: in this case, the killing was accomplished with a razor. In other cases, how tells us that interest rates were lowered by increasing the money supply, the football victory was achieved via a new formation, the political candidate won through superior precinct organization. The how is clearly of less importance than the what and, in our culture, the who, and can be relegated safely to subsequent sentences and paragraphs.

At another, and deeper, level, answering how requires detailing the actual sequence of acts, actors, and events that leads to a particular conclusion. How fills in a space; it tells us how an intention (the why) becomes an accomplishment (the what). How puts the reader in touch with the hard surfaces of human activity, the actual set of contingent circumstances. Loeb did this; Day did that—a blind chain of events, finally detailed for a jury, leading to a hideous outcome. When the description becomes fine-grained enough, how merges into why: a description becomes an explanation.

Why answers to the question of explanation. It accounts for events, actions, and actors. It is a search for the deeper underlying factors which lie behind the surfaces of the news story. "A story is worthless if it doesn't tell me why something happened," says Allan M. Siegal, news editor of the *New York Times*. Well, Mr. Siegal goes too far. If we threw out all the stories in the *Times* that failed to answer the question "why," there wouldn't be much newspaper left beyond the advertisements. Nonetheless, the why element attempts to make things sensible, coherent, explicable. It satisfies our desire to believe that the world, at least most of the time, is driven by something other than blind chance.

How and why are the most problematic aspects of American journalism: the dark continent and invisible landscape. Why and how are what we most want to get out of a news story and are least likely to receive or what we must in most cases supply ourselves.

Both largely elude and must elude the conventions of daily journalism, as they elude, incidentally, art and science. Our interest in "what's new," "what's happening," is not merely cognitive and aesthetic. We want more than the facts pleasingly arranged. We also want to know how to feel about events and what, if anything, to do about them. If they occur by luck or blind chance, that is a kind of explanation, too. It tells us to be tragically resigned to them; indeed, luck and chance are the unannounced dummy variables of journalistic thought, as they are of common sense. We need not only to know but to understand, not only to grasp but to take an attitude toward the events and personalities that pass before us. But to have an understanding or an attitude depends upon depth in the news story. Why and how attempt to supply this depth, even if honored every day largely in the breach.

The fact that news stories seldom make sense in this larger context is the most frequent, punishing, and uncharitable accusation made of daily journalism. Listen to one comment, this about daily reporting from Washington, among the many that might be cited:

> The daily news coverage travels over surfaces of words and events, but it rarely reaches deeper to the underlying reality of *how* things actually happen. Its own conventions and reflexes, in large measure, prevent the news media from doing more. Until this changes too, citizens will continue to be confused by the daily slices of news from Washington. Periodically, they will continue to be shocked by occasional comprehensive revelations of what's really happening, *deeper accounts which explain the events* they thought they understood.

This obsessive criticism of daily journalism is true as far as it goes, though it is unforgivably self-righteous. What it overlooks is that depth—the how and the why—are rarely in any individual story. They are properties of the whole, not the part; the coverage, not the account. To expect the dramatic unity of a three-act play in a twelve-paragraph story in a daily newspaper is to doom oneself to perpetual disappointment. But if a story can be kept alive in the news long enough, it can be fleshed out and rounded off. Journalists devote much of their energy to precisely that: keeping significant events afloat long enough so that interpretation, explanation, and thick description can be added as part of ongoing development. Alas, management and the marketing department devote much of their energy to precisely the opposite—making each front page look like a new chapter in human history.

Journalism must be examined as a corpus, not as a set of isolated stories. The corpus includes not only the multiple treatments of an event within the newspaper—breaking stories, follow-ups, news analysis, interpretation and background, critical commentary, editorials—but also the other forms of journalism that surround, correct, and complete the daily newspaper: television coverage, documentary and docudrama, the newsweeklies and journals of opinion and, finally, book-length journalism. It is a decade after the Vietnam War that its why is being established in books such as Loren Baritz's *Backfire*. The story of busing and racial desegregation in Boston—the how and the why—cannot be found in the *Boston Globe*'s massive coverage that won the paper a Pulitzer Prize. The story wasn't remotely complete until the publication of J. Anthony Lukas's *Common Ground,* though even that remarkable book subordinated the why of the busing story to the how—to the close-grained, personified flow of events. The story behind the story was that there was no story at all. All the standard explanations—racism, bureaucratic incompetence, political manipulation, journalistic irresponsibility—ebb away under the relentless detail of Lukas's narrative. Similarly, the story of apartheid in South Africa can never be adequately described or explained in the *New York Times* no matter how many stories are devoted to it or how relentlessly Anthony Lewis bangs away at it in his columns. Joseph Lelyveld's *Move Your Shadow* deepens our understanding beyond that provided in breaking stories of this riot or that, this government action or that, but it hardly explains either the origins or trajectory of that political system. If anything, the book makes apartheid politically more ambiguous, as it deepens our moral revulsion.

Journalism is, in fact, a curriculum. Its first course is the breaking stories of the daily press. There one gets a bare description: the identification of the actors and the events, the scene against which the events are played out and the tools available to the protagonists. Intermediate and advanced work—the fine-grained descriptions and interpretations—await the columns of analysis and interpretation, the weekly summaries and commentaries, and the book-length expositions. Each part of the curriculum depends on every other part.

It is a weakness of American journalism that the curriculum is so badly integrated and cross-referenced that each story starts anew as if no one had ever touched the subject before. It is also a weakness of American journalism that so few of the students ever get beyond the first course. But keep things in perspective. It is similarly a weakness, say, of American social science that the curriculum is incoherent and badly cross-referenced and so few of the students take more than the introductory course. It is worse. Most students think the introductory course is the curriculum, and this naive assumption is reinforced by the pretensions of teachers and textbook writers.

The weaknesses of American journalism are systemic; they are of a cloth with the weaknesses of American institutions generally, including education. Both journalism and education assume the constant student and the constant reader. American journalism assumes the figure who queues up every day for his dose of news and beyond that the commentary, analysis, and evidence that turn the "news" into knowledge. American education assumes the "constant student" who engages in lifelong learning; who, unsatisfied by the pieties and simplicities of Sociology I, goes on to explore subjects in depth and detail and along the way acquires a mastery of theory and evidence. This is both wrong and self-serving. But, to rephrase Walter Lippmann, more journalists and scholars have been ruined by self-importance than by liquor.

I

Many of the relations between the course and curriculum of American journalism, and many of the problems of description and explanation, are exemplified by an episode within the "big story" of recent years, the story of the American economy. Since at least 1980, we have been treated to a daily saga of runaway budget deficits, high unemployment, tax reform and reductions, roller-coaster stock market prices, corporate takeovers and consolidations, mounting trade deficits, rapidly rising military expenditures, and high, though moderating, interest rates.

An instructive episode in this larger story opened in January 1982 when William Greider, then of the *Washington Post,* published a long essay in *The Atlantic* entitled "The Education of David Stockman." The piece was based on eighteen "off-the-record" interviews with the then director of the Office of Management and Budget taped during the first nine months of the presidency of Ronald Reagan. The essay revealed Stockman's growing doubts about the wisdom of the economic policy Reagan was pursuing. Stockman early recognized that no matter how cleverly numbers were massaged, the president's economic policy would produce massive budget deficits and the economic stimulus from tax reduction would not generate sufficient revenue to offset increased expenditures for defense. The doctrines of supply-side economics on which Reagan had conducted his successful campaign were, in Stockman's estimation, naively optimistic or "voodoo economics," as George Bush had called them during the heat of the Republican primaries. The supply-side tax reduction of Ronald Reagan turned out to be no different from the demand-side tax reduction of President John Kennedy, except it was much more skewed toward the rich and powerful. Reagan's economic policy was a return to traditional Republican "trickle down" economics that helped the poor by first benefiting the rich.

Greider's essay revealed in stark terms the considerable pulling and hauling within the administration and Congress over economic policy. It underscored the compromises and trade-offs, the caving in to special interests, the triumph of expediency over principle that is inevitable in putting together a revenue and expenditure program. It set out the terms on which the private debate among presidential advisers was conducted and defined in "brutal terms" the genuine problems which Congress and the president would have to confront. It took us behind the calm exterior of the federal bureaucracy into a war of conflicting opinions where political choices were made amid ambiguity and uncertainty. To a certain extent, it

demystified the process of budget-making by demonstrating that
the experts had no magic wand or profound insight into the economy. They turned out to be pretty much like everyone else: confused about what was going on in the economy; badly divided
among themselves as to remedies; not much more in control of the
situation than the rankest amateurs. The piece revealed as well, at
least as Greider saw it, an awesome paradox: Reagan's stunning
legislative victories, which had dominated the news during the first
months of his term, trapped him in the awesome fiscal crisis with
which we still live. At least one of the roots of the paradox was in
the Greider-Stockman revelation that the one impregnable, off-
limits part of the budget was defense. This was the biggest peacetime arms buildup in the history of the republic—one which in five
years would more than double the Pentagon's annual budget.

Despite the picture of conflict, indecision, and uncertainty over
economic policy the *Atlantic* essay revealed, Reagan himself presented a confident image on television and in the newspaper: an
image of fiscal control and responsibility, of a new era of stable
growth, balanced budgets, stock market expansion, and lowered
inflation: a calm and eloquent reassurance despite privately held
doubts of many of his advisers, including Stockman.

For anyone familiar with bureaucracies, Greider's article rang
true, particularly in contrasting the smooth and reassuring exterior
of certainty and an interior space of policy-making dominated by
conflict and disarray. But did the article explain anything? Hardly.
It did account for Stockman's position on economic policy by showing something of the ideological commitments from which it derived. The essay, however, was primarily an answer to the question
"how," a thick description of the actual process of policy-making,
an etching of the space between intention and accomplishment that
eludes so much of daily journalism. Greider's publisher, E. P. Dutton, described the essay this way when it reprinted it in book form:
"*The Education of David Stockman* is a narrative of political action
with overtones of tragedy as the idealistic young conservative re-
former discovers the complexities of the political system and
watches as his moral principles are undermined by the necessities of
compromise." It sounds like a soap opera; indeed, the sentence has

the cadence of the introduction to the old radio soap opera "Our Gal Sunday." And it is, in a way, a soap opera. While the essay is flat-footed and straightforward, it does have a strong narrative line. It opens with its one literary twist: a tour of the Stockman farm in western Michigan, situating the protagonist in his native habitat, among the conditions and people that formed him. The essay thereby sets up a contrast between a quasi-heroic protagonist who has learned solid ideological lessons in the outlands and the administration insiders who defeat him in the cloakrooms and boardrooms of Washington. The essay's revelatory power is in its consistent narrative focus—from David Stockman's point of view—and a dramatic line—from Michigan innocence to Washington defeat—which, while an exaggeration, makes the entire episode coherent and the descriptive detail informing.

But the story had an additional twist. Although the Greider-Stockman conversations were "off-the-record" (not for publication in any form), certain details were put on "background" (for anonymous publication only). *Washington Post* reporters pursued the leads the private discussions opened up and published the results. They found White House sources to corroborate important information in the Stockman interviews so they could write independent stories. Other Washington journalists were covering and writing about these same matters. Therefore, the essential facts in the Greider essay appeared in the daily press attributed to those ubiquitous characters of Washington journalism: administration sources, senior officials, senior White House aides, key congressional aides, Defense Department advisers, etc. The key point, in Greider's mind, was that the *Atlantic* essay contained nothing that was not widely known among Washington journalists, nothing that had not already appeared in the daily press. Nonetheless, the article created one of those brief storms typical of a Washington season: a squall of comment, charges, and recriminations that dissipates as quickly as it appears. Stockman was called into the president's woodshed for a licking and emerged striking his breast intoning many *mea culpas*. Greider was pilloried for betraying principles of the press. He had, so it was charged, withheld information from his own paper and the public to publish it where it would get more attention.

When the *Atlantic* article appeared, Greider was transformed from a reporter to a source: he was now a who, the subject of a story. Some reporters who called for interviews obviously hadn't read the piece and wanted Greider to summarize it. They showed little interest in the substance of the article—the depiction of the process of policy-making, the specific policies developed, the paradox of legislative triumph and fiscal crisis—but much interest in the specific personalities inhabiting the story. They wanted to know about motive: Why did Stockman give the interviews? Why did Greider conduct them? Why did Stockman tell Greider the things he did? Why did Greider withhold such information from his own paper?

Greider tried to explain the ground rules for the interviews and the content of the article, but he found that sophisticated explanations did not hold up well in telephone interviews with reporters writing to deadline and in search of a pithy lead. Press accounts of the article by journalists who had read it were "brutal summaries" that sacrificed psychological nuance, character, plot, subtlety, and ambiguity—all those qualities which Greider thought made his piece distinctive and useful.

As I said earlier, the perplexing thing about the controversy was that the essential information contained in the *Atlantic* piece had been earlier reported in the daily press, though attributed to "senior budget officials." All Greider had done was to thicken the narrative and put Stockman's name in place of the anonymous source. It was now Stockman revealing his private doubts about the administration program. But if the information was already available, why the controversy? The answer is simple: in American journalism, names make news, and explanations in the news pretty much come down to the motives of the actors in the political drama.

Greider concluded that the conventions of daily journalism "serve only a very limited market—the elite audience of Washington insiders—while obscuring things for the larger audience of ordinary citizens." Such insiders can read names into the anonymous sources and can ferret out motives from the interests lying behind the innocence of the text. The text may answer how and why, but in ways accessible only to those who already know the rules of Washington and the reportorial game, those who already understand the background of government policy-making: the players and interests at loose in the process, the alliances that exist between officials and reporters. Greider came to believe that his *Atlantic* article refuted the simple and shallow version of reality that the news created when complex episodes were carved into daily slices. He also rediscovered an old lesson of journalism, a lesson recently restated by the journalist-turned-historian Robert Darnton: journalists write not for the public but for one another, for their editors, for their sources, and for other insiders who are part of the specialized world they are reporting. It is in this context that the deeply coded text of the daily news story develops. Such stories provide a forum in which "participants in political debates can argue with each other in semi-public disguises, influencing the flow of public dialogue and the content of elite opinion without having to answer directly for their utterances." Journalists and other insiders become so adept at the deep reading of veiled messages that they forget they are unintelligible to the ordinary reader, or, if intelligible, convey an entirely different message. Washington news is valued precisely because it is an insider's conversation, one interest group speaking to another, with reporters acting as symbol brokers coding stories into a conversation only the sophisticated few can follow. Greider summarizes:

> This inside knowledge provides a continuing subtext for the news of Washington; very little of it is conveyed in intelligible terms to the uninformed. The "rules" prevent that, and so also do the conventions of the press, how a story is written, and what meets the standard definition of what is news. The insiders, both reporters and government officials, will read every news story with this subtext clearly in mind. Other readers are left to struggle with their own translation.

The *Atlantic* article broke through this coded text; it presented the "unvarnished private dialogue of government" that was supposed to remain private, implicit, known only to insiders capable of penetrating the bland, reassuring rhetoric of the official news story and the official handout. By making the private public, the Greider piece diminished the value of every insider's knowledge and revealed the rules of the game to a wider audience. Greider attempted, in short, to give a lesson in how to read the daily news and how to add description and explanation to accounts that regularly omit them. In doing so, his piece contradicted the reassuring image of order and progress conveyed by breaking stories.

What are the lessons to be learned from the Greider-Stockman episode? First, daily journalism offers more description and explanation than one would ordinarily think, but they are not transparently available on the surface of the text. Despite the commitment of journalists to objectivity and facticity, much of what they have to report is obliquely stated, coded deeply into the text, and recoverable only by "constant readers" who can decode the text and who bring to it substantial knowledge of politics, bureaucracy, and, as here, budgets. Second, the most important descriptions and explanations of journalism are lost when they are sliced into daily fragments, thin tissue cultures of reality, disconnected from a narrative framework. Third, the reader can discover such descriptions and explanations only when the separate stories are reintegrated into a more coherent framework and when the episodes of the news have a narrative structure that contains elements of drama, nuances of character, and precise chronological order. Finally, the episode demonstrates how overwhelmingly dependent American journalism is on explaining events by attributing motives. What the essay displays throughout are the motives, purposes, and intentions of the actors in the budget struggle and, then, in the newspaper accounts, the motives of Stockman and Greider themselves. The origins of these habits, including the habit of relying on motives for explanations, is revealed in some commonplace history of American journalism.

II

A *Wall Street Journal* radio ad says something like the following: "The business section of the daily newspaper will give you the 'Who, What, When, and Where' but only the *Wall Street Journal* gives you the 'Why and How.' " This is the hyperbole of advertising, of course, but the claim holds some truth. The *Journal*'s feature stories are not written against a deadline, and consume luxurious amounts of space. They allow for a certain lushness of detail and description and use a variety of literary devices, particularly person-ification, that give a certain illusion of explanation. At the other extreme, the staple of the *Journal* is the endless columns of price quotations from the financial and commodity markets and these numbers are, in a way, the archetype of the news story. The num-bers tell a sophisticated reader what has happened (the market is down), how he should feel about it (that's bad), and what he should do about it (it's time to get out). The reader can extract a description and explanation from the statistics. The numbers merely signal an event; the description and explanation are within the knowledge of the reader, and this knowledge constitutes the paper's collaborative counterforce.

What is unexceptional about the *Journal* ad is its heroic and naive realism. The ad assumes that the stories in the *Journal* record a transparent truth of an objective reality. Perhaps this naive realism still flourishes only among journalists. The essays in this book argue, to the contrary, that the stories written by journalists mani-fest the reality-making practices of the craft rather than some objec-tive world. Journalists need not apologize for this. All writing, even scientific writing, is a form of storytelling aimed at imposing coher-ence on the otherwise chaotic flow of events. That is the point, after all, of the George Eliot quote that heads this essay. Even scientists must start with the make-believe of a beginning: the fatal pause between the tick and the tock, a moment of unfilled silence in which the scientist's story of the universe can begin. Journalism, then, is a fiction in the sense that all stories are fictions. They are made by the journalist out of the conventions, procedures, ethos, and devices of his craft. The language of journalism is not transparent to nature or the world. Journalists speak an invented code, often, as the Greider-Stockman story indicates, a densely compacted code, and in this sense participate in a making, a fiction. As I previously suggested, the raw data of journalism are always slipping away toward the story forms, the genres, the structures of consciousness with which the journalist tries to grasp hold of the suicide at the bridge or the bureaucrat in the policy conference. The raw materials of the making, the events, the data of journalism, maintain their own unblessed existence outside the news columns. Well, one must retreat. Press conferences, pseudoevents, and media events are now so inextricably knotted into the world that the issue is as complicated as our sex lives. Nonetheless, journalism, like all fictions, is a creative and imaginative work, a symbolic strategy, a way of rendering the world reassuringly comprehensive or, failing that, of assigning events to fate, luck, and chance. Journalism, like everything else, often fails, but journalists do not accept, because we will not tolerate, mystery for very long, particularly if it involves politics and economics, matters of ultimate threat or reassurance. So the initially unintelligible is bashed at until it is in some kind of shape.

News is not, then, some transparent glimpse at the world. News registers, on the one hand, the organizational constraints under which journalists labor: the processes by which beats are defined, stories selected and edited, the random eruption of events reduced to routine procedure, the editorial resources of a publisher allocated, and "authorities" defined and consulted. The news registers, on the other hand, the literary forms and narrative devices journalists regularly used to manage the overwhelming flow of events. These devices are partly economic and bureaucratic. They guarantee the production of a certain number of words and stories every day. They guarantee that the journalist, under the most outrageous circumstances of time and situation, can instantly turn an event into a story. These literary devices are tropisms; the journalist turns to them as a plant to light. Writing has to be virtually that automatic if he is to produce stories on demand. They guarantee that the daily newspaper will be full of news at a cost that ensures a product salable to advertisers and readers. There is a harmonics to journalism; the stories write themselves. Yet the stories slip away toward the literary devices and dramatic conventions that are part of the culture as a whole. If, for example, one can earn a profit selling "ideological stories" in European newspapers but cannot in the United States, it tells us, at the least, that the dramatic conventions of the ideological are not sufficiently resonant with American culture as a whole. They do not seem to get at the truth as we understand it.

The forms of American journalism are receptacles into which can be poured the disconnected data of everyday life. As Carlin Romano says, journalists present to the world not a mirror image of truth but a coherent narrative of the world that serves particular purposes. Even that must be amended. As a rule, the newspaper presents a disconnected and often incoherent narrative—in its individual stories and in its total coverage. If the newspaper mirrors anything, it is this disconnection and incoherence, though it contributes to and symbolizes the very condition it mirrors. In fact, journalism can present a coherent narrative only if it is rooted in a social and political ideology, an ideology that gives a consistent focus or narrative line to events, that provides the terminology for a thick description and a ready vocabulary of explanation.

The crucial events, the shaping influences, in the history of American journalism were those that stripped away this ideological context: the decline of the partisan press, the emergence of the penny papers, and the deployment of the telegraph as the nervous system of the news business.

The *Wall Street Journal* is, in a sense, the archetype of the American newspaper: a paper for a commercial class interested in and with an economic interest in the news of the day. The American newspaper of the eighteenth and early nineteenth centuries was a producer good for a commercial class rather than a consumer good for a consumer class. It reflected the economic, political, and cultural orientations of that class. News of the day was primarily news of the rudimentary and disjointed markets of early American capitalism: of prices, transactions, shipping, the availability of goods, and events which affected prices and availabilities in markets near and far. There was political news, too, but it was political news in a restricted sense: news that could influence the conduct of commerce, not news of every conceivable happening in the society. Much of what is today called news—burglaries, fires, for example —was inserted in the paper as paid advertisements; much of what is today called advertising—the availability of goods, for example —appeared in the news columns. It was no coincidence that the most popular name for American newspapers in 1800 was *The Advertiser*. But the word "advertising" had a special meaning: not the purchase of space but the unpurchased announcement of the availability of merchandise.

The commercial and trading elites and the papers and newsletters

representing their interests were central to fomenting conflict with
Britain when the crown hampered their commercial activities. Following independence, the commercial press retained its interest in
politics; that is, it "reported" on matters affecting the fate of merchants and traders. But this class was deeply divided over issues
such as the national bank. The partisan press, aligned with different
factions of the commercial class, gave venomous expression to these
differences. But the thing to remember is this: because the press
was organized around articulate economic interests, the news had
meaning, could be interpreted through and explained by those interests. A partisan press created and utilized an ideological framework that made sense of the news.

The second critical fact concerning the partisan press concerns
the matter of time. The cycle of business is the cycle of the day: the
opening and closing of trade. The press of the eighteenth and early
nineteenth centuries was not technologically equipped to report on
a timely, daily basis, but it shared with businessmen the understanding that time is of the essence of trade. As a result, the natural
epoch of journalism became the day: the cycle of work and trade for
a business class. The technological impetus in journalism has been
to coordinate the cycle of communication with the cycle of trade.

While journalism lives by cycles ranging upward from the hour,
its natural métier is the stories of the day, even if it recycles them
over longer or shorter units of time. Journalism is a daybook that
records the significant happenings of that day. Its time frame is not
posterity, and the journalists' flattering, self-protecting definition
of his work as the "first rough draft of history" does not alter that
fact. The archetype of journalism is the diary or account book. The
diary records what is significant in the life of a person for that day.
The business journal records all transactions for a given day. The
news begins in bookkeeping. Commerce lives by, begins and ends
the day with, the record of transactions on, say, the stock and
commodity markets. The news begins as a record of commercial
transactions and a tool of commerce. Every day there is news; every
day there are stories to be told because every day there is business
to be done and prices to be posted. In this sense, the origins of
journalism, capitalism, and bookkeeping are indissoluble.

In the 1830s, a cheap, daily popular press—a "penny press"—was created in the major cities. The penny press did not destroy the commercial press. The latter has continued down to this day not only in the *Wall Street Journal* and the *Journal of Commerce, Barron's* and *Business Week, Forbes* and *Fortune,* but in private newsletters and private exchanges that grew after the birth of the penny press. Such publications have edged closer to the popular press with the enormous expansion of the middle class. The *Wall Street Journal* doesn't call itself "the daily diary of the American dream" for nothing. But the penny press did displace the commercial-partisan press in the 1830s as the model of a daily newspaper.

While scholars disagree over the significance of the penny press, one can safely say three things about it. First, the penny press was a consumer good for a consumer society; it reflected all of society and politics, not just the world of commerce and commercial politics. The retreat from partisanship meant that any matter, however minor, qualified for space in the paper: the details not only of trade and commerce, but the courts, the streets, the strange, the commonplace. The penny papers were filled with the odd, the exotic, and the trivial. Above all, they focused on the anonymous individuals, groups, and classes that inhabited the city. They presented a panorama of facts and persons, a "gastronomy of the eye"; in another of Baudelaire's phrases, they were a "kaleidoscope equipped with consciousness."

Second, the penny press displaced not merely partisanship but an explicit ideological context in which to present, interpret, and explain the news. Such papers choked off, at least relatively, an ideological press among the working class. At its best, the penny press attempted to eliminate the wretched partisanship and factionalism into which the press had degenerated since the Revolution. It tried to constitute, through the more or less neutral support of advertising, an open forum in which to examine and represent a public rather than a merely partisan interest.

Third, the penny press imposed the cycle and habit of commerce upon the life of society generally. Because in business time is money, the latest news can make the difference between success and failure, selling cheap or selling dear. Time is seldom so important in noncommercial activity. The latest news is not always the best and most useful news. Little is lost if the news of politics or urban life is a little old. Nonetheless, the cycle and habit of beginning and ending the day by reading the latest prices was imposed on social activities generally. Beginning in the 1830s, the stories of society were told on a daily basis. The value of timeliness was generalized by the penny press into the cardinal value of journalism.

The events of journalism happen today. The morning reading of the *New York Times* is important because it establishes the salience of stories for the day. It also determines salience for the television networks, the newsmagazines, the journals of opinion issued weekly and monthly. And the stories of books begin in the announcements in news columns: a family named Clutter was murdered in Holcomb, Kansas, yesterday. With the penny press, all forms of writing became increasingly a parasite of "breaking news."

The telegraph cemented everything the "penny press" set in motion. It allowed newspapers to operate in "real time" for the first time. Its value was insuring that time became irrelevant for purposes of trade. When instantaneous market reports were available everywhere at the same moment, everyone was effectively in the same place for purposes of trade. The telegraph gave a real rather than an illusory meaning to timeliness. It turned competition among newspapers away from price, even away from quality, and onto timeliness. Time became the loss leader of journalism.

The telegraph also reworked the nature of written language and finally the nature of awareness itself. One old saw has it that the telegraph, by creating the wire services, led to a fundamental change in news. It snapped the tradition of partisan journalism by forcing the wire services to generate "objective" news that papers of any political stripe could use. Yet the issue is deeper than that. The wire services demanded language stripped of the local, the regional and colloquial. They demanded something closer to a "scientific" language, one of strict denotation where the connotative features of utterance were under control, one of fact. If a story were to be understood in the same way from Maine to California, language had to be flattened out and standardized. The telegraph, therefore, led to the disappearance of forms of speech and styles of journalism and storytelling—the tall story, the hoax, much humor, irony, and satire—that depended on a more traditional use of language. The origins of objectivity, then, lie in the necessity of stretching language in space over the long lines of Western Union.

Similarly, the telegraph eliminated the correspondent who provided letters that announced an event, described it in detail, and analyzed its substance. It replaced him with the stringer who supplied the bare facts. As the telegraph made words expensive, a language of spare fact became the norm. Telegraph copy had to be condensed to save money. From the stringer's notes, someone at the end of the telegraphic line had to reconstitute the story, a process that reaches high art with the newsmagazines: the story divorced from the storyteller.

If the telegraph made prose lean and unadorned and led to a journalism without the luxury of detail and analysis, it also brought an overwhelming crush of such prose to the newsroom. In the face of what was a real glut of occurrences, news judgment had to be routinized and the organization of the newsroom made factorylike. The reporter who produced the new prose displaced the editor as the archetype of the journalist. The spareness of the prose and its sheer volume allowed news, indeed forced news, to be treated like a commodity: something that could be transported, measured, reduced, and timed. News because subject to all the procedures developed for handling agricultural commodities. It was subject to "rates, contracts, franchising, discounts and thefts."

Together those developments of the second third of the nineteenth century brought a new kind of journalism, a kind that is still roughly the staple of our newspapers. But, as explained earlier, this new journalism made description and explanation radically problematic: "penny" and telegraphic journalism divorced news from an ideological context that could explain and give significance to events. It substituted the vague principle of a public interest for "class interest" as the criterion for selecting, interpreting, and explaining the news. It brought the newsroom a glut of occurrences that overwhelmed the newspaper and forced the journalist to explain not just something but everything. As a result, he often could explain nothing. By elevating objectivity and facticity into cardinal principles, the penny press abandoned explanation as a primary goal. Simultaneously, it confronted the reader with events with which he had no experience and no method with which to explain them. It filled the paper with human interest material that, however charming, was inexplicable. And, finally, it divorced the announcement of news from its analysis and required the reader to maintain constant vigilance to the news if he was to understand anything.

III

The conditions of journalistic practice and the literary forms journalists inherited together strictly limit the degree to which daily journalism can answer how and why. How something happens or how someone accomplishes something demands the journalist's close, detailed attention to the flow of facts which culminate in a happening. The dailiness and deadline of the newspaper and the television news show usually preclude the opportunity to adequately etch in the detail which intervenes between an intention and an accomplishment, a cause and its effect. Moreover, the journalist's typical tools, particularly the telephone interview, are inadequate to a task that demands far more varied resources. Journalists cannot subpoena witnesses; no one is required to talk to them. As a result, "how," the detail, must await agencies outside of journalism such as the grand jury, the common trial, the blue-ribbon commission, social surveys, congressional investigating committees, or other, more leisured and wide-ranging forms of journalistic inquiry: the extended series, magazine article, or book.

Explanation in daily journalism has even greater limits. Explanation demands that the journalist not only retell an event but account for it. Such accounting normally takes one of four forms: determining motives, elucidating causes, predicting consequences, or estimating significance. However, the canons of objectivity, the absence of a forum or method through which evidence can be systematically adduced, and the absence of an explicit ideological commitment on the part of journalists renders the task of explanation radically problematic, except under certain well-stipulated conditions.

First, the problem of objectivity. Who, what, when, and where are relatively transparent. Why is invisible. Who, what, when, and where are empirical. Why is abstract. Who, what, when, and where refer to phenomena on the surface of the world. Why refers to something buried beneath appearances. Who, what, when, and where do not mirror the world, of course. They reflect the reality-making practices of journalists. Answering such questions depends upon conventions that are widely shared, even if infrequently noted. The other essays in this volume attest to the conventionality of these elements. We no longer, for example, identify figures in the news by feminine nouns: poetess, Negress, Jewess, actress. The who, the identification, now obeys a different set of conventions which attempt to depress the importance of "race" and gender, conventions which journalists both use and legitimate. But for all the conventionality of who, what, when, and where, they are accessible and identifiable because our culture widely shares a gradient against which to measure them. As Michael Schudson's essay demonstrates, the notion of when, of time in journalism, is not as transparent as phrases like "recent," "immediate," or "breaking" seem to suggest. Nonetheless, time in journalism is measured against a standard gradient of tense, of past, present, and future, which is widely shared in the culture.

There is no accessible gradient for the measurement of causes, the assessment of motives, the prediction of consequences, or the evaluation of significance. No one has seen a cause or a consequence; motives are ghostly happenings in the head; and significance seems to be in the eye of the beholder. Explanations do not lie within events or actions. Rather, they lie behind them or are inferences or extrapolations that go well beyond the commonsense evidence at hand. Explanation, then, cuts against the naive realism of journalism with its insistence on objective fact.

The first injunction of journalists is to stay with the facts; facts provide the elements of the story. But causes, consequences, and motives are not themselves facts. Because journalists are above all else empiricists, the why must elude them. They lack a framework of theory or ideology from which to deduce evidence or infer explanations. To explain is to abandon journalism in the archetypal sense:

it is to pursue soft news, "trust me" journalism. Explanatory journalism is, to use an ugly phrase, "thumbsucker journalism": stories coming from the journalist's head rather than the facts.

Something is philosophically awry about all this, of course. While the first law of journalism is to stick to hard surfaces, the essays in this volume present enough evidence for the mushiness of all facts. The facts of the case are always elaborate, arbitrary cultural constructions through which who, what, when, and where are not only identified but judged, not only described but evaluated. But such constructions and identifications can be pinned down by ordinary techniques of journalistic investigation. Not so with why. For it, one must go outside the interview and the clip file. It drives one to the library, the computer, government documents, historical surveys. But there are no conventions to guide journalists in sifting and judging evidence from such sources and no forum in which conflicting evidence can be weighed.

More than the organization of the newsroom, the nature of journalistic investigations and the professional ideology of journalism suppress a journalism of explanation. The basic definitions of news exclude explanation from the outset. News focuses on the unusual, the nonroutine, the unexpected. Thus, it necessarily highlights events that interest us precisely because they have no explanation. This is part of the meaning of human interest: deviation from the accepted routine of ordinary life. News of novel events must strain causality and credibility. News is when man bites dog. Unfortunately, no one knows what possessed the man who bit the dog; even psychiatrists are not likely to be much help.

Much of journalism focuses on the bizarre, the uncanny, the inexplicable. Journalism ritualizes the bizarre; it is a counterphobia for overcoming objects of fear. Such stories of the bizarre, uncanny, horrible, and unfathomable are like roller coasters, prizefights, stock car races—pleasurable because we can be disturbed and frightened without being hurt or overwhelmed. Where would we be without stories of UFOs and other such phenomena, stories at once intensely pleasing and intensely disturbing? In the age of the partisan press, such stories were consigned to folklore, the oral tradition, and other underground modes of storytelling. With the penny press, they came into the open and took up residence in newspapers as the unexplained and unexplainable desiderata of our civilization.

The impossible French have even given such stories a name: *faits-divers*. This most easily translates as "fillers," but we might better render it idiomatically as "random, uncanny occurrences." Such stories, according to Roland Barthes, preserve at the very heart of modern society an ambiguity of the rational and the irrational, of the intelligible and the unfathomable. In his essay, Carlin Romano cited one such story: "Guest Drowns at Party for 100 Lifeguards." But think of some other newspaper staples: "Chief of Police Kills Wife"; "Psychiatrist's Son Commits Mayhem"; "Burglars Frightened Away by Other Burglars"; "Thieves Sic Their Police Dog on Night Watchman." We are here in the realm of perversity, chance, accident, coincidence. "Man and Wife Collide with One Another in Auto Accident"; "Father Runs Over His Child in the Driveway"; "Man Drinks Himself to Death at Party to Celebrate His Divorce." Every such story is a sign at once intelligent and indecipherable.

The factors of coincidence, unpredictability, and the uncanny float some events to the surface of the news from the many which fit a type, explaining why a few murders get reported of the many committed, a few accidents detailed of the many occurring. Consider this from the Associated Press:

A confirmed AIDS victim who allegedly spat on four police officers during a traffic arrest was charged Friday with assault with intent to murder.

John Richards of Davison, Ohio, was charged with the felony warrant because "it appears the man knows he has AIDS and was trying to transmit it by spitting on the officers," said Assistant Genesee County Prosecutor John McGraw.

What is going on here? This is of course the season for stories about AIDS because of the menacing potential of the disease. But what did Mr. Richards think he was up to? And what, even more, was going on with the police? It is precisely the bizarre and inexplicable quality of the event that makes it a story. It gives new mean-

ing to the phrase "deadly weapon"; it conjures up a time when our
saliva will be registered.

Or, consider the following from the *Chicago Sun-Times* of January
7, 1986:

Tale of True Love
He Expects Death, Gives Girlfriend His Heart

PATTERSON, Calif. (AP) A 15-year old boy who learned that
his girlfriend needed a heart transplant told his mother three
weeks ago that he was going to die and that the young woman
should have his heart.

Felipe Garza Jr., who his half-brother said had seemed to
be in perfect health, died Saturday after a blood vessel burst in
his head.

His family followed his wishes, and Felipe's heart was trans-
planted Sunday into Donna Ashlock.

His half-brother, John Sanchez, 20, said Felipe told their
mother, Maria, three weeks ago: "I'm going to die, and I'm
going to give my heart to my girlfriend."

This is the type of story that *faits-divers* defines; as a result, it
appeared everywhere: the straight press; the weekly tabloids; television news, national and local; the newsweeklies; even many of the
prestige papers. It is the generality of its distribution and the un-
canniness of its content that makes it so informing an example.
Naturally, as the story travels from the most to the least respectable
journal, the bizarre elements in the story become more pronounced.
But its appeal and significance are universal.

Stories like those cited appear in the daily press, where they are
oddment and filler. They are the main news of the tabloid weeklies.
In the *National Enquirer,* the *Star,* and the *Weekly World News,* the
limits of the bizarre are pushed out one standard deviation, but the
type is common to the press in general. From the tabloid weeklies:
"She Became Great Granny Three Times in One Day"; "Dog Eats
Boy's Nose"; "Chinese Genius is Only Five and Ready for College";
"I Won't Be a Fat Farm Flop—700 Pound Behemoth Vows." What
is filler in the straight press is feature in the tabloids. What is filler
in the evening news, often designed to give an upbeat if totally

improbable ending to a half hour of mayhem and melancholy, is feature for Charles Kuralt's "On the Road." As we shall see, the same instructive relation between the straight press and the weekly tabloids occurs in the realm of motives.

The world of the inexplicable contrasts sharply with the foreground of daily news, the world of politics and economics. In the latter domains, we are unwilling to leave events to chance or dismiss happenings as bizarre, mysterious, or coincidental. The world of politics and economics is a world of threat in which we can lose our lives, our possessions, our freedom, our entire sense of purpose. In that world, we seek reassurance that someone or something is in control. We are intolerant of mystery in politics even when politics is mysterious, for this is the sphere of the menacing. Whenever such threat and reward systems confront us, we demand explanation, coherence, significance, and intelligibility. So once we leave the realm of *faits-divers*, the how and why get answered by one device or another despite the limitations of daily journalism.

IV

We start from this proposition: when matters of fundamental importance surface in the news, they cannot be treated as secular mysteries and left unexplained. They must be accounted for, must be rendered sensible. The economy and the political system form the sacred center of modern society. With them, we are unwilling to sit about muttering "It's fate" or "So be it." We insist that the economy and the polity be explicable: a domain where someone is in control, or natural laws are being obeyed, or events are significant and consequential, or that despite all the bad news of the moment, the signs in the headlines augur well for the future.

The importance of economics and politics to each individual's life chances guarantees that people will come up with explanations— ideological explanations—even if the press and the politicians are silent on these issues. As a result, explanation is an arena of struggle within journalism, a struggle to control the natural ideological forces set in motion by the appearance of disturbing and perplexing events. The press explains such events by elucidating motives, dem-

onstrating causes, predicting consequences, or divining significance. The order of these forms of explanation is logical, not
chronological. Different events are explained in different ways; any
given story will mix these forms of explanation together; and the
same story will be subjected at different times to different forms of
explanation. But the order of explanation runs as follows: if you can
find a motive, state it; if you can't find a motive, search for a cause;
if you can't find a motive or a cause, look for consequences; if you
can find none of the above, read the tea leaves of the event for its
significance. Motive explanations, however, dominate American
journalism and create, as we shall see, all sorts of havoc.

To unpack these complicated matters, I will use one extended
example. In March 1985, the Department of Commerce issued its
monthly report on the balance of payments of the American economy. These monthly statements had regularly shown a deteriorating
American position in the international economy. The March statement was unexceptional; indeed, it was a considerable improvement
over the report of the previous October. Here is the AP story which
opened this chapter in the trade crisis:

> The nation's trade deficit climbed to $11.4 billion in Febru-
> ary, the worst showing since September, as export sales fell
> 7.7 percent, the government reported Thursday.
>   The deficit was 11 percent higher than the $10.3 billion
> deficit in January and was the biggest monthly imbalance
> since the $11.5 billion deficit in September, the Commerce
> Department said.

Then, after one more paragraph of description, the story offered
this unattributed explanation:

> The poor performance has been blamed in part on the dollar's
> high value, which makes U.S. goods more expensive and
> harder to sell overseas while whetting Americans' appetite for
> a flood of cheaper exports.

This explanation undoubtedly came from the Department of
Commerce briefing, but interestingly it did not carry the argument

a step further: the high value of the dollar could have been blamed on the large federal deficit, continuing high interest rates, the need for enormous federal borrowing, and the influx of foreign currency chasing investments.

The monthly stories of the trade deficit normally do not receive much attention beyond the business and financial press and usually disappear within a day or two. However, the March 1985 report showed, among other things, a further worsening of our trade balance with Japan. This story might have disappeared except that the voluntary import restrictions on Japanese automobiles were about to expire. The question on the political agenda was whether the import restrictions should be kept at the same level, raised, lowered, or eliminated altogether. Action on automobile import restrictions was but a prelude, however, to overall trade policy on a number of American products—shoes, textiles, steel—that had been faring badly in international trade. The Reagan administration generally supported free trade, but it was also negotiating with the Japanese to gain greater access to Japanese markets for American manufacturers of, among other things, telecommunications products. The second matter which made the March Commerce Department report of greater-than-normal significance was that planning was under way for an early May "economic summit" in Bonn, West Germany, between Japan, the United States, and the other major Western countries. At that conference, trade policy was to be a principal item of discussion.

The story of the balance of payments and trade policy was continuously at the "front" of the news from early March until it was pushed aside by the controversy surrounding President Reagan's visit to the Bitburg cemetery containing the graves of World War II German soldiers, including the burial sites of members of the SS. The trade story declined in prominence through an odd conjunction of circumstances: the attention to German-American relations symbolized by the cemetery visit offended President Mitterrand of France, who largely sabotaged attempts to plan a series of future meetings on trade policy.

One of the early reactions to the trade crisis was a 92–0 vote in the Senate condemning the Japanese for restrictive trade practices.

A flurry of charges and countercharges allowed journalists to keep the trade story alive for a protracted period and to examine it from every conceivable angle. Many other interest groups also wished to keep the story in the headlines, and there was considerable behind-the-scenes struggle to define and explain the trade crisis. The struggle was an attempt to control public sentiment toward the Japanese and toward tariff and trade policy generally.

The question facing journalists was this: why was there an increasingly negative balance of payments with Japan and other countries? The significance of the journalist's attempt to answer the questions was this: the answer arrived at would be one of the central elements determining the course of government economic policy.

The first explanation offered was based upon motives. Such stories pitted wily Japanese against innocent Americans. The Japanese in their desire to dominate international markets were playing by unacceptable rules of the game. Through a variety of devices, they were securing access to American markets and technology, engaging in unfair competitive practices, and excluding American products and producers from Japan.

This explanation was advanced by leaders of declining industries, Senators Robert Packwood and John Danforth, and congressmen from districts economically depressed by the flood of imports. Senator Packwood wrote in the *New York Times* that, to cite the headline, "Japan's Not Entitled to 'Free Lunch.' " He argued that "America can successfully compete in the Japanese market—if we can get into it. The problem is the jaded Japanese bureaucracy." The *Chicago Tribune* reported a speech by Lee Iacocca, the Chrysler Corporation chairman, in which he demanded that the "Japanese Play Fair With Us." He claimed that "Americans see it as a one-way trade relationship, a well-ordered plan by Japan to take as much as it can and put very little back." Joseph A. Reaves of the *Chicago Tribune* reported from Tokyo that "Americans see the Japanese as conniving protectionists who want to get rich exporting their goods around the world while buying only Japanese products at home." The troubles of individual industries in dealing with the Japanese were reported. James Mateja, the automotive writer of the *Chicago Tribune,* interviewed a representative of the automotive replacement parts industry who argued that neither low quality nor high price kept his industry out of the Japanese market. It was restrictive trade practices: ". . . if you have equal access to specifications, and if you can retain business at the best price, then our prices would knock their socks off. I don't know how they accept price quotes now." A consensus position offered on Japanese motives was summarized by a *Tribune* business writer: "They [U.S. officials in Tokyo] say the Japanese simply aren't playing fair in the trade game. American companies trying to do business in Japan face an impenetrable wall of government-imposed barriers designed to protect Japanese firms."

The "motive story" of trade was not restricted to analyzing the Japanese. Clyde Farnsworth of the *New York Times* reported that pressing "trade issues are reshaping the political lineup in the United States as Democrats and Republicans maneuver for advantage while trying to deal with an influx of imports from Japan and other countries." He claimed that "Democrats now smell blood on the issue" and were going after twenty-two Republican Senate seats. The Democrats were going to tie trade problems to Republican free market economic policy that was causing an overvalued dollar.

Farnsworth's story hints at a shift in the form of explanation of the trade crisis story: from motives to causes. It was the Japanese themselves who pointed out not only the restrictive trade practices of the United States but, more importantly, that the trade deficit was caused by the overvalued dollar, the poor quality of American goods, the taste standards of the Japanese market, or the fact that the strength of the recovery of the American economy set unprecedented demand by Americans for foreign products. The explanation, in other words, did not reside in the motives of the Japanese or in individual Americans but in collective international economic conditions: the more or less natural laws of modern economics or the unintended consequences of normal economic activity.

Ronald Yates of the *Chicago Tribune* reported the comments of Toshiaki Fujinami, president of a small Japanese paper products company: U.S. senators "are just trying to shift the blame for the declining American economy away from the huge U.S. budget deficit and the over-valued dollar to Japan." Edwin Yoder in the Providence *Journal* warned against "Misreading Causes of the U.S. Trade Deficit" and claimed that "Reagan-Congress fiscal policy" and the ludicrous budget deficit of $200 billion a year "is the sword we throw ourselves on every day." He offered his own quick explanation:

> The budget deficits generate historically high "real" interest rates, adjusted for inflation. They suck prodigious sums of foreign capital into the United States, keeping the dollar drastically overvalued against other major currencies.
>
> The stark weighting of the terms of trade to our disfavor functions as an export tax on U.S. goods, an import subsidy to foreign goods and an incentive to U.S. employers to move plants "offshore" if they can. Those that can't move close. In this witch's brew, one partner's trade practices, even Japan's, are a piddling ingredient—the equivalent of one eye of newt.

Chicago Tribune editorials and editorial columns by Stephen Chapman pointed out that the "real" motives of Lee Iacocca and others like him were less in gaining access to Japanese markets and more in restricting foreign competition. They pointed out that Japan's trade restrictions are "just handy excuses for American ones." Chapman argued that the Japanese had not refused to buy American goods. "American exports to Japan had risen by 9 per cent last year." What, then, caused the trade deficit? The strong dollar. "Foreigners, including the Japanese, are eager to buy a share of our booming economy. As long as foreigners invest more here than Americans invest abroad, Americans will have to import more goods than they export. That's not bad trade." Another reason: the American economy recovered faster than Japan's and Western Europe's. "Consequently, American businesses and consumers have more money to spend than their foreign counterparts. So the U.S. imports more than they do."

Hobart Rowen of the *Washington Post* reported that a study by the Institute of International Economics showed that each country had roughly equivalent barriers to trade. The study attributed trade tension to the distorted relation between the dollar and the yen. Rowen noted that the institute's conclusion "conflicts with frequent assertions by administration officials and business executives that the imbalance in trade is a result of Tokyo's barriers to U.S. imports."

As this example shows, journalists writing about causes depend upon "experts," "think tanks," and other organizations attempting to influence policy. Journalists can often handle motive explanations based upon only their own knowledge or a few well-placed sources. But with causes, journalists are largely at the mercy of others, not because the subject is necessarily more technical but because the form of the explanation is one in which social scientists specialize and therefore have an overwhelming advantage.

United States and international economic conditions were not the only causes cited for the trade deficit. A slowly emerging crop of stories admitted to Japanese trade barriers but rooted those barriers not in the motives and intentions of Japanese leaders but in Japanese cultural habits. The *New York Times's* Nicholas Kristof argued that "even without intentional restrictions the Japanese market remains more elusive than most because of deep cultural differences—the way Japan organizes its society, arranges its economy, and views the world." Kristof suggested that the cultural barriers to trade "cannot be easily negotiated away." Even Japanese often have difficulty breaking into the Japanese market. He cited Jon K. T. Choy, an economist at the Japan Economic Institute in Washington, who explained that the "Japanese system doesn't simply discriminate against foreigners—it discriminates against newcomers." The Japanese "place a premium on a long-term relationship with suppliers, doing business with those who have faithfully performed their obligations in the past. This is what makes it difficult even for new Japanese companies to break into the market." Even more: Americans don't speak Japanese, whereas the Japanese speak English and understand American culture; the Japanese resist foreign goods because they consider their own superior; American products have incomprehensible instructions and are not sized and detailed to the Japanese market. (Pampers, for example, were inappropriately shaped to the Japanese bottom.)

The cultural cause of the trade deficit was elaborated in other articles which examined the shopping habits of the Japanese ("The

Wary Shoppers of Japan," *New York Times*) and Japanese attitudes toward everything foreign ("The Hideous Gaijin in Japan," *Newsweek*).

There was something disingenuous about cultural explanations of trade deficits. Most of those reporting such explanations were advocating free trade in one way or another. However, the theory of free trade assumes the absence of cultural barriers to trade. Buyers and sellers in Japan and the United States are assumed to operate in terms of a purely rational model of economic activity where price and quality govern the terms of trade.

While such stories increasingly emphasized the causes of the trade deficit, other reports continued to analyze motives. The motives in question were those of the Reagan administration. A long wrap-up story in the *Chicago Tribune* relied on an expert on Japan, Chalmers Johnson of the University of California. He linked the trade deficit to the fact that "U.S. foreign policy is controlled by the State Department which, like Reagan, sees Japan more in terms of the Soviet-American rivalry than in its economic role." As long as Prime Minister Nakasone was seen as a firm ally against the Soviets, "his inability to produce real Japanese concessions on trade will be forgiven." Similarly, the economist Robert Solow, writing in the *New York Times,* suggested that the Reagan administration did not really care about the economic effect of budget deficits. The Reagan administration did not really favor investment, productivity, or growth. "Its goal is to shrink the Federal Government, to limit its capacity to provide services, at least civilian services, or to redistribute income to the poor or to regulate private activity." In other words, the trade crisis was a nonstory because the budget deficits driving the terms of trade derived from Reagan's intention to reshape domestic politics.

These multiple explanations of the trade deficit, and the blizzard of stories reporting them, were made more complicated by two other types of stories concerning Japanese-American relations. First were stories about the personal relations of Reagan and Nakasone, a "Ron" and "Yasu" show: two embattled leaders trying to control angry forces of economic warfare at loose beneath them, sending delegations from one capital to the other to soothe relations. The other set of stories transmitted messages between the Japanese and

American bureaucracies: charges, recriminations, demands for concessions, threats of what was ahead if this practice or that was not abandoned.

The causes of an event are intimately linked to its consequences. Therefore, every story that explains an event by elucidating causes also states, more or less directly, the consequences that flow from it. If the balance of payment problem is caused by budget deficits, and if the budget deficits are to continue for some time, then a train of consequences follows—at least until the Gramm-Rudman deficit controls kick in. But the Gramm-Rudman mechanisms have their own consequences. Causes are usually emphasized more than consequences because consequences are in the future and thus as much a matter of prophecy as of knowledge. Even so, many stories cited the predicted consequences of the trade imbalance for employment, basic manufacturing industries, regional economic development, and even the future of United States–Japanese relations. Edwin Yoder's piece, previously cited, evoked a reenactment of World War II: "Only fools underrate the mischief of . . . cultural barriers in history and the teaching of this sad history is that the United States and Japan have had difficulty understanding one another before. . . . No one is looking for a reprise of those old enmities. . . ."

If all else fails, find the significance in the event. What does the trade crisis tell us about ourselves? What is the larger meaning of the event? Bill Neikirk in the *Chicago Tribune* told us: "Here is what's happening: They [the Japanese] sacrifice more than we do. . . . They anticipate and manage better than we do. . . . Their system of compensation promotes worker loyalty and holds down welfare payments . . . they have maintained higher efficiency . . . better management and lower wages . . . we have been outperformed." In short, the real significance of the trade crisis is that ours is a declining economy and civilization, having lost the habits of character that made us once a great nation.

V

I have argued that "why" is the question most often left unanswered, or answered with an insinuation. Attempting to answer "why" places American journalists on soft ground, where they are subjected to and reliant on experts. When explanations do appear, they are of particular types consonant with American culture as a whole. That should not surprise us. Despite everything said about the political biases of American journalists, they are, John Chancellor says, "pretty much like everyone else in their basic beliefs."

I earlier suggested that American journalism always begins from the question of "who." Although I exaggerate, you will not go far wrong assuming that "names make news." The primary subject of journalism is people—what they say and do. Moreover, the subject is usually an individual—what someone says and does. Groups, in turn, are usually personified by leaders or representatives who speak or act for them, even when we know this is pretty much a fiction. Edward Kennedy speaks for liberals, Jesse Jackson for blacks, Gloria Steinem for liberated women. Sometimes a composite or a persona speaks for a leaderless or amorphous group: "scientists say"; a suicide note from a teenager stands for all unwritten notes. Their sayings and doings are representative of a class. If journalists cannot find a representative individual, they more or less invent one, as leaders were invented or selected by the press during the 1960s for the student and antiwar movements.

Because news is mainly about the doings and sayings of individuals, why is usually answered by identifying the motives of those individuals. Why tells us why someone did something. This is the sense in which American culture is "individualistic": We assume that individuals are authors of their own acts, that individuals do what they do intentionally, they say what they say because they have purposes in mind. The world is the way it is because individuals want it that way. Explanation in American journalism is a kind of long-distance mind reading in which the journalist elucidates the motives, intentions, purposes, and hidden agendas which guide individuals in their actions.

This overreliance on motive explanations is a pervasive weakness of American journalism. Motive explanations are too easy. It takes time, effort, and substantial knowledge to find a cause, whereas motives are available for a phone call. And motives are profoundly misleading and simplifying. Motive explanations end up portraying a world in which people are driven by desires no more complicated than greed.

Journalism is not the only forum in which motives are established. The courtroom is the great American scene in the drama of motives. To compare journalism to the courts is not farfetched. The adversary model of journalism, with the press as prosecutor and public representative, is clearly derived from the courts. The journalist is the detective, the investigator, trying to establish the facts of the case and the motives of the actors. The "detective story" and the journalism story have developed in tandem since the emergence of the penny press.

A *New Yorker* cartoon of a few years back featured two quizzical detectives staring at a corpse. One remarked to the other that "it is an old-fashioned crime—it has a motive." The cartoon is testimony to a demand we make of the courtroom and the press: they present little episodes in what Max Weber called the "quest for lucidity," the demand that the world make sense.

In a murder trial, for example, there will be two points of contention. First, what was the act and was it committed by the accused? But the answer to those questions depends critically on a third: what was the motive? The nature of the act and the assignment of guilt cannot be made until the act is motivated, until a statement of intention is attached to it that makes it intelligible to us. In fact, to make acts intelligible is the greatest demand of the courtroom. We make acts intelligible by showing the grounds a person had for acting. These grounds are, however, not the cause of an act. If I make a person's murderous act intelligible by portraying his motive, I do not mean the motive caused the murder. After all, many people have such motives, but they do not commit murder. The motive makes intelligible but it does not cause; it is understanding action without understanding causation. Because I understand the motive behind a murderous act, I do not necessarily approve of it. It merely means that the motive is a plausible ground for the act. Acts must be placed within learned interpretive schemes so that we might judge them as being murder, suicide, manslaughter, self-defense, first degree, etc. And those terms are not exactly unambiguous.

Let us take the matter a step further. Suppose in our hypothetical crime a husband murders his wife. What interpretations might be made of his behavior? How will it be motivated? How will the action be made intelligible to us (which is also an attempt, let us remember, to make it intelligible to the accused)? We have a standard typology of motives we can bring to bear. He did it for her money—a technically rational motive in a utilitarian culture. He did it because he found her sleeping with another man—the motive of honor. He did it out of anger—it was an act of passion, of emotion. Finally, we might even imagine that he did it because this is what men always do in this society under such circumstances—it is explained by tradition.

This example illustrates a number of things. First, the courtroom is simply a compacted scene of the most ordinary and important aspects of social life: it consists of interpreting experience, attaching explanations to ambiguous phenomena, using cultural resources— standard typologies of motives, for example—to explain human activity.

Similarly, American journalists explain actions by attributing motives. The motives they attribute are, in the first instance, rational, instrumental, purposeful ones. We can understand murder for money much better than murder for honor. Similarly, journalists attribute rational motives to politicians. In 1980, the *New York Times* explained that Jimmy Carter was opening his campaign on Labor Day in the South because of what Mr. Carter's campaign advisers "concede to be a serious effort by Ronald Reagan to win votes here." Carter had many reasons to begin in the South: tradition, his affection for his native region, the honor he wished to bring to his associates. Nonetheless, the motive selected was the one that showed it was a rational act designed solely to win the election.

The explanation of conduct by rational motives is a literary and cultural convention. Just how conventional it is is revealed when we encounter, for example, Soviet journalism, where stories are framed in terms of large collective forces—capitalism, history, imperialism —rather than individual motives. Individuals merely personify these larger forces which are in the saddle driving the actions of individuals. But for us, individuals act. Individuals make history. Individuals have purposes and intentions. Therefore, to answer the question "why" in American journalism, the journalist must discover a motive or attribute one to the actor.

Explanation by rational motives is the archetype of journalism as it is of the culture. But such explanations are often too arbitrary. William Greider, for example, was dismayed when journalists asked about the motives behind his *Atlantic* article rather than about the substance of the article itself. Similarly, the questions put to political candidates are less about what the candidate is saying than why he is saying it, leading to the well-known complaint that no one writes about the issues anymore. It is simply assumed that everything a candidate does is designed to win the election, and that pretty much exhausts the meaning of what is said. Indeed, it seems at times that journalists and political candidates are in a silent conspiracy to focus attention on the hidden states of mind and intentions of politicians and away from what they are concretely up to and saying. When a story breaks this mold, it is often refreshing in its candor. A *New York Times* story from Moscow by Serge Schmemann on December 10, 1985, was striking precisely because it reported directly on what Gorbachev said about U.S.-Soviet relations without one word of speculation as to motives:

> Mikhail S. Gorbachev told 400 American business executives today that while the Geneva summit meeting had opened the way to better Soviet-American relations, trade would remain limited until Washington lifted "political obstacles."
>
> "I will be absolutely frank with you," the Soviet leader told the representatives of about 150 American companies in Moscow . . . , "so long as those obstacles exist . . . there will be no normal development of Soviet-U.S. trade and other economic ties on a large scale. This is regrettable but we are not going to beg the United States for anything."
>
> . . . Mr. Gorbachev held out the carrot of "major long-term projects and numerous medium and even small business deals." But first, he said, Washington would have to lift the restrictions imposed on trade with the Soviet Union.

The obstacles he listed included legislation denying most favored nation status and export-import credits to Moscow unless it permitted emigration of Jews and restrictions on high-technology exports. Mr. Gorbachev also cited what he called "the policy of boycotts, embargoes, punishments and broken trade contracts that has become a habit with the United States."

The story conveys the sense of Russian rhetoric that is, one imagines, the real substance of summit diplomacy.

Motive explanations are not only arbitrary but easy. They deflect attention rather too quickly and casually away from the what and onto the why. Sometimes the motive is incorporated into the very definition of the who, as when the *New York Times* in a breaking story from Japan mentions that "saboteurs today knocked out key rail communications and signal systems, forcing the shutdown of 23 commuter trains. . . . The saboteurs, described by authorities as left-wing extremists . . ." Similarly, Bernhard Goetz quickly became known as the "subway vigilante," an identification that told us immediately what he did and why he did it. More to the point, journalists approach the action of politicians as drama critics at a play, looking for a subtext in the script. The *Wall Street Journal* tells us that Representative Daniel Rostenkowski, chairman of the House Ways and Means Committee, had "several motives" behind his enthusiasm for tax reform: "He isn't eager to get ambushed by the White House again; tax revision can be a vehicle to reassert his committee's and his own imperatives"; the average voter supports tax simplification; and it is "an issue that can move the Democratic party closer to the political center." In short, Rostenkowski is interested in everything but tax reform.

This tendency to focus on motive explanations led Leon Sigal to complain that news stories focus on the who rather than the what and the why of disputes. As he said, journalists tend to ask who was responsible for an event rather than what was the cause. It is not that journalists substitute who for why but rather that they substitute one kind of why—a motive statement—for another kind of why—a cause statement.

In continuing stories, motives are often reduced to boilerplate, a continuing thread of standard interpretation inserted in every story. Since 1969, for example, we have had a steady stream of stories about political violence in Northern Ireland. A recent one was carried in the *Times* from the AP:

> BELFAST, Northern Ireland, Jan. 1—Just one minute into the new year, Irish Republican Army guerrillas killed two policemen and wounded a third in an ambush that the I.R.A. said opened a renewed campaign against British security forces.

After five paragraphs describing the killings, the following boiler-plate paragraph was inserted:

> The predominantly Roman Catholic I.R.A. is fighting to drive the British from Northern Ireland and unite the Protes-tant-dominated province with the overwhelmingly Catholic Irish Republic.

That paragraph appears in virtually every story from Northern Ireland with little or no variation. It is the explanatory paragraph, the motive paragraph, the paragraph that sets the story in context. The trouble is that it is a gross, oversimple, and unchanging explanation for complex and changing events. Not even the IRA is that simple, internally unified, or unchanging. The boilerplate acts to select stories as well as to select explanations. Stories from Ireland are selected, at one point in the transmission system or another, that fit into the one overarching boilerplate explanation available for all events in the province.

Rational explanations by motives—and here the IRA is rational on an American model—commit journalists to viewing individuals, particularly political actors, as possessing far clearer and more artic-ulate purposes than they usually do. As a result, they create a picture that renders politics far more orderly and directed than it ever is for the participants. Journalists introduce a clarity into events that rarely exists for those caught up in the muddled flow of happenings, the ambiguities of situations, and the crosscutting and contradictory nature of purposes and intentions.

That motives obey literary and even legal conventions rather than simply mirroring what is going on can be seen in the contrasting treatment of two New York killings. In December 1985, Paul Castellano and Thomas Bilotti were gunned down on a mid-Manhattan street. Before the blood was dry on the sidewalk, the *Times* had identified the killer and the motive. "John Gotti, a fastidious, well-groomed forty-five-year-old resident of Queens, is believed by law-enforcement officials to be a central figure in an internal fight for leadership of the Gambino crime family." The law enforcement officials were then quoted to round out the explanation: "John Gotti is a major organized crime figure in the Gambino crime family and heir apparent. . . . Gotti will emerge as the head of the other capos—that's what this struggle is all about. Bilotti was Gotti's rival and he's gone, and there may well be some more killings before it's settled." Well, we know why members of the Mafia commit murder, and they normally do not bring libel suits.

That case contrasts nicely with a more mysterious one. In June 1985, a seventeen-year-old Harlem resident, Edmund Perry, a graduate of Phillips Exeter Academy, a member of the freshman class at Stanford, was killed by an undercover police officer near St. Luke's Hospital on Manhattan's Upper West Side. It was an improbable killing, and the *Times* covered the case very circumspectly. The paper was cautious in attributing motive, was hesitant to convict anyone involved. The case did not fit the type. Racism is one non-rational motive we all understand. As a result, the episode was dramatically awry. It should have been the racism of the police officer that motivated the killing. Why should a successful black youth on his way to great things mug and attempt to rob an undercover officer as alleged? The killing did not fit an acceptable, sensible pattern of motivation, and so the *Times* awaited the grand jury investigation and, even when charges were dismissed against the officer, was careful not to resolve the case for its readers.

Motive explanations work only when they fit a certain ideal type of rational, purposeful action. But when they are made to fit the type, they are often too simple or radically misleading or generate an unnecessary cynicism. In anticipation of the first celebration of Martin Luther King's birthday as a national holiday, NBC reported that President Reagan was to visit a school named after the slain civil rights leader. It described it as "part of his attempt to improve his image among blacks," an image, we were told, that was "on the rise." Even Ronald Reagan is more complicated than that.

It is not the literal truth of the motives journalists unmask that is in question. Surely, people are driven by self-interest. But that is not the only motive that drives them; all self-interested action is knotted into and contained by other, larger, and often more honorable motives. The real problem is that the motives journalists describe and report are the motives that we live. The notion of the "hidden agenda" is now so destructively widespread in the culture because we have so unfailingly described our political leaders as possessed by undisclosed and manipulative intentions. Paradoxically, Marxism has become the ideology of late bourgeois America because our vocabulary of motives pretty much comes down to "whose ox gets gored." Therefore, journalism becomes the unmasking and revealing of the "true" motives behind appearances. Power, wealth, control become the primary objects of people's actions because we assume that everyone is driven by selfish interest. This compulsive explanation excludes the possibility that anyone can be motivated by the common good or the public interest, and so we should not be surprised if individuals are not so motivated. Greed, in the most general sense, explains everything. The one state of mind with which we feel comfortable is the rational, instrumental one. Actions which do not fit this scheme largely confuse and befuddle us.

The final and most unfortunate aspect of motive explanations is the overwhelmingly technical bias they give to journalism. If people are uniformly out to better their own self-interest, and what they say and do is designed to further that end, the only sensible questions are: Are they successful? Are their means well adapted to their ends? Are they pursuing a rational course of action? We therefore ask: How is pacification going in Vietnam? What is the body count? Who is winning the election? What do the opinion polls say? Is the antiwar movement gaining or losing ground? Technique becomes all-important because we assume that all individuals, groups, and institutions care about is winning and that the technical success of their strategies is all that is in question. All life becomes a horse race in which the press reports the progress of the contestants to the wire and announces the winners and the losers. Meanwhile, everyone forgets what the race is about and the stakes we have in the outcome.

It is often said that the press reduces politics to a clash of personalities, wills, and ambitions. The only purpose of politics becomes the desire to win elections. The real meaning of objectivity is that the press takes that desire, and all such rational desires, as given and assesses everything a politician does in its light. We get, therefore, stories of success or failure, victory or defeat, cleverness or ineptness, achievement or mismanagement, defined by technical expertise, not by the content of character or nobility of purpose.

Journalists pretty much keep their own counsel on rational motives. Sources are used to "objectify" what the journalist already knows. Other actions and other motives cannot be fully explained because, while conscious, they are not rational or believable. The old saw that men kill for money and women for love simply argues that while both men and women are motivated by conscious motives, men are motivated by reason, women are not. Claus von Bülow, innocent, makes sense; Jean Harris, guilty, does not. If individuals announce they are motivated by honor, loyalty, duty, or other nonrational motives, the journalist cannot quite take them seriously, nor can we; therefore, they have to be unmasked. Actions motivated by tradition, values, and affections pretty much escape our understanding and end up as the human interest exotica which fill the space between the self-interest stories and provide the features for the *National Enquirer* and Charles Kuralt.

When we move to nonrational motives, we move, in fact, into the domain of causes. Nonrational motives move people as irresistible forces over which they have no control. To deal with them, journalists must call on the experts. Experts play the same role in journalism as they do in the courts. They straighten out minor technical matters such as ballistics and resolve major matters of cause and interpretation. If journalists cannot find a rational motive, they have to bring in psychiatrists, psychologists, sociologists, and other experts on national character and the behavior of strange people to provide an irrational one. English rioting in Brussels, blacks rioting in Brixton, terrorists "rioting" everywhere pretty much fall outside rational assessment, so only the experts can make them comprehensible. This is particularly pronounced on television, where breaking stories on the evening news are explained by experts on "Nightline" or the morning news. Unfortunately, the experts do not always agree, and it usually comes down to whom the journalist chooses to trust.

If the irrational is the first domain of causal explanations, the statistical is the second. Explanation by causes is particularly well adapted to the periodic reports of government and the significant findings that turn up in scientific journals. Youth suicide is up, and the *New England Journal of Medicine* has an explanation based on the "rate" of depression in all age groups. Child abuse is on the rise, and a sociologist tells us of the disorganization of the American family. Mortgage rates hit a six-year low, and an economist informs us of the money supply and the Federal Reserve Board. Auto sales are down 15 percent, and an expert in consumer behavior tells us about the psychology of consumer expectations. The homeless are filling up the city, and a bureaucrat reminds us of the consequence of "de-institutionalizing" the mentally ill.

Stories of causation turn the journalist to the experts, even though the experts are not always disinterested. In fact, organizations are often created for the sole purpose of providing journalists with explanations. When a new and perplexing report comes out, someone has to be found with an explanation, and, therefore, "institutes of explanation" are available for every problem affecting the national interest.

A few years back, there was a move afoot to increase the amount of what Philip Meyer called "precision journalism," the application of social science methods to the problems journalists regularly report. Precision journalism was designed to get at aggregate motives of large numbers of people so that journalists would not be always guessing at the motives of voters, or of racial groups or other subclasses of the population. It was also designed to free journalists

from relying on experts by making them more self-sufficient inves-
tigators of large-scale problems for which statistics and computers
provide the only answers: problems of population, migration, collective behavior, or problems of analyzing public records from the
courts, the police, and the assessors's office. The movement has
pretty much come to naught, except that newspapers conduct horse
race polls in elections. Otherwise, given the nature of breaking
news, journalists still pretty much rely on experts for the stipulation
of causes.

Causal stories are often personified, of course. The growth of
population, shifts in migration patterns, changes in the composition
of the labor force or the mix of occupations are often exemplified in
individuals and the reasons they have for migrating, changing jobs,
having children, etc. For example, the increasing rate of suicide
among young males is often rendered by focusing on a particularly
tragic death or a group of suicides in a community overcome by
grief. But such suicides represent a class of acts that must be accounted for by larger historical forces than simply the motives of
individuals.

When a farmer in Hills, Iowa, killed three people and then
committed suicide, the *New York Times* headlined the story "Deaths
on the Iowa Prairie: Four New Victims of the Economy." The
deaths were "but the latest in a series of violent outbursts across the
Middle West" caused by the sagging farm economy.

The reverse side of cause stories are consequence stories, and they
frequently are embedded one in the other. Youth suicide, falling
interest rates, and declining sales all have consequences in addition
to causes. They are fateful signs with which to read the future of
the community and the nation. When Chrysler and Mitsubishi
signed an agreement to build a new joint production plant in
Bloomington, Illinois, the newly formed company, the Diamond
Star Motors Corporation, announced that the workers to be hired
would be recent high-school graduates. A television story of the
announcement did not emphasize the motives of the company—
new workers are cheaper and less given to unionization—or the
cause of the policy—the problems of training older workers without
automotive experience. Instead, the story emphasized the conse-

quence: The opening of the plant would not reduce unemployment. It would merely siphon off new entrants to the job market.

A decision to emphasize consequence over causes and motives is a decision to emphasize the future over the past. Consequences are predictions of what will happen rather than a recounting of what has happened. They open up the future and often unintended consequences of events. As they are as much matters of prophecy as prediction, consequence stories also throw the journalist into the arms of the expert: the futurologists of one kind or another who are able to divine the far horizons of human life.

The final form of explanation in journalism is significance. Events surface all the time which are in no way the result of intentional human acts nor the result of vast historical causes. Their consequences are opaque and unknowable. They are, nonetheless, signs that must be read, portents of something larger, events to be prized and remembered as markers, as peculiar evidence of the state of civilization, or the dangers we face or the glories we once possessed.

Any event can be read for its significance. Carlin Romano calls these "symbolic events" and cites the spate of stories about President Reagan on horseback following his surgery for cancer of the colon. Such stories show that the presidency continues, the ship of state, forgive the pun, rests on an even keel. At such a moment, only the most cynical ask why he is on horseback. People treat it for what it is—a sign full of meaning for the body politic.

The murder and suicide victims in Hills, Iowa, mentioned earlier, were treated by the *Times* as casualties of the economy. The *Iowa City Press-Citizen* admitted that explanation but tried to see in the event a larger, tragic significance:

> There are accounts of bank transactions and economic explanations and other hypotheses as the murder and suicide story unravels. But that's not what it is really all about. It's about people—alone, desperate, and powerless with nowhere to turn. . . .
> Target prices, price supports, ceilings, sealing crops. The terminology doesn't matter. It's welfare. Farmers know it.

And farmers are proud people. Nobody really wants to live that way. But for now there is no choice. . . .

But if there's one thing that is clear from Monday's tragic series of murder and suicide, it is that the farm crisis is *not* numbers and deficits and bushels of corn. It is people and pride and tears and blood.

The time has come for the state and the country to reach out to farmers who are suffering—not because they are failed businessmen and women but because they are human beings whose lives are falling apart—fast.

Significance can be found in a grain of sand—indeed, in any episode, however minor, that surfaces in a community. But as a form of explanation, significance is most manifest in stories of deaths, birthdays, anniversaries, inaugurals, coronations, weddings —in, to twist a phrase of Elihu Katz, the high holy days and the high holy events of the press. The inauguration of a president, the death of a beloved public figure, the two-hundredth anniversary of the Revolution or the Constitution, the commemoration of the onset of World War II or the invasion of Normandy—these become rituals of reflection and recollection: symbols of unity and disunity, triumph and tragedy, hope and despair. They are marked by an altered role for the journalist. While writing about them, he abandons his pose as critic, adversary, and detective and becomes a member of the communty, a citizen: reverent and pietistic. In these events, he aids us in the search for meaning rather than motives, consolation rather than causes, symbolism rather than consequences.

Two events of the recent past demonstrate aspects of the search for significance. The first was the tenth anniversary of the evacuation of Saigon and the "loss" of the war in Vietnam. The war is still too close, the memory still too green, to completely abandon the question of why we lost the war. Nonetheless, the widespread and often enormously expensive coverage of the anniversary took the form of a stocktaking: Where were we ten years later? What did we learn from it? What does it reveal to us about ourselves?

The second event says something about the struggle over significance rather than its mere elucidation: the visit of Reagan to the cemetery at Bitburg. In one sense, this was a harmless ceremonial event amid a busy European tour. But it came to bear significance as a gesture of contrasting meaning: a gesture of final reconciliation with an old enemy now a valuable ally and, simultaneously, a gesture of forgiveness for that which could not be forgiven—the Holocaust. The struggles over whether Reagan should make the ceremonial stop and over the meaning of going or not going reveal the power of presidential gestures and the way in which the press collaborates in the quest for meaning while innocently reporting the news.

Perhaps the best and most revealing recent example of a "significance story" started out as a far more ordinary event. In the late fall of 1984, a seventeen-year-old black man was shot on the South Side of Chicago. The murder perhaps wouldn't have been reported or have received any particular play except that Ben Wilson happened to be one of the best high-school basketball players in the country. Destined for stardom, he had already signed a tender with the basketball program at the University of Illinois. He was about to embark on an education, an escape from the ghetto, and perhaps a life of fame and riches.

The first stories concentrated on what had happened on a Friday afternoon after school: Who killed him and why did he do it? Was Wilson responsible in any way for his own death?

Between the time of the stories of the murder of Ben Wilson and the stories of the trial, conviction, and sentencing of his killer, the fate of this young man gave rise to other kinds of stories.

At first, Ben Wilson became the personification of the problems of growing up black, of the constant threat of gang violence, and of the toll taken by ghetto life. Wilson became a "news peg," a tragic death to be explained by the impersonal causes of poverty, unemployment, ignorance, illiteracy, and hopelessness. Ben Wilson's death, in a way, explained his killer. Distinguished reporting of these conditions even had an effect. Gang violence was reported to be down 40 percent in the wake of Wilson's death and the coverage of it.

The coverage, however, also looked for the significance of the death of this young man. The significance was found in public forgetfulness a generation after the civil rights struggle and a half generation after the War on Poverty. In an era of affluence, concern for private gratification, and disinterest in the problems of public life, stories of the "ghetto" were not in. The *Chicago Tribune* used the death of Ben Wilson to forcefully remind its readers of the meaning of life in urban America. The tragedy of the stories was that it took the misfortune of Ben Wilson to bring these persistent concerns and problems back into the newspaper.

VI

I have emphasized throughout this essay that journalism is a curriculum and not merely a series of news flashes. Everything can be found in American journalism, generously understood, but it is disconnected and incoherent. It takes an astute and constant reader —such as journalists are themselves—to connect the disconnected, to find sense and significance in the overwhelming and overbearing glut of occurrences.

American journalism is deeply embedded in American culture. Its faults and its triumphs are pretty much characteristic of the culture as a whole. The forms of storytelling it has adopted are those prized and cultivated throughout much of our literature. The explanations it offers are pretty much the same offered in the intellectual disciplines. As journalists move from explanations by motives to causes to consequences to significance, they roughly mirror the movement of scholars from utilitarian to causal to functional to hermeneutic explanations. Journalists, however, obsessively rely on motive explanations and thereby weaken the explanatory power of their work.

Journalists, because of their professional ideology and the industrial conditions under which they work, offer thick descriptions pretty much between the lines. They explain events by insinuating, often sotto voce, motives typical of our obsessively practical culture. Otherwise, they rely on experts, not always of their own choosing, to supply them with causes and consequences, or they sum up the folk wisdom and commonsense significance of the community. This renders journalists active participants in reality making and not merely passive observers. It also makes them frequent victims of the forces around them rather than defenders of a public interest or a common good.

As a wise man once said, journalism has taken its revenge on philosophy. As the unloved child of the craft of letters, journalism concentrates on the new, novel, transient, and ephemeral. Philosophy, the crown of the literary craft, once concentrated on the eternal, enduring, momentous, and significant. Journalism's revenge has been to impose the cycle of the news on philosophy, indeed, on all the literary arts. Everyone looks for their subject in today's headlines.

Many have argued that the overriding problem of American culture is that it has no sense of time. American managers administer for the short run; American politicians look no further than the next election. Whether one looks at the fashionability of our scholarship, the transience of our interests, the length of our memories, the planning of our institutions, or even, Reagan aside, the tenure of our presidents, everything seems to have the life span of a butterfly in spring.

The daily news bulletins report this spectacle of change: victories, defeats, trends, fluctuations, battles, controversies, threats. But beneath this change, the structures of society—the distribution of income and poverty, the cleavages of class and status, race and ethnicity, the gross inequalities of hardships and life chances—remain remarkably persistent.

If you look at the entire curriculum of journalism, you will find much reporting of the enduring and persistent, the solid and unyielding structures of social life. It is the part of journalism that offers genuine description and explanation, compelling force and narrative detail, and yet it is not the part of journalism we generally honor. At some lost moment in our history, journalism became identified with, defined by, breaking news, the news flash, the news bulletin. When that happened, our understanding of journalism as a democratic social practice was impossibly narrowed and our habits of reading, of attention, of interpretation were impaired. Journalists came to think of themselves as being in the news business, where their greatest achievements were defined by being first rather than

best, with uncovering the unknown rather than clarifying and interpreting the known. Scholars too often take journalists at their word
and neither read nor analyze anything beyond the wire services.
They are as ignorant of the curriculum of journalism as the most
addled teenager. We are then doubly betrayed. To restore a sense of
time to both journalism and scholarship is going to take a lot of
work and a lot of luck. All of us might begin by reading more
wisely.

Writing the News (By Telling the "Story")

ROBERT KARL MANOFF

"**D**ebate Goes on Over Nature of Reality," the *New York Times* reported in its science section not long ago. Although the story concerned events at the frontier where physics and philosophy meet, such a headline could have been affixed to a story about the *Times* itself, to a story about any American newspaper, or indeed to a story about the whole of the American press. For we read the news our papers deliver each day believing that it is an index to the real, and, indeed, judgments about reality do give us the news. For this reason, judgments about the news are always to some extent judgments about reality. Any reading of the news must question the press concerning the truth claim that gives it its privileged status.

To ask the questions of the news that the news customarily asks of reality is to discover that the nature of reality itself is only one of the conditions shaping the reports about it. Stories also reflect the identities of the people reporters talk to, the places they go, the things they believe, the routines that guide how they work, and the conventions that govern what they write. Perhaps most important, they reflect the fact that the news account often achieves its unity prior to the answers it provides to any one of the questions it poses.

The unity of the story is not necessarily as self-evident as it seems the next day, when it appears with all the authority that attends the morning's headlines. What the real story would be was certainly unclear to the five reporters who had been delegated to accompany the president on *Air Force One* during his routine flight to the summit meeting with Mikhail Gorbachev on Saturday, November 16, 1985. Members of the first pool of the summit trip, they had been designated to cover the flight for the rest of the White House press, which had left almost an hour before the president to be in position to report his arrival when he landed in Geneva. The sky was still bright outside when Larry Speakes, the president's deputy press secretary, made his way to the back of the plane, where the pool was keeping watch. He handed out the schedule for the summit ("the bible") and talked to the pool about the president's mood ("upbeat"), popularity ("extraordinarily high"), and plans for a public appearance with Mikhail Gorbachev ("we've had discussions"). He also offered comments on the story that had broken that morning in the *New York Times* and the *Washington Post*. Both papers had carried reports about a letter on Soviet treaty violations which Secretary of Defense Caspar Weinberger had delivered to the president only a few days before, along with a memorandum on the same subject. Both papers had obtained copies of the letter and had reported the secretary's eleventh-hour warning against any commitment to abide by the unratified SALT II treaty or to compromise on the "Star Wars" antimissile defense at the summit. In the words of the report which members of the pool later composed for their colleagues, during the discussion Speakes "expressed irritation" that Weinberger's letter had found its way into the morning papers. It had all the earmarks of a Pentagon leak, he seemed to suggest; in any case, he said, "the President would have preferred to read it in the privacy of the Oval Office." The trip was starting to get interesting.

A couple of hours passed before Robert McFarlane wandered back to the pool. The national security adviser stood in the aisle and chatted with the group—Helen Thomas, United Press International; Michael Putzel, the Associated Press; James McCartney, Knight-Ridder; Gary Schuster, CBS; and Morton Kondracke, *Newsweek.* McFarlane had spent a year in Geneva between tours in Vietnam and, Putzel said later, he seemed to be feeling sentimental. "He was unusually relaxed and sort of warm and personal. We chatted about his addiction to chocolate, how nice it was going back to Geneva, where he had a favorite chocolate shop. He was standing there talking to us, and my impression is that he was about to leave —when Helen asked him."

Seated across from Putzel, Thomas had been thinking about the leak of the Weinberger letter. "The story as we took off was in both the *Post* and the *Times,* so of course we would ask about that," she said the next day. "I mean, that's the minimum. I thought it was an important question to ask what they thought about it." She turned to McFarlane: was the leak, she wanted to know, "sabotage"?

"When Helen asked him that, he sort of stopped short," Putzel recalls. "He paused and thought for a moment. Then he turned and said, 'On background—sure it was.' Then *very* hastily, he turned on his heel and walked to the front. You could see his eyes narrow when he said it. I wouldn't call it fury, but his eyes narrowed."

"Wow!" Thomas remembers thinking, "not the usual pap. . . . You know, I said, 'Oh, my goodness, that's it,' and I think we all felt we had gotten something definitive."

Following pool custom, Putzel picked up a phone and called the Washington bureaus of both wire services with an account of the conversation; Kondracke and McCartney prepared a six-hundred-word report on the flight for distribution when the pool caught up with the rest of the White House press in Geneva. The report identified Speakes and McFarlane as the two administration officials who had talked to the pool on the flight, but in the ninth paragraph, where it reported the "sabotage" question, the answer was attributed solely to a "senior American official."

In Washington, the wire services immediately went to work rewriting Putzel's dictation and getting reactions from other officials. "We recognized that it was a significant story," says Charles J. Lewis, the AP's Washington bureau chief. "There were a lot of people running around the world saying that the release of the

Weinberger letter was going to do serious damage. Everybody was interested in the motive of the leaker. That's why the comments from *Air Force One* received such attention."

By the time the White House press straggled into the Intercontinental Hotel about 10 P.M. Geneva time, stories pegged to the "sabotage" comment had already arrived on the wires. Before reporters reached the press center set up in the hotel ballroom by the presidential staff, the UPI story was already up on the board where wire copy was hung. It began:

ABOARD AIR FORCE ONE, NOV. 16 (UPI)—A TOP ADMINISTRATION OFFICIAL SATURDAY ACCUSED SOMEONE IN THE U.S. GOVERNMENT OF TRYING TO SABOTAGE THE SUPERPOWER SUMMIT BY LEAKING CONFIDENTIAL ADVICE FROM DEFENSE SECRETARY CASPAR WEINBERGER URGING PRESIDENT REAGAN TO TAKE A TOUGH LINE ON SOVIET TREATY VIOLATIONS.

Although most of the hundred journalists who had made their way to the room had not yet noticed the story, some of them soon got calls about it from their editors, and word of the "sabotage" comment spread quickly. As they settled into their seats at the long, felt-covered tables facing a podium and TV monitors, the reporters were already talking about the White House reaction. Some of the more restless went to the board and started taking notes from the UPI story, but the monitors soon flickered on with a live feed of the president's arrival at the Geneva airport, and all eyes turned to the business at hand. They had the arrival story to write for the evening news and the Sunday papers, a genre of set-piece journalism so routine that the Reuters team had its lead on the computer even before the president's plane rolled to a halt. Fifteen minutes later, when the exchange of remarks between the presidents of Switzerland and the United States had been completed, the monitors again went blank, and Jack Nelson, the *Los Angeles Times* Washington bureau chief, was out of his seat, searching the room, in vain, for the pool report. Not long after that, a White House staff member appeared with a stack of the reports, placed it on a table near the door, and retreated demurely. There followed a dignified but determined scramble for copies. Now everybody had the story.

Word was already out that McFarlane was the man behind the "sabotage" remark, and although everyone realized that the national security adviser and the press secretary had pumped life into what might otherwise have been something of a one-day affair, the White House reaction to the leak of the letter had become the first news out of the summit. Most reporters were now on deadline: the evening news programs had to go on the air within minutes, and reporters writing for morning papers had at best a few hours. Nelson, for one, picked up his copy of the pool report and headed for the *Los Angeles Times*'s temporary office, established in an Empire salon at the elegant Beau Rivage Hotel in downtown Geneva.

"We called the Washington bureau and Norm Kempster, who covers the State Department for us, was going to be writing a story because somebody in Weinberger's office was reacting," Richard Cooper, the assistant chief of the *Los Angeles Times*'s Washington bureau, recalled when he joined Jack Nelson a few days later in a conversation about the story. Their paper had been beaten by the *Post* and the *New York Times* on the original Weinberger-letter story, so for Sunday's paper they felt obliged to backtrack and fill in their readers.

"Kempster wrote what was going to be, for us, the catch-up for the first day's story. And then the White House arrived and had these comments from the pool report about sabotage," Cooper continued.

"So we took the story over," said Nelson.

"Jack sat down and started writing sort of an 'arrival story,' saying that Reagan arrived for the summit with Gorbachev sounding an upbeat note, or something like that."

"Despite the fact that behind the scenes it was just blood all over the rug," Nelson added.

"We had to write an arrival story," Cooper went on. "We had to get Reagan into Geneva for the Sunday paper. That was the spot news. And so Jack wrote a story that in effect said: Reagan arrived for the summit amid dismaying new evidence of discord and disarray within his own ranks. And then we said, at the airport Reagan said, 'I come in peace for all mankind,' or whatever he said—but that American advisers were distraught over the public disclosure of the letter. And then we had the 'sabotage' quote and we had Speakes saying tartly that the president would rather have read it in his office. And then we had some analysis.

"Now Kempster had written the story strictly on the letter from Washington, and in talking back and forth to Los Angeles, the assistant foreign editor and I concluded that there was so much overlap between these two stories that it would be better to just have one. (Both of us were going to have to explain what Weinberger's positions and urgings meant, what the ABM Treaty says, what's in SALT II and what the letter's effect might be on it.) It requires a certain amount of unselfishness on the reporter's part, because Kempster did a lot of work, wrote an eight-hundred-word story. So on the computer they sent us the Washington story and we put the two together."

The headline over the piece the next morning, "Advisers' Discord Clouds Reagan's Arrival in Geneva," caught the spirit of this synthesis. The lead "got Reagan into Geneva," but beginning in the second paragraph, the story backed up to inform readers about the leak of the Weinberger memo, Weinberger's position concerning arms control issues, the White House reaction, and to provide a long explanation of the Weinberger letter and extensive quotations from the document. The story concluded with thirteen paragraphs, tied to the rest of the story only by a "meanwhile," that described negotiations to shape the meetings between Reagan and Gorbachev that were still forty-eight hours away.

Having broken the letter story the day before, the *New York Times* and the *Washington Post* took a somewhat different tack. Reporters writing for both papers simply assumed that their readers knew about the letter and only needed to be reminded about it in general terms in the context of the next day's developments. Bernard Weinraub, one of the *Times*'s White House reporters, said that he had heard about the "sabotage" comment by word of mouth Saturday night even before he got his copy of the pool report. He wrote a twenty-four-paragraph story which the *Times* ran on page one the next morning. The *Post* played Lou Cannon's account of the day's events the same way. Here are the portions of both stories that ran on the front page, before the reader was required to jump to page 16 in the *Times* and page A31 in the *Post*—the point at which journalists assume that they lose many, if not most, of their readers:

By Bernard Weinraub

Special to The New York Times

GENEVA, Nov. 16—President Reagan arrived here today for the Soviet-American summit meeting amid a dispute over the disclosure of a letter written by Defense Secretary Caspar W. Weinberger urging that no accords be made on two key arms issues.

En route to Geneva, a White House official said he was "astonished" and "perplexed" at the letter, which was published in The New York Times today. An article about the letter, which was not made public officially, also appeared in The Washington Post.

The letter was attached to a Defense Department report to the President on purported Soviet violations of arms control agreements. The letter and the report were obtained by The New York Times from an Administration source.

The White House official who said that the letter "astonished" him was asked whether, in his view, the release of the letter to the press had been intended to sabotage the summit talks.

"Sure it was," the official said. Larry Speakes, the White House spokesman, said: "The President would have preferred to

By Lou Cannon

Washington Post Staff Writer

GENEVA, Nov. 16—President Reagan's arrival here for the superpower summit was marred by the eruption of a bitter battle within the administration over the unauthorized disclosure of a letter to Reagan from Defense Secretary Caspar W. Weinberger. One White House official said the leak was viewed as an attempt to sabotage the summit.

The three-page letter from Weinberger warning the president of the dangers of continued adherence to the SALT II treaty was delivered to the White House on Wednesday as the cover to a long-awaited study of Soviet arms control violations. Copies were obtained Friday by The Washington Post and The New York Times, The Times printed a full copy of it in Saturday's editions.

Pentagon officials said yesterday that the Defense Department had not been the source of the leak, and an official traveling with President Reagan said that Weinberger had ordered an investigation into the matter.

Officials said that Reagan, en route to Geneva, summoned aides to a midair conference in an attempt to determine whether Weinberger or one of his aides read it in the privacy of the Oval Office and not in The New York Times."

[In Washington, Mr. Weinberger's spokesman, Robert Sims, said the Defense Department "had absolutely nothing to do with the release of the letter." Mr. Sims said that it was Mr. Weinberger's policy not to publicly discuss any advice to the President and that the Secretary was "outraged at the disclosure and ordered an immediate investigation."

[When asked about the comment of the White House official that the disclosure was intended to sabotage the summit meeting, Mr. Sims said, "The Secretary would agree that the public release of this private letter to the President was not helpful and feels equally disturbed and concerned."]

Mr. Weinberger, who will not be at

Continued on Page 16,
Column 5

had leaked the letter. A senior official aboard Air Force One was asked whether he regarded the leaked letter as an effort to sabotage Reagan's summit with Soviet leader Mikhail Gorbachev.

"Sure it was," the official replied.

Another senior official called the release of the letter "egregious" and said it was "a blatant attempt to undermine the president just before the summit," which begins here Tuesday.

But Weinberger's spokesman, Bob Sims, denied that the secretary of defense was responsible for the disclosure.

"Department of Defense had nothing to do with the release of the text of Secretary Weinberger's letter to the president to any publications," Sims said. "It is Sec-

See Weinberger, A31, Col. 1

We can see how these stories differ in an instant:

Weinraub's lead for the *Times* is written in the active voice that journalists are urged to employ ("Reagan arrived here today" instead of Cannon's construction, "Reagan's arrival here . . . was"). The leads as a whole suggest a slightly different relationship between the events described: Cannon's subordinates the arrival to the dispute, while Weinraub's makes the dispute an aspect of the arrival.

Weinraub's constructions are also slightly more "objective" in the sense in which journalists typically understand the term, for in his story Reagan arrived "amid a dispute" while in Cannon's his arrival was "marred" by that same dispute. Weinraub, that is to say, describes the circumstances, while Cannon's lead suggests a judgment concerning their consequences. In his third paragraph, Weinraub also carefully describes Soviet violations of arms control agreements as "purported," while Cannon in his second seems to refer to them as an established fact. Weinraub also uses less inflected language to suggest how the *Times* came into possession of the Weinberger letter. He merely says it was "obtained" (and on the jump inside the paper refers to the event itself as a "disclosure"), while Cannon is willing to label this transfer of knowledge a "leak."

Certain facts appear in one story but not in the other. The *Times* has officials being "astonished" and "perplexed" by the publication of the letter, while the *Post* has an official calling it "egregious" and the president calling a meeting to discuss it. The *Post* tells us the name of the treaty that was the object of Weinberger's efforts (SALT II), and tells us that his letter was three pages long, that it was delivered on Wednesday and obtained by the press on Friday. The *Times* adds that it came from an "administration source," and also adds brackets around the remarks of Robert Sims, the Pentagon spokesman, to make it clear that they were interpolated by the editors.

That's it. In all other respects, two of the senior political reporters in the country had produced stories which for all intents and purposes were identical. The short account of the differences above, in other words, virtually exhausts the contrasts in order to highlight the resemblances. How similar the stories actually are becomes clear if we compare the structure of the information that each imparts to the reader. Here, for example, is a breakdown of the order in which information is presented on both front pages:

The Washington Post	The New York Times
Reagan arrival ————————	Reagan arrival
White House reaction	Letter content
Letter content	White House reaction
Letter purpose	Letter published
Letter obtained	Letter purpose
Letter published	Letter obtained

The Washington Post	The New York Times
Pentagon reaction	
White House reaction——————White House reaction
"Sure it was"——————————"Sure it was"
White House reaction——————White House reaction
Sims reaction————————————Sims reaction

The rhythms of both pieces are strikingly similar. McFarlane's response to Thomas's question, attributed to an "official" in accordance with the background rule he invoked, occurs as the climax of the first part of both stories, "Sure it was" being set off as a fifth and separate paragraph in both. Moreover, the stories contain almost the same information, weighted in almost the same way, presented in nearly identical order. Both papers included the same information in the lead (Reagan's arrival, White House reaction, and the content of the letter), in their reprise of the letter (its purpose and how it was obtained and published), in the description of White House reaction setting up and following the McFarlane comment, and in their reporting of the comments of Pentagon spokesman Robert Sims. The similarities are so striking, in fact, that they seem to suggest that there was a certain inevitability in the way the papers reported the news, or, perhaps more accurately, that the facts such stories contain naturally formed themselves into "the news." "The leak happened in Washington, but it mattered in Geneva," Richard Cooper said of the Weinberger-letter story, explaining why it commanded the attention of the *Los Angeles Times* bureau at the summit. President Reagan had just gotten off the plane Saturday night as well, and, of course, that was news, too. The stories that put these things together appeared as the apparently natural outcome of the day's events. The similarities appear to be the natural product of two crack reporters who let the facts speak for themselves.

This appearance, however, is somewhat deceptive. To see why, we have to look at the newspapers of the day before, the *Post* and the *New York Times* editions of Saturday, November 16, which were delivered to offices all over Washington as the president was preparing to board *Air Force One* for the flight to Geneva. Saturday's papers broke the story of Secretary Weinberger's letter to the president, sent over to the White House several days earlier as the cover to a report outlining possible responses to alleged Soviet violations of SALT II and the Antiballistic Missile Treaty of 1973. The *Times* article, written by Michael R. Gordon, the paper's new national security correspondent, began on the front page and jumped to page 7, where the paper also ran the entire text of the letter across four columns at the top of the page. Together, the story and the text ran fifty-five inches, ten of them on the front page, which signaled the importance with which the editors regarded this story. *Post* editors, in contrast, buried their account, written by Walter Pincus, a veteran on this beat, on page A11, gave it only twenty inches, and did not run the text of the letter. Even in Washington, accordingly, it was the *Times* story which many people saw first, and it was the play the *Times* gave the story that suggested the importance of the Weinberger letter to other correspondents. The question that Helen Thomas asked McFarlane on the way to Geneva, for example, echoed the last paragraph of the *Times* article, which quoted a charge by Spurgeon Keeny, Jr., president of the Arms Control Association, that "it is clear that the Secretary of Defense is trying to sabotage those areas where they [*sic*] might be some agreement."

However differently they played the original story of the leak on Saturday, by Sunday the two papers were speaking with a single voice. The twenty-four hours between constitute a study in differences overcome. For the *Post,* the story of the leak was the shortest of six summit-related articles in Saturday's paper, two of which ran on page one. It was also considered less important than a story about Secretary Weinberger's efforts to protect the defense budget from congressional action to reduce it, which the paper ran on page A3. The Pincus story itself seemed to treat the leak of the letter as a footnote to the long-running story about the Pentagon's attempt to line up the president behind the Pentagon's plans to respond to alleged Soviet treaty violations. The fourth paragraph of the story noted that the study which the letter accompanied found that Soviet violations were continuing, "as previously reported." There was not much new here, in the opinion of Pincus and the *Post.* The *Times's* page-one play of the story suggested a very different view. Yet even the *Times* noted on the jump that the report merely seemed to repeat earlier Pentagon charges of Soviet violations "in stronger terms," although it did charge additional violations of the "spirit" of the 1972 accord in the Soviet deployment of SS-19 ICBMs. The letter was described by unnamed administration officials as a "last-minute effort to influence Mr. Reagan's arms control positions" at the summit, and for the *Times* it was the timing of the letter rather than its content that seems to have made it important.

In the initial furor over the letter, the fact that it contained little new was largely lost from view. The White House press corps, comfortable with the genre of story that reports dissension in administration ranks, quickly saw the letter as a sign that such discord had indeed increased. Such "disarray stories" have long been a staple of Washington reporting, and have, in fact, been written about nuclear policy since the month after Hiroshima, when the press reported disarray in the Truman administration over whether to share the atomic secret with the Allies. Struggles within the Reagan administration over its arms control policies have provided the White House press with ample opportunities to write such stories over the preceding several years, and there had been a flood of reports on the eve of the summit itself describing heightened disorder: *Time* reported "deep divisions among the President's men"; Evans and Novak, "an administration in confusion"; and Leslie H. Gelb, in the *New York Times,* "disarray" on arms control policy "caused mainly by the fact that President Reagan has not yet decided on his own general approach to the meeting, let alone on the specifics." "Disarray" is a tale that Washington reporters know how to write and that readers are used to reading. It is a story form well suited to reporting a city whose principal feature is bureaucracy—a genre that subordinates discussion of the issues to reports on the status of the important players. Like the "arrival story," the "disarray story" was a readily available device with which facts could easily be arranged into a narrative.

Stories written upon arrival in Geneva Saturday night for the next day's paper were shaped by the "disarray" genre, and on Sunday the angle suggested by this story was the principal one pursued by the press. Reporters grilled Larry Speakes at his 11 A.M. briefing, followed the comments of administration spokesmen on the morning news programs (the transcripts of which were distributed by the White House), and sought out their sources in the bars and byways of the Intercontinental Hotel. By evening, the strands of the story were coming apart: the letter was not unusual, the leak was unfortunate, the president's plans were unchanged. "The Secretary of Defense['s] views, as expressed in his cover letter which was printed in the newspapers of yesterday and today, are not new," Larry Speakes had said at the morning briefing, and at the end of the day, the press could do little but concede that he was right. "Mr. Weinberger's positions on the two questions coincide with those of the White House," R. W. Apple, Jr., concluded in Monday's *New York Times*.

If it took two days for the facts to catch up with the "disarray story," the story of the leak itself never got into print. As Charles J. Lewis, the AP Washington bureau chief, put it, "The identity and motive of the leaker were major parlor games in town." Had it been somebody on Weinberger's staff—Richard Perle, the controversial assistant secretary of defense, for example—trying to put additional pressure on the White House on the eve of the summit or signaling a victory on the issue to conservative constituencies on the Hill and in the hustings? Or had Weinberger's enemies on the White House staff leaked the letter in the hope of embarrassing the secretary and injuring his relations with the president? Or, as yet others speculated, had the leak come from a congressional source, motive unknown, even one working, as others have done, merely to demonstrate his own importance? If there was little new in the letter, if the timing was a peg but not really the news, the identity and motive of the leaker remained very much a story, but one that could only be written by the reporters who had first gotten access to the letter. Although Walter Pincus made an effort to get his source to go on the record, he failed, and his identity and motive— the real story in this incident—remained mostly unknown and universally unreported.

Since Weinberger's letter took on real importance only when it was leaked to the press, however, with an additional phone call or

two both the *Times* and the *Post* in theory could have reported
something like the following at the top of their Saturday stories:

> Washington, Nov. 15—A recent letter from Secretary of De-
> fense Caspar W. Weinberger to President Reagan urging him
> not to compromise on SALT II and the ABM Treaty was made
> available to [the *New York Times*/the *Washington Post*] today.
> The letter reiterates the secretary's well-known positions on
> alleged Soviet treaty violations, according to administration
> officials, but with the source of the leak requesting anonymity,
> the disclosure of the letter has put the administration on the
> defensive on the eve of the Geneva summit, other sources say.

Such a lead would have removed the emphasis from the "disarray
story"—for which the Weinberger letter was poor or in any case
relatively uninteresting evidence—in order to place it where it belonged: on the leak itself and its implications for the summit. To
have written it would have been to provide the most limited of the
alternative readings which could have been justified by the affair,
but the story such a lead suggests would have taken a better measure
of the events than those which in fact appeared. To have written it,
however, would have been to suggest that journalists had helped
make the news that convention dictates they only admit to covering.
It would have been to violate the canon according to which the
objectivity of the news is ensured by removing any reference to the
journalist as an agent in its creation. But if it had been written, it
would have put the real "who," the leaker, back in the center of the
story where he belonged. It would have put the act of leaking in
the center of the story, where it, too, belonged as the "what." The
answer to "when" would have been "today"—Friday—the day of
the leak, rather than Wednesday, when the letter was delivered to
the White House. The answer to "where" would have remained
much the same—Washington—although with the story now incor-
porating the leak, its significance for the events unfolding in Geneva
could have been established more explicitly. Finally, answering the
"why" inherent in the story suggested by this lead would have
required reporting not only on Weinberger's intentions but on the

leaker's motives—as well as on why this disclosure would have the impact suggested in the lead.

Even with the letter in hand on Friday, therefore, the story to be written about it could not yet be taken for granted. It involved a complex military and diplomatic matter in which one bureaucratic maneuver—the secretary's letter—had been trumped by another— the leak itself. What the papers presented as "the news" about it on Saturday was really a selection of what might have been reported, a selection shaped above all by the way the events of the day intersected with the conventions journalists had available to report them. The president had embarked on a journey with the kind of palpable physical and ceremonial attributes that suggested it had reality as an event. Something, in other words, did indeed take place, and did indeed present itself in sequence. It was a fact that "the president left Washington," as it was a fact that "the president arrived in Geneva." These facts demanded to be reported, but to do so journalists had to represent them through textual forms that made demands of their own. In the process, such "facts" became a "story." But *which* story did not depend solely on the facts. A "departure story" could have been constructed, for example, and it would have begun: "President Reagan left Washington today on his trip to the Geneva summit amid a dispute over the disclosure of a letter . . ." But it was the "arrival story" which best met the narrative requirements imposed by the nature of the events and the routines of journalism. As Richard Cooper explained, sounding for all the world like an author plotting out his novel, "We had to get Reagan into Geneva for the Sunday paper."

He also recognized that storytelling requirements made it necessary to put the "arrival story" together with the "Weinberger-letter story," since to do otherwise would have meant telling important parts of the same story twice. For the *Los Angeles Times* but also for the *New York Times* and the *Washington Post,* the "arrival story" thereby became charged with the greater drama of this other story which (after convention ruled out reporting the facts in other ways, such as in a story featuring the leak itself) naturally seemed to resolve into a story about "disarray." The *Post* had been closer to the mark when it downplayed the story on Saturday, but the *Times,* by putting it on the front page and running the complete text of the letter, had created a news event which the *Post* could not afford to ignore. Despite unresolved ambiguities concerning the significance of the letter and the leak, Sunday's stories in both papers presented a uniform account. In the midst of this complex affair, the source of this similarity, however, lay not in the facts themselves but in the way events with structures of their own (the trip and the leak) were shaped by journalistic convention (the "objective" standard of non-self-referential reporting) and transformed by narrative forms ("arrival" and "disarray") into what all concerned agreed was "the story."

Reality does not always provide materials so well suited to narrative form as a president's "quest for peace," nor events so seemingly dramatic as the leak of a confidential letter written for his eyes on the eve of his departure. Not all events lend themselves so well to appropriation by narrative; and forms are not always so readily available as those of the "arrival" and "disarray" stories. When, as at the beginning of the summit trip, events and narrative forms seem to intersect, reporters working at this temporal and literary conjunction find it natural to report the story they do and unsurprising that other reporters may have made the same choices. But when events and narrative forms share less of an affinity, reporters are faced with more decisions to make and tend to make them differently.

Although almost any day's papers can provide interesting material with which to test this proposition, a revealing case in point dates from the postsummit period when Robert McFarlane announced his resignation as the president's national security affairs adviser and shortly thereafter delivered what was billed as his farewell address to the World Affairs Council in Washington, D.C. "McFarlane Says More Effort Needed to Put Down Spying," read the headline over the story about the speech in the *Washington Times* the next day, December 10, 1985, while Lou Cannon's story in the *Washington Post* carried the head "McFarlane Optimistic on Arms Control; But Outgoing Reagan Aide Sees U.S.-Soviet Accord on Afghanistan Less Likely." The heads suggested that the stories were not so much in disagreement over what McFarlane had said as about different speeches entirely.

This impression was confirmed by the stories themselves. Bill Gertz's piece in the *Times* reported that McFarlane had said that "the United States should make greater efforts to reduce spying even at the cost of straining U.S.-Soviet relations" and continued with twelve more paragraphs on espionage and counterespionage activities before adding that McFarlane had said it was "too soon to tell" how the summit would affect arms control negotiations. Cannon's piece in the *Post* devoted not a single word to reporting the remarks on espionage. Its entire length was devoted to expanding upon McFarlane's judgment, quoted in the lead, "that the United States and the Soviet Union 'are at a real moment of opportunity in arms control' and have the chance to achieve an interim agreement that would limit intermediate-range ballistic missiles in Europe."

Two reporters had taken a speech, the kind of event that a hundred years ago would have been covered by a stenographer, and come up with completely disparate accounts of it. Ironists tend to make sport of such divergent readings. The *New Republic* regularly runs clashing headlines ("White House Backing C.I.A. on Prosecuting Publications" [*New York Times*], "White House Shuns Casey's Proposal to Prosecute Press" [*Washington Times*]) in order to make it clear that someone, yet again, got the story wrong. But the reporters covering McFarlane's speech provided something other than ironic contrast—in effect, they wrote different stories, one predominantly about espionage, the other completely about arms control. The last three paragraphs of Cannon's story, moreover, diverged markedly not only from Gertz's piece but from McFarlane's text as well. They did so after Cannon quoted McFarlane as saying that "new opportunities" existed for agreements between the United States and the Soviet Union. "However," wrote Cannon at the beginning of the next paragraph, "the departing security affairs adviser made no mention in his 25-minute address of Reagan's favorite proposal, the missile defense plan formally known as the Strategic Defense Initiative and often called 'Star Wars.' " Cannon then went on to fill in the negotiating background on the "Star Wars" issues in another paragraph, and, lastly, to explain that the phrase "interim agreement," which he, following McFarlane, had used in his lead, was a term of art employed by Soviet negotiators to refer to an understanding that might be reached on the subject of intermediate-range missiles (U.S. cruise and Pershings, Soviet SS-20s)—but only in the context of controls on the development of "Star Wars."

In these last three paragraphs of the story, Cannon seemed to be providing the context and background that journalists are often asked to supply by their critics. The process, in this case at least, is not particularly elegant. The background about "Star Wars" is tied to the preceding story by an introductory adverb—"However"—which at first seems argumentative. Not unless the reader knows that McFarlane has been a less than enthusiastic supporter of "Star Wars" will he realize that the reporter is not so much arguing with the speaker as pointing out what he considers to be a significant, and intentional, omission in his remarks. Cannon then explains that the USSR is insisting on the limitation of SDI as the quid pro quo for a treaty on offensive missiles. Having laid this groundwork for the knowledgeable reader, the last paragraph of the piece brings it full circle to the lead by raising the question of the "interim agreement." In the context of the conflict between the United States and the USSR over limitation of offensive missile systems, it suggests to those who read it carefully that McFarlane's omission of "Star Wars" and his use of Soviet terminology may have suggested certain initiatives that the departing national security affairs adviser, for one, might have considered it in the interest of his government to pursue.

Such a close reading is what national security journalism very often requires. What it reveals in this instance is something more than the nuances of McFarlane's positions on the issues. For in order to make these clear, Cannon has in effect sketched a three-paragraph outline for a story that would embed the speech in a broader narrative. It would be one that would recount the history of McFarlane's relations with the other members of the Reagan team and especially the friction between him and the new chief of staff, Donald T. Regan; would describe the evolution of his arms control positions; and would detail his role in the development of the "Star Wars" concept and his interest in using it to strike an arms limitation deal with the Russians. This story, in turn, would be part of a greater narrative, a portion of which Cannon did indeed write six days later in the *Post*. Naturally enough, it carried the head "Disarray Under Regan." Like all speeches, however, McFarlane's was an event with a weak narrative line, and it was an inadequate vehicle for such a story. Moreover, the repertory of narrative forms for reporting speeches is small, particularly when the speech is not part of some larger ceremonial occasion the story of which subsumes the speech itself. In reporting a speech such as McFarlane's, the reporter has fewer conventional narrative resources on which to draw. If he does not merely want to transcribe or summarize the remarks—vaguely demeaning tasks for the contemporary journalist—the reporter gets fewer clues from the event itself about how to play it than he does, for example, from Reagan's arrival in Geneva. The weakness of the narrative structure of the speech means that the reporter covering a speech must in effect discover "the story" for himself. Gertz did so by writing it into the "espionage story" which the *Times*, like many papers, had been featuring. Cannon did so by making it part of the "arms control story," which the *Post* follows closely. The "disarray story" that Cannon sketched in his last three paragraphs was a sign of tension between the rest of his text and the weakly structured event it reported. The nominal story was that motivated by what McFarlane said, and Cannon wrote it. The real story, one may hazard, was motivated by what he did not say, and Cannon permitted it to erupt through the text despite one of journalism's important conventions: stories are about what happened, not what didn't.

A weakly structured event may nevertheless provide the occasion for a more fully realized narrative, as had been demonstrated a month earlier, when members of the White House press corps, Cannon among them, reported an interview which five Western European television correspondents conducted with President Reagan several days before he was due to leave for the summit. The event produced major stories, all of which were featured on the front pages of the next morning's newspapers.

"President Reagan yesterday downplayed the chances for arms control progress at the Geneva summit next week, and all but ruled out a joint communiqué with Soviet leader Mikhail S. Gorbachev at the summit's conclusion," Walter V. Robinson wrote in the *Boston Globe* of November 13. Under the head "Reagan Cool on Prospects for Arms Progress," his lengthy story quoted the president's bearish assessment in detail, and bolstered the report with similar comments offered by presidential spokesman Edward Djerejian and by "a senior U.S. official" at a briefing earlier in the day. Jack Nelson's story for the *Los Angeles Times* took another tack, accurately reflected in the headline affixed to it by the desk in Los Angeles: "President Is Upbeat on Summit; Sees Many Areas for Accord; Europe Missiles Stressed." Nelson's lead reported that during the interview the president had offered "one of his most optimistic statements about the outlook for next week's summit" and in his second paragraph elaborated on this point by mentioning negotiations to eliminate medium-range missiles in Europe and to establish a "nuclear-free zone in Europe." The rest of the piece developed this theme, citing remarks by Paul H. Nitze, the senior arms control adviser, Secretary of State George Shultz, and Senators Bob Dole and Robert C. Byrd, who spoke after they met with the president and his advisers to receive a briefing on the summit.

Cannon teamed up with Don Oberdorfer and adopted an entirely different approach for the story in the *Washington Post* which was headed, "U.S. Offers to Extend SALT II Compliance; Reagan Would Sell SDI to Soviets 'at Cost.'" Their lead reported that the administration had informed the Soviets the week before of its willingness to continue to abide by the Salt II Treaty even though it had not been formally ratified by the United States (the very policy, incidentally, that Secretary Weinberger challenged in his letter to the president delivered and leaked the very week this story appeared). The second paragraph of the story reported that "meanwhile," the president had held an interview with European journalists during which he had modified his "Star Wars" plans, offering to sell the technology, once it was developed, to the Soviet Union "at cost." The story's third paragraph began this way: "Reagan's interview came on a busy day of presummit activity, most conducted by 'administration officials' who asked for anonymity." The rest of the lengthy account discussed this activity by category, two long sections being devoted to summarizing developments concerning SALT II policy and human rights and a third being devoted to the president's interview with the European press. The account of the interview itself avoided the characterization of Reagan's arms control expectations, which played such an important role in the accounts in the *Globe* and the *Los Angeles Times*. It focused, instead, on his apparent willingness to discuss a nuclear-free zone in Europe, something Nelson had mentioned, but only in passing, pointing out that it "appeared to be a new statement of policy."

The most significant sentence in the *Post*'s account is that which begins the third paragraph of the story and places the president's interview in the context of "a busy day of presummit activity." Despite the fact that it is not the lead, this statement contextualizes the day's events using an apparently neutral device for organizing interviews, briefings, and other developments that were merely mentioned seriatim in the two other papers. Juxtaposing them in this fashion, however, is something more than the neutral organizational technique it may seem to be. For in doing so, Cannon and Oberdorfer are in fact assimilating the "interview story" to a more powerful one, thereby effecting a shift in both its importance and its meaning: Ronald Reagan (a who) is removed from the center of the account and replaced by "a busy day of presummit activity" (a what). The answer to "when" is no longer "during the president's interview" but "throughout the day of summit preparations"; the answer to "where" is no longer "the president's office" or "the White House" but wherever presummit preparations are under way; the answer to "why" can no longer be supplied by scrutinizing the president's activities but must be deduced with reference to those of an entire administration preparing to present its case to the Soviet Union, world opinion, and its own people.

Constructing the story of "a busy day of presummit activity" is a way of knitting apparently disparate events together into a single narrative. To do so is to use the power that narrative possesses to suggest that the story's unity mirrors reality's and to suggest that the events of the day, separate in space and time, share a meaning which the narrative has restored to them. The reader is invited to understand that the intentions of those directing and participating in the events ("administration officials," for example) are to be grasped not through any of their individual actions (the interview, for example), but through the pattern they create, which is grasped by the story. Although such a story may report the events of the day, it also interprets them, even if it does so under the colors of giving the news.

This choice of narrative structure, in fact, is among the most important journalistic decisions, less noticeable than the thumbs-up, thumbs-down judgments of the *Boston Globe* or *Los Angeles Times* stories, but far more significant since it determines the shape of the event to be judged and thereby often the judgment that is to be rendered. In fact, journalism can be seen as an activity that judges events while it reports them by juxtaposing, amalgamating, or separating facts, events, and opinion in order to find in them their "story."

Just how radical this process can be is established by a group of stories reporting a speech delivered by Secretary Weinberger to a Washington luncheon sponsored by the Carnegie Endowment for International Peace on January 9, 1986, some eight weeks after the summit. The news reports the following day were largely in agreement about what the secretary had said: he had warned that increased Pentagon spending was necessary to drive the Soviet Union to the bargaining table and that the USSR had recently added eighteen SS-25 ICBMs to the twenty-seven it had already deployed, in violation of the ceilings being observed under the SALT II Treaty (which the United States, despite the secretary's earlier efforts, was still honoring). The facts of the matter seemed to be clear to all and the accounts of the lunch provided no discrepant headlines for the *New Republic*. But the next day's spot news accounts, agreeing as they did about what Weinberger had said, nevertheless conveyed thoroughly different impressions of why he had spoken and what his remarks had meant. They did so by virtue of the larger narrative into which they inserted the speech itself. Looking over the accounts of the speech that ran in *USA Today*, the *Philadelphia Inquirer*, the *New York Times*, the *Boston Globe* and the *Los Angeles Times*, it is clear that none of them merely reported it. All juxtaposed it to extratextual information in the interest of creating a story.

Fred Kaplan of the *Globe* juxtaposed the charge of Soviet SS-25 deployments with earlier statements by the secretary on the same general subject, demonstrating that he had made similar accusations concerning Soviet violations before. Kaplan also provided details of the SALT II agreement (for example, that under its terms a "new type" of missile is one whose principal dimensions or weight differ from those of existing systems by more than 5 percent), which he then used to evaluate the charges that the SS-25 deployments were violations of the agreement or a threat to American security. By virtue of the information Kaplan brought to bear on the speech on his own authority, the speech was assimilated to a "deployments story" and used to demonstrate that the story itself was nothing new. Using a different temporal horizon, Johanna Neuman's account in *USA Today*, headlined "Arms Talks to Start Amid New Charges," looked ahead. It began: "The USA's arms control negotiators return to Geneva this weekend—after new Pentagon charges that the Soviets have deployed 18 new missiles in 'clear violation' of SALT II." In her hands, Weinberger's speech became the beginning of a new chapter in the "negotiations story" that had yet to be written.

James Gerstenzang presented the speech as part of the "budget story," his report in the *Los Angeles Times* being dominated by an account of the fiscal pressures on the defense budget. It juxtaposed specific congressionally mandated budget ceilings for fiscal 1986 and 1987, details of the politics that shaped the budget-making process, and information concerning how the Pentagon was likely to wield the knife on its own programs should it come to that. (It would protect its strategic weapons systems.) The story reported the SS-25 deployments and the speech as a whole as part of the long-running "budget-struggle story." Mark Thompson also framed the speech as a budget story in the *Inquirer*, emphasizing the secretary's argument that only increased defense spending could get the Soviets to the bargaining table. But his lead gave the story another twist. It began: "Defense Secretary Caspar W. Weinberger, seeking to revive the Pentagon's faltering budget buildup, said yesterday that the Soviet Union had deployed 18 new intercontinental ballistic missiles in 'clear violation' of the 1979 Strategic Arms Limitation Treaty." The subordinate clause tucked into this lead nicely attributed a motive to the secretary, and in doing so tended to make Gerstenzang's "budget story" into one featuring the secretary himself.

Bill Keller's piece for the *New York Times* also emphasized the budget but did so in order to scrutinize Weinberger's claim that its size would directly affect the arms control process. It cited the Gramm-Rudman-Hollings deficit-reduction act in lieu of the generalized pressures suggested in Thompson's story, and, like Kaplan's, juxtaposed earlier statements by the secretary and other Pentagon officials with those contained in the text of the speech. Midway through the account, however, Keller reported that many in the audience "were stunned by Mr. Weinberger's comment, in an off-the-record question session after his speech, that he had played no part in a recent Administration arms control proposal to ban mobile intercontinental missiles." Keller reported that "members of the audience said the remark, if true, amounted to an admission that Mr. Weinberger wields little influence in the Administration's arms negotiating policy. Another said it 'indicates the confusion inside the Administration' on arms issues." Although missing from the lead, this material in fact dominated the story, since, as Keller himself made clear, other administration officials had already disclosed the SS-25 deployments in November. In this fashion, the speech was assimilated into a story about Weinberger himself, a variety of the "influence-waxing-or-influence-waning story" that is as much a staple of Washington reporting as the "disarray story," which was also echoed here.

One measure of the diversity of these narrative strategies is the nature of the extratextual material that is juxtaposed with the speech in order to make the strategies work. Since the event itself was narratively weak and the speaker and his subject semantically complex, the speech could serve as the narrative vehicle for diverse stories, all of them, in their own way, being true. The complete list of materials brought into play in order to write these stories is impressive and, in simplified form, looks like this:

- Earlier Weinberger statements on SS-25 deployments:
  Last October *(Globe)*
  November *(New York Times)*
  December 6 *(Globe, Inquirer, Los Angeles Times)*
- Report in the *New York Times* last week *(Globe)*
- Background on SALT II:

History and provisions *(Globe, New York Times, Los Angeles Times)*

Terminology *(Globe)*

- Forthcoming SALT II compliance issues *(Globe)*
- Soviet military activities not mentioned in the speech:
    SS-24 testing *(Globe, Los Angeles Times)*
    SS-11 dismantling *(New York Times)*
- U.S. military activity not mentioned in the speech:
    Midgetman missile *(Globe, New York Times)*
- Soviet reactions to American charges *(Globe, Inquirer, New York Times, Los Angeles Times)*
- Budget process *(Inquirer, New York Times, Los Angeles Times)*
- Congressional budget projections *(Inquirer)*
- Gramm-Rudman-Hollings act *(Inquirer, New York Times, Los Angeles Times)*
- Administration position on SALT II *(Inquirer, Los Angeles Times)*
- Resumption of Geneva talks *(USA Today)*
- November summit agreements *(USA Today)*
- Pentagon budget-cutting strategy *(Los Angeles Times)*
- Weinberger's role in mobile-missile proposal *(New York Times)*
- NATO's antiterrorism position *(Los Angeles Times)*
- Additional comments by (partial listing):
    Weinberger aides *(Los Angeles Times)*
    Administration officials *(Los Angeles Times)*
    Brent Scowcroft, administration adviser *(New York Times)*
    Thomas Longstreth, Edward Kennedy adviser *(New York Times)*
    Russell Murray, congressional aide *(New York Times)*
    Larry Speakes, president's deputy press secretary *(USA Today)*
    Michael Krepon, Carnegie Endowment *(Globe)*

Substantially different accounts of the speech emerged in each of the papers. By juxtaposing different information with the text of the address, by assimilating it to different narrative texts, the speech became either a military and arms control document, a budgetary maneuver, or part of American negotiating strategy. The audience for which each of these reports presumed the speech to have been intended was different in each case, comprising different constituencies in Congress, the executive branch, the Pentagon, and within the Soviet military, economic, and political leadership. The desire to reach different audiences, of course, implies different motives, and each of these speeches was presumably motivated in different ways, although only the *Boston Globe* suggested how explicitly. Creating narratives by juxtaposing information was therefore an act that "created" the speech—or recreated it—in each case with reference to its intentions and therefore its meaning. None of these accounts was necessarily incompatible with the others, it should be said; but by virtue of what they chose to juxtapose with the speech itself, five reporters writing five news stories about a single speech created markedly different impressions concerning its thrust and significance. They did so, moreover, within the conventions of daily journalism. None seemed to breach the divide between interpreting and reporting, and none of the stories were set apart with a "News Analysis" slug. Inasmuch as they were narratives, however, all of them were indeed interpretations.

Moreover, the deftness with which Mark Thompson used a subordinate clause in his budget story to recast it as one about Weinberger suggests a process that is worth examining in some detail. For although every news story is shaped by the demands of a narrative, some are shaped by those of more than one. Like Thompson's, that is, many stories contain fragments of other narratives that shade the meaning of the principal one. On February 4, 1986, for example, during the slight thaw in superpower relations that followed the Geneva summit, *L'Humanité,* the newspaper of the French Communist Party, reprinted the text of an interview with Mikhail Gorbachev, the Soviet leader. Although it ranged across a number of issues in East-West relations, the interview, coming as it did on the eve of an exchange of spies that was expected to include the Russian dissident Anatoly Shcharansky, created a slight stir because Gorbachev seemed to rule out the prospect of a similar swap involving another prominent dissident, Andrei Sakharov, living in internal exile in the city of Gorky. Sakharov, he said, "still has knowledge of secrets of special importance to the state and for this reason cannot go abroad."

This statement, as Celestine Bohlen reported in the *Washington Post* the next day, constituted "Gorbachev's first public justification of the treatment of Sakharov." But although her account of the interview ran some twenty inches, she did not elaborate on his explanation. In this respect, her treatment of the question of "secrets of special importance" was minimalist: it repeated what had been said but no more. It was left to the reader to supply his own information, should he have it, or to remain in the dark as to whether Gorbachev's allusion had substance.

The *San Diego Union* provided such information directly, drawing on news service accounts and writing its story at the desk. The story's first four paragraphs conveyed the basic facts about Gorbachev's statement, the context of the interview, the plight of Sakharov's wife, Yelena Bonner, who had recently been permitted to go abroad for medical treatment. It then quoted the statement about "secrets of special importance," and followed it with a paragraph that read as follows: "It was the first time that Gorbachev publicly referred to Sakharov by name and accused the human rights activist, known as the father of the Soviet hydrogen bomb, of being a criminal." What matters here is the information which the paper inserted between Sakharov's human rights activities and Gorbachev's accusation. That he worked on the Soviet H-bomb suggests the kind of "special secrets" he might be considered to possess in Soviet eyes. In this respect, it is an elaboration that clarifies the meaning of Gorbachev's statement. But it does more than that. For the information juxtaposed—that he was the bomb's "father"—establishes something of a moral equivalence on his behalf with George Washington, known as "the Father of His Country," and with Edward Teller, the Manhattan Project physicist who is universally known as "the Father of the H-bomb." San Diego being a city with a large naval base and strong military ties, and the *Union* being a paper with strong defense coverage and hawkish editorial views, for the paper to call Sakharov the father of his country's own bomb is to honor him.

In the *Union*'s story, "the father of the Soviet hydrogen bomb" is a phrase that seems to modify the preceding one, "human rights activist"—something that Sakharov also is. Inasmuch as Sakharov's scientific discoveries do not bear on his human rights activities, his work on the bomb appears to be something of a non sequitur in logical terms. In narrative terms, however, it is not. What we have here in fact is the germ of a biography, a narrative fragment which is fulfilling an informational role, it is true, but a rhetorical and political one as well. Although it is here by virtue of its nominal news value, its presence adds to the contrast between Sakharov the "human rights activist" (for us) and the "criminal" (for them). The fragment weights the scales of judgment in favor of Sakharov the activist, adding to his moral standing in the eyes of the reader by suggesting the story that is to be told about him and, by implication, about his persecution at Soviet hands.

It is in this fashion that the interpolation of a single narrative fragment can carry as much semantic weight as an entire editorial. "Thiokol Engineers Tell of Being Overruled," the *Washington Post* reported on its front page of February 26, 1986, over an account detailing how the management of Morton Thiokol, "apparently responding to pressure from the National Aeronautics and Space Administration," had recommended the launch of the space shuttle *Challenger* that had exploded upon lift-off a month before. A straight news account of testimony before the presidential commission investigating the accident, the article by Boyce Rensberger and Kevin Klose obeyed the conventions governing such stories throughout the fifty inches of its length. They reported that engineers for Thiokol, which manufactured the solid-fuel boosters for the shuttle at its Utah plant, all opposed the launch on the night before it took place. According to the testimony, however, NASA officials were "appalled" at the engineers' recommendation, and pressured Thiokol management to overrule its own people. Robert K. Lund, the company's vice president for engineering, supported his staff, the paper reported. But he was told by his superiors to "take off your engineer hat and put on your management hat," and he thereupon approved the launch.

For the most part, the story was a straightforward one based on the testimony: Who? Thiokol managers. What? Approved the launch over the recommendation of their engineers. Where? Brigham City, Utah; the Marshall Space Flight Center, Huntsville, Alabama; and the John F. Kennedy Space Center, Cape Canaveral, Florida. When? During the conference call the night before the

launch. Why? NASA pressure. But the testimony itself left part of
the story untold, and the reporters, working within narrative convention, moved to tell it in the interstices of their text: it was the
story of why Thiokol caved in to NASA pressure. On the night
before the launch, they wrote, "when the engineers stood firm, their
company's management, then trying to win a new booster contract
from NASA, overruled them and gave NASA the go-ahead it
sought." A mere fact about a contract, of course. But one behind
which everyone can read the story about how hardball is played—
how deals are struck, business is lost or won, careers are made or
ruined. The subordinate clause in this sentence, in other words, the
narrative fragment inserted in the text, supplies the motive which
the presidential commission had not. Four days later, the *New York
Times* supplied it explicitly. "Thiokol is said to have had no reason
to fear for the renewal of its NASA contract," the paper wrote, "but
if not, what did its reconsidering executives mean when they asked
their chief engineer 'to take off your engineer hat and put on
your management hat'?" This *Times* piece, however, was an
editorial.

Narrative fragments interpolated in this fashion do not dominate
an account such as this, but they inflect it. They are signs of the
eruption of another story through the text of an existing one. They
are pieces of a shadow text that force their way into the nominal
one, fugitive presences that testify to unresolved tensions between
the event reported and the narrative that is doing so. But when
event and narrative form coincide, when narrative fit is good, such
tension resolves itself in the flow of the story, the news account
takes on its particular authority, and reality seems to be captured
by the text. News stories, in fact, exploit the privileged relationship
they are assumed to share with reality. In one sense, every news
story takes this relationship for granted, just as all readers do, and
it is the tacit agreement of journalists and readers to regard the news
as truth that makes reading the news *as news* possible at all. But
while this is an assumption that informs the reading of all the news,
certain stories depend for their effect more than others on the tacit
claim that the form assumed by the narrative is the shape that events
demanded to take.

William E. Geist wrote a representative piece of this sort for the

New York Times on the day after Hands Across America held a briefing at a midtown hotel in the winter of 1986. The organization was then trying to mobilize 6 million people to pay for the privilege of standing palm-to-palm in an unbroken chain across 4,152 miles of American countryside, 510 communities, 10 rivers, and 2 deserts in order to benefit the hungry and homeless. From all appearances, the briefing was a typical one: the event was described, the plans were hyped, endorsements were announced, and refreshments were served. It was "a fashionable audience," Geist wrote, that "sipped Tab and decaffeinated coffee and tapped their toes to 'We Are The World.' " It heard "talk of starvation and moral obligations," he wrote, and received a list of dozens of celebrity endorsers (it "sometimes read like a 'Who's Who' of show business, at other times like a 'Who's *That?*' " he wrote). Then everyone went home—and Geist went for the kicker: "After the briefing," his last paragraph read, "people leaving the Sheraton Centre walked past a man outside wearing filthy, tattered clothes and begging for quarters. They gave him a wide berth."

Just the facts. Or, more precisely, just the story: people went to the briefing and then they left. The events described here seemed to arrange themselves naturally into just this order. It is the events themselves, it seems, that expose the pretensions of the audience, the events that contrast its members' concern about homelessness and hunger with their aversion for the homeless and hungry. In reality, other things probably went on after the briefing as well. Some people probably returned to offices, where they have labored for years to prevent human suffering, and went back to work. Dedicated Hands Across America staff members may have gone to sleep for the first time in forty-eight hours now that the press conference was over. Perhaps some in the crowd went to church. Who knows? This little tale, simple as a bedtime story, depends for its effect on excluding such possibilities. It depends for its effect on its implicit claim that this is what happened, that this is all of what happened that mattered, and that the facts in the world naturally formed themselves into the story that expressed their meaning.

Such ironic juxtapositions are employed in much news writing. They provide details such as those that Joan Didion found herself noting when she visited the Metrocenter in San Salvador, "Central America's Largest Shopping Mall," in the midst of a civil war—the Muzak ("I Left My Heart in San Francisco"), the pâté de foie gras, "the young matrons in tight Sergio Valente jeans, trailing maids and babies behind them and buying towels, big beach towels printed with maps of Manhattan that featured Bloomingdale's." The shopping center, she wrote in *Salvador,* the memoir of her trip, "embodied the future for which El Salvador was presumably being saved, and I wrote it down dutifully, this being the kind of 'color' I knew how to interpret, the kind of inductive irony, the detail that was supposed to illuminate the story." She kept writing until she realized that it would do nothing of the sort, "that this was a story that would not be illuminated by such details, that this was a story that would perhaps not be illuminated at all, that this was perhaps even less a 'story' than a true *noche obscura*"—a dark night of the soul.

Didion's final refusal of irony, her refusal of narrative itself, is something unique, however, particularly in daily journalism. Inductive ironies discovered in the interest of the story find their way into many news accounts, particularly those which are most aware of their own narrative form. Although an especially powerful device, the ironic juxtaposition is in fact but one privileged and heightened technique among those by which all news is constructed. It is privileged because it creates a particularly literary effect in a body of writing where the use of other self-consciously literary devices is discouraged. It is heightened because the effect intended is direct and overt. Otherwise, the dynamics of the stories it creates are much the same as those of any narrative that creates a sense of its own inevitability.

As with other forms of journalistic narrative, the ironic account seems to enable the world to speak for itself. The writer appears to be merely the medium for the story and takes no responsibility for shaping it. "Complete objectivity and suppression of all explicit moral judgments are essential to his method," Northrop Frye has written of the ironist, and although he did not, he might well have had the journalist in mind. "Irony," he says, "is born from the low mimetic; it takes life exactly as it finds it." Not quite. The power of irony, we should say, depends rather on its ability to convince the reader that this is what it has done.

For although explicit judgments are suppressed, ironic narrative seeks to establish a bond between writer and reader in order to persuade the latter that he has discovered judgments for himself. As a genre, we might say, this is its work. Wayne C. Booth, another of the literary critics who have turned their attention to irony, has even argued that ironic discourse has assumed this task because it has displaced the theological. Secular culture, he has argued, no longer provides a center; it is not governed by a logos which guides its behavior and provides standards by which to judge its conduct. Yet because the need for such an order exists—even in the absence of the faith that could found it—irony serves as a means to make the very judgments that once would have been referred to the highest authority. As he puts it, "Can you imagine a syndicated columnist saying, not 'ironically enough,' but rather 'in the eyes of God the result must have appeared amusing'?"

Journalists undoubtedly have more modest intentions than replacing what Booth calls "traditional God-language" with "modern irony-language." Whatever their intentions, however, their texts obey the laws of the genre even when they are not, in the pure sense of the word, ironic. For although newswriting operates according to an objective canon that emphasizes the facts, it does so within the requirement that it represent the events it reports in the form of stories. Journalists have always been aware of this, have always known that they were out to get "the story," but have not always considered the consequences. Readers have often understood that they were getting more than the facts they were promised, but have not often stopped to consider that in reading the news they were being told a tale.

Narratives are organizations of experience. They bring order to events by making them something that can be told about; they have power because they make the world make sense. The sense they make, however, is conventional. No story is the inevitable product of the event it reports; no event dictates its own narrative form. News occurs at the conjunction of events and texts, and while events create the story, the story also creates the event. The narrative choice made by the journalist is therefore not a free choice. It is guided by the appearance which reality has assumed for him, by institutions and routines, by conventions that shape his perceptions and that provide the formal repertory for presenting them. It is the interaction of these forces that produces the news, and it is their relationship that determines its diversity or uniformity. In no case, however, does reading the news, really reading the news, confirm the impression that narrative seeks to convey: that there is but one story to tell and but one right way to tell it. Journalistic narrative depends for its effect on this impression, and all stories are in this measure ironic. The real irony, however, is that this impression, the most basic one both writers and readers share about the news, is wrong.

Notes

Reading the News, BY ROBERT KARL MANOFF and MICHAEL SCHUDSON

PAGE

3 **swift oblivion:** Edwin L. Shuman, *Practical Journalism* (New York: Daniel Appleton & Co., 1903), p. 60. Eighty-three years later, the only change in this formula is the addition of "how" and the flipping of the order of what and who, reflecting, as the authors of several of these essays note, the increasing importance of the personality in American society and the institutionalizing of an ongoing relationship with sources—the whos— in American journalistic practice.

WHO? *Sources Make the News*, BY LEON V. SIGAL

10 **one of the officers:** Leonard Buder, "Police Kill Woman Being Evicted; Officers Say She Wielded a Knife," *New York Times,* October 30, 1984.

11 **the back rent:** Selwyn Raab, "Police and Victim's Daughter Clash on Shooting," *New York Times,* November 1, 1984.

12 **four times as often:** Herbert Gans, *Deciding What's News* (New York: Vintage, 1980), pp. 8–10.

12 **the human interest story:** Michael Schudson, *Discovering the News* (New York: Basic Books, 1978), chaps. 1–3; Helen MacGill Hughes, *News and the Human Interest Story* (New Brunswick, N.J.: Transaction Books, 1981), chap. 1.

18 **Martha Kumar:** Michael Grossman and Martha Joynt Kumar, *Portraying the President* (Baltimore: Johns Hopkins University Press, 1981), pp. 190– 96.

20 **in a convincing tone:** Walter Lippmann, *Public Opinion* (New York: Free Press, 1965), pp. 157–58.

21 **authoritativeness of its sources:** Carl Bernstein and Bob Woodward, *All the President's Men* (New York: Simon & Schuster, 1974), pp. 33–34.

23 **with American policies:** Lou Cannon, "Reagan Aides Clash Over Europe Speech," *Washington Post,* April 30, 1985.

Evans and Robert Novak: Rowland Evans and Robert Novak, "Springing to Buchanan's Defense," *Washington Post,* May 6, 1985.

25 **official proceedings:** Leon V. Sigal, *Reporters and Officials* (Lexington, Mass.: D. C. Heath Co., 1973), chap. 4.

PAGE

27 **have been listening**: John Darnton, "A Letter from Warsaw: 'Fear Can Come Back As Quickly As a Door Slamming,' " *New York Times*, December 18, 1981.

28 **"pleasant atmosphere"**: James McCartney, "The Vested Interests of the Reporter," *Reporting the News*, ed. Louis Lyons (Cambridge, Mass.: Belknap Press, 1965), p. 99.

29 **a convincing case**: Daniel Patrick Moynihan, "The Presidency and the Press," *Commentary* 51 (March 1971): 10. A more recent statement of the thesis by S. Robert Lichter and Stanley Rothman also leaves the key relationship between reporters' beliefs and news content up in the air. In "Media and Business Elites," *Public Opinion* 4, no. 5 (October/November 1981): 60, they say, "The crucial task that remains is to discover what relationship, if any, exists between how these individuals view the world and how they present the world to the public." A year later, they were still not up to the task of demonstrating the relationship. In "Media and Business Elites: Two Classes in Conflict," *Public Interest* 69 (Fall 1982): 124, they say, "Our results suggest that journalists' perceptions of social reality are influenced by their political attitudes, so it is not unreasonable to infer that their news judgments may reflect both the 'progressive' values they hold and 'the new sensibility' they represent." See also the critical analysis of the Lichter and Rothman work by Herbert J. Gans, "Are U.S. Journalists Dangerously Liberal?" *Columbia Journalism Review*, November/December 1985, pp. 29–33.

30 **resistant to change**: Fred Greenstein, *Children and Politics* (New Haven: Yale University Press, 1969), chap. 2.

considerably overtime: Seymour Martin Lipset and William Schneider, *The Confidence Gap* (New York: Free Press, 1983), pp. 48–49.

34 **"know I'm famous"**: Todd Gitlin, *The Whole World Is Watching* (Berkeley: University of California Press, 1980), p. 149, n. 8. Edie Goldenberg, *Making the Papers* (Lexington, Mass.: Lexington Books, 1975) looks at the interaction between local opposition groups and the press.

36 **question its sustainability**: For an example in the best tradition of traditional news coverage, see John Herbers, "Vietnam Moratorium Observed Nationwide by Foes of War; Rallies Here Crowded, Orderly," *New York Times*, October 16, 1969.

WHAT? *The Grisly Truth about Bare Facts*, BY CARLIN ROMANO

39 **"Spiked"**: Patrick Brogan, *Spiked: The Short Life and Death of the National News Council* (New York: Priority Press, 1985).

"a mirror and a painting": Editorial, "Docudrama Strikes Again," *New York Times*, February 10, 1985.

"an item newsworthy": Vicki Hay, "Libel Law: Panel Discusses a Hypothetical Case," *Editor and Publisher*, August 10, 1985, p. 16.

PAGE
41   **about a fact:** Alan White, *Truth* (Garden City, N.Y.: Anchor/Doubleday,
     1970), p. 80.
     "worst of times": Erik Braidy and Mark Celender, "Drugs Throw Baseball
     a Curve," *USA Today*, September 12, 1985.
     "sub-1300 market": Charles Koshetz, "Market May Drop Below Bench-
     mark," *USA Today*, September 12, 1985.
42   **"Richard Nixon and so on":** By "press" in this article, I mean major
     commercial daily newspapers.
     "on which men can act": Walter Lippmann, *Public Opinion* (New York:
     Free Press, 1965), p. 226.
44   **city pool:** AP, "Guest Drowns at Party for 100 Lifeguards," *Philadelphia
     Inquirer*, August 2, 1985.
45   **in U.F.O.:** Arnold Sawislak, *Dwarf Rapes Nun; Flees in U.F.O.* (New York:
     St. Martin's, 1985).
     "Since 1962": John Woestendiek, "Thornburgh Approves 3 Executions,"
     Philadelphia Inquirer, August 2, 1985.
46   **syndicated:** Los Angeles Times Service, "Israeli Jets Retaliate, Hit Militia,"
     Philadelphia Inquirer, August 2, 1985.
     "are news": Inquirer Wire Services, "Jetliner Crashes Near Dallas," *Phila-
     delphia Inquirer*, August 3, 1985.
47   **"the Thames":** Mort Rosenblum, *Coups and Earthquakes* (New York: Harper
     & Row, 1979), p. 124.
     "happens in Chile": Ibid.
48   **plans for one:** The standard media reference to Seale in recent years has
     been along the lines of Bruce Olson's UPI story of July, 4, 1983, "Catch-
     ing Up with the Chicago Seven: Bobby Seale . . . is now writing a cook-
     book in Denver." Even former allies like Angela Davis have been quoted
     as assuming that Seale has totally changed—she has referred to him as
     one of those "spokespersons during the late '60s and early '70s . . . who
     have since left" (Murray Dubin, "A '60s Activist Who Remains Active,"
     Philadelphia Inquirer, October 8, 1984).
          Yet Seale has also worked in Philadephia Mayor W. Wilson Goode's
     campaign, a nonprofit jobs program in Philadephia, and a community
     organization in Washington, D.C., in recent years. He has been quoted
     as saying that the sixties "is a lamp by which I guide my feet to the
     future" (*Philadelphia Inquirer*, July 7, 1984).
50   **far from ideal:** Ze'ev Chafets, *Double Vision: How the Press Distorts America's
     View of the Middle East* (New York: Morrow, 1985), p. 18.
     "discovering one": Ibid., p. 36.
     "journalists": Ibid., p. 451.
51   **"the newspaper resented it":** Joanne Ambrosio, "It's in the Journal. But
     This Is Reporting?" *Columbia Journalism Review*, March/April 1980,
     p. 34.
     "public relations counsel": Michael Schudson, *Discovering the News: A*

Social History of American Newspapers (New York: Basic Books, 1978), p. 138.

54 **"sit on it":** Thomas L. Friedman, "Disclosure of Secret Airlift Opens Rift at Israeli Agency," *New York Times,* January 5, 1985.

55 **the cooperation:** Joe Shoquist, "Editors Back AP Request to Delay Kidnapping Story," *Associated Press Managing Editors News* (hereafter, *APME News*), April 1974, p. 1.

from objective: Tom Goldstein, *The News at Any Cost* (New York: Simon & Schuster, 1985), p. 14. A full account of the *Times's* coverage of Judge Kaufman would require a study of its own—one that might start with the judge's role in the trial of Ethel and Julius Rosenberg.

56 **Richard Severo:** Papers that covered the story included the *Village Voice* (February 12, 1985) and the *Philadelphia Inquirer* (February 3, 1985). Severo, a science reporter, had been transferred to the paper's metropolitan desk after he refused to sell his book to Times Books, then the paper's in-house publishing firm. He accepted a higher offer instead from Harper & Row.

editor's note: Perlez's original story ran on August 5, 1985.

57 **of his column:** The *Times* announced Schanberg's dismissal as columnist in a two-paragraph story at the bottom of a local news page in the second section of August 20, 1985. It did not take note of his resignation in December after he declined the offer of a job on the Sunday magazine.

primitive superstition: The style book of the *Philadelphia Inquirer,* like those of many other papers, typographically institutionalizes the belief in his divinity by requiring that all pronominal references to him be uppercase. This convention obtained even in a review of a book (Jaroslav Pelikan's *Jesus Through the Centuries*) specifically noncommittal as to his divinity.

58 **"doctrine":** Edward Said, *Covering Islam: How the Media and the Experts Determine How We See the Rest of the World* (New York: Pantheon, 1981), pp. 29–30.

"Western press": Ibid., p. 31.

59 **poor do not:** Herbert Gans, *Deciding What's News* (New York: Vintage, 1980), p. 26.

rarely mentioned: Ibid., pp. 26–27.

of deaths: Ibid., p. 58.

"multinationals": Ibid., p. 37.

62 **"about the fact":** Wilbur Schramm, *Responsibility in Mass Communication* (New York: Harper & Brothers, 1957), p. 92.

"investigation cease": Pamela Ridder, "There Are TK Fact-Checkers in the U.S.," *Columbia Journalism Review,* November/December 1980, p. 62.

"cast on things": Rosemary Righter, *Whose News?: Politics, the Press and the Third World* (London: Burnett Books, 1978), p. 9

63 **"which is true":** Ernest Gellner, "Fact," *The Dictionary of the Social Sciences,*

ed. Julius Gould and William L. Kolb (New York: Free Press, 1964), p. 255.

"and say this"): Ludwig Wittgenstein, *Philosophical Remarks* (Chicago: University of Chicago Press, 1980), p. 302.

64   **Theater:** Curtis MacDougall, *Newsroom Problems and Procedures* (New York: Dover, 1963), pp. 126–27.

"that is news": In his book *American Journalism* (New York: Macmillan, 1950), Frank Luther Mott attributed the classic line to *New York Sun* editor John B. Bogart: "When a dog bites a man, that is not news; but when a man bites a dog, that is news." In *The Newspaperman, News and Society* (New York: Arno Press, 1980, p. 254), Warren Breed cites the saying and writes, "The illustration is usually credited to Charles A. Dana, but [Stanley] Walker asserts the originator was actually Amos Cummings, one of Dana's editors."

British: Doris A. Graeber, "Coping with the Daily Flood of News," *Nieman Reports,* Spring 1985, p. 21.

particular premises: Richard Swinburne, ed., *The Justification of Induction* (New York: Oxford University Press, 1974), p. 1.

66   **"in 49 B.C.":** Lester King, *Medical Thinking: An Historical Preface* (Princeton: Princeton University Press, 1982), p. 255.

67   **Indian language:** I am grateful to Professor Judith Shapiro of the Bryn Mawr anthropology department for bringing this to my attention.

68   **its genesis:** " 'Star Wars Plan': How Term Arose," *New York Times,* September 25, 1985.

69   **upon the movies first:** The president, nonetheless, has tried to fight back, declaring that "the Force is with us" in a speech to the National Space Club about the Strategic Defense Initiative (March 1985).

70   **"subway vigilante":** UPI, "Most Americans Back Goetz, Newsweek Survey Indicates," *Philadelphia Inquirer,* March 4, 1985.

counterrevolutionaries: Shirley Christian, *Nicaragua: Revolution in the Family* (New York: Random House, 1985), p. 202.

" 'terrorists' ": Thomas L. Friedman, "Israelis Offer Little Information on 21 Slain in Lebanon Sweep," *New York Times,* March 22, 1985.

overboard: Samuel G. Freedman, "Across the Country, a Sense of Euphoria and Cries for Blood," *New York Times,* October 12, 1985.

71   **"63 days":** Roger Morris, "Beirut—and the Press—Under Siege," *Columbia Journalism Review,* November/December 1982, p. 30.

72   **"a personal one":** John Hellmann, *Fables of Fact: The New Journalism as New Fiction* (Urbana: University of Illinois Press, 1981), p. 4.

73   **convention center:** *New York Times,* October 15, 1985.

"begun to wiggle": John Hersey, "The Legend of the License," *Yale Review,* Autumn 1980, p. 2.

"nation of morons": Reinhold Niebuhr, "The Role of the Newspapers in America's Function as a Great Power," in Ralph D. Casey, ed., *The Press* *in Perspective* (Baton Rouge: Louisiana State University Press, 1963), p. 44.

     "Facts consist": Ibid., p. 43.

74 "Soviet society": Paul Lendvai, *The Bureaucracy of Truth: How Communist Governments Manage the News* (London: Burnett Books, 1981), p. 55.

     "Canadian news": Dean Shacklett, "Papers Do a Lousy Job of Covering Canada," *APME News,* January 1982, p. 7.

75 who voice them: Anthony Smith, *The Geopolitics of Information: How Western Culture Dominates the World* (New York: Oxford University Press, 1980), and Righter, *Whose News?*

76 no newspaper copy editors exist: William Porter, *The Italian Journalist* (Ann Arbor: University of Michigan Press, 1983), p. 14.

     and those more recent: Charles R. Eisendrath, "France," in *World Press Encyclopedia,* ed. George Thomas, 2 vols. (New York: Facts on File, 1982), 1: 349.

     course of a broadcast day: John Lent, "Thailand," in ibid., 2: 869.

77 to be conquered: Thomas S. Kuhn, *The Structure of Scientific Revolutions* (Chicago: University of Chicago Press, 1971).

     "in its domain": Paul Feyerabend, *Against Method* (London: Verso Editions, 1975), p. 55.

     ideas and theories: Richard Rorty, *Philosophy and the Mirror of Nature* (Princeton: Princeton University Press, 1979); *Consequences of Pragmatism* (Minneapolis: University of Minnesota Press, 1982).

WHEN? *Deadlines, Datelines, and History,* BY MICHAEL SCHUDSON

79 David Sarnoff: Erik Barnouw, *Tube of Plenty* (New York: Oxford University Press, 1975), p. 18.

     Walter Trohan: Walter Trohan, *Political Animals* (Garden City, N.Y.: Doubleday, 1975), p. 25.

80 On November 22, 1963: Timothy Crouse, *The Boys on the Bus* (New York: Ballantine, 1973), p. 207.

     Daniel Schorr: Daniel Schorr, *Clearing the Air* (Boston: Houghton Mifflin, 1977), p. 1.

     Dan Rather: Dan Rather with Mickey Herskowitz, *The Camera Never Blinks* (New York: Morrow, 1977), p. 46.

81 E. L. Godkin: E. L. Godkin, "Newspapers Here and Abroad," *North American Review* 150 (February 1890): 200.

     The news organization: Philip Schlesinger, "Newsmen and Their Time-Machine," *British Journal of Sociology* 28 (1977): 336–50.

91 part of a megastory: "Megastory" is a term I borrow from William Blakemore, correspondent for ABC News.

97 seven-day week developed: Eviator Zerubavel, *The Seven Day Circle* (New York: Free Press, 1985), p. 1.

PAGE

100 State of the Union message: For a study of changes in the way the press
has reported the State of the Union message, including changes in the
temporal contexts the press provides for the message, see Michael Schudson, "The Politics of Narrative Form: The Emergence of News Conventions in Print and Television," *Daedalus* 111 (Fall 1982): 97–112.

104 Available social research: Jack Whalen and Richard Flacks, "Echoes of
Rebellion: The Liberated Generation Grows Up," *Journal of Political and
Military Sociology* 12 (Spring 1984): 61–78.

WHERE? *Cartography, Community, and the Cold War,* BY DANIEL C. HALLIN

113 Kim Willenson: Kim Willenson, "Frolic in Honduras," *Washington Journalism Review* 7 (July 1985): 17–20.

120 market surveys: Katharine Seelye, "Al Neurath's Technicolor Baby," *Columbia Journalism Review* 21 (March/April 1983): 27–35.

122 Warren I. Susman: Warren I. Susman, *Culture as History: The Transforma-
tion of American Society in the Twentieth Century* (New York: Pantheon
Books, 1984), pp. 212–13.

124 "upscale" readers: Félix Gutiérrez and Clint C. Wilson II, "The Demographic Dilemma," *Columbia Journalism Review* 17 (January/February
1979): 53–55.

135 role played by maps: Daniel C. Hallin, *The "Uncensored War": The Media
and Vietnam* (New York: Oxford University Press, 1986), pp. 51–58.

138 perspectives on world politics: Daniel C. Hallin, "The Media Go to War
—From Vietnam to Central America," *NACLA Report on the Americas* 17
(July/August, 1983).

140 Av Westin: Av Westin, *Newswatch: How TV Decides the News* (New York:
Simon & Schuster, 1982), pp. 198, 200.

141 Third World rarely appears: Johan Galtung and Marie Ruge, "The Struc-
ture of Foreign News," *Journal of International Peace Research* 2 (1965): 64–
91; Sophia Peterson, "International News Selection by the Elite Press: A
Case Study," *Public Opinion Quarterly* 45 (Summer 1981): 143–63; Peter
H. Dahlgren with Sumitra Chakrapani, "The Third World on TV News:
Western Ways of Seeing the 'Other,' " in William C. Adams, ed., *Tele-
vision Coverage of International Affairs* (Norwood, N.J.: Ablex Publishing
Corp., 1982), pp. 45–65.

WHY AND HOW? *The Dark Continent of American Journalism,* BY JAMES W. CAREY

146 Men can do nothing: George Eliot, *Daniel Deronda,* ed. Graham Handley
(Oxford: Clarendon Press, 1984), p. 1. I am indebted to Howard Ziff of
the University of Massachusetts for calling this quote to my attention.

147 with a proposition: A slightly different version of the lead appears in Dick

Griffin and Rob Warden, eds., *Done in a Day: 100 Years of Great Writing from the Chicago Daily News* (Chicago: Swallow Press, 1977), pp. 405–7.

149 "A story is worthless": As quoted by Gerald Lansom and Mitchell Stephens in "'Trust Me' Journalism," *Washington Journalism Review*, November 1982, p. 43.

150 The daily news coverage: "Publisher's Note" to William Greider, *The Education of David Stockman and Other Americans* (New York: E. P. Dutton, 1982), p. xii.

154 "the necessities of compromise": Ibid., p. xi.

156 "a very limited market": Greider, *The Education of David Stockman*, p. xv.

journalists write: Robert Darnton, "Writing News and Telling Stories," *Daedalus* 104, no. 2 (Spring 1975): 175–94.

157 "participants in political debates": Greider, *The Education of David Stockman*, p. xxiv.

This inside knowledge: Ibid., p. xxv.

163 "kaleidoscope equipped with consciousness": As cited by Walter Benjamin in *Illuminations* (New York: Harcourt, Brace & World, 1968), p. 177.

169 an ambiguity: Roland Barthes, "Structure of the *Faits-Divers*," in *Critical Essays*, trans. Richard Howard (Evanston: Northwestern University Press, 1972), pp. 185–95.

A confirmed AIDS victim: *Champaign-Urbana News-Gazette*, December 7, 1985.

170 Tale of True Love: *Chicago Sun-Times*, January 7, 1986.

From the tabloid weeklies: *National Enquirer*, January 7, 1986; *Weekly World News*, January 7, 1986.

172 The nation's trade deficit: *Chicago Tribune*, March 29, 1985.

174 Senator Packwood wrote: *New York Times*, April 24, 1985.

Iacocca: "Japanese Play Fair with Us," *Chicago Tribune*, April 18, 1985.

"Americans see the Japanese": Joseph A. Reaves, "In Trade Fight, Perceptions Are Bottom Line," *Chicago Tribune*, April 14, 1985.

175 "if you have equal access": James Mateja, "U.S. Auto Parts Sellers Find Japan a Tough Market to Crack," *Chicago Tribune*, April 14, 1985.

"Japanese aren't playing fair": Joseph A. Reaves, "U.S. Trade Complaints," *Chicago Tribune*, April 7, 1985.

"Democrats now smell blood": Clyde H. Farnsworth, "Debate On Trade . . . ," *New York Times*, April 11, 1985.

"shift the blame": Ronald Yates, "Japan Split on Trade Gap . . . ," *Chicago Tribune*, March 31, 1985.

176 "The budget deficits": Edwin Yoder, "Misreading Causes of the U.S. Trade Deficit," *Providence Journal*, April 19, 1985.

"just handy excuses": Stephen Chapman, "Why Such an Uproar Against Japan?" *Chicago Tribune*, April 5, 1985.

PAGE

176–77   "barriers to U.S. imports": Hobart Rowen, "Experts Deny Japan's Barriers Cause Imbalance in U.S. Trade," *International Herald Tribune,* July 12, 1985.

177   "Japanese market remains elusive": Nicholas D. Kristof, "Japan Trade Barriers Called Mainly Cultural," *New York Times,* April 4, 1985.

177–78   "The Wary Shoppers of Japan": Susan Chira, *New York Times,* April 12, 1985.

178   "The Hideous Gaijin in Japan": Marjorie Smith, *Newsweek,* April 22, 1985, p. 22.

A long wrap-up story: R. C. Longworth, "Collision Course with Japan," *Chicago Tribune,* April 7, 1985.

"shrink the federal government": Robert M. Solow, "Why People Make Fun of Economists," *New York Times,* December 29, 1985.

179   "Here is what's happening": Bill Neikirk, "We Really Don't Want to Beat Up the Japanese, Just Beat 'Em," *Chicago Tribune,* April 7, 1985.

182   "to win votes here": Cited in Lansom and Stephens, " 'Trust Me' Journalism," p. 47.

183   Mikhail S. Gorbachev told: Serge Schmemann, "A Gorbachev Trade Warning," *New York Times,* December 11, 1985.

"saboteurs today knocked out": Clyde Haberman, "Sabotage Cripples Japan Rail Lines," *New York Times,* November 30, 1985.

184   "He isn't eager": Jeffrey H. Birnbaum, "Rostenkowski Looms as Key to Tax-Revision Fight," *Wall Street Journal,* March 29, 1985.

Just one minute: *New York Times,* January 2, 1986.

186   "John Gotti": *New York Times,* December 18, 1985.

the *Times* covered the case: M. A. Farber, "A Shattering of Destinies," *New York Times,* July 4, 1985.

189   "precision journalism": Philip Meyer, *Precision Journalism* (Bloomington: Indiana University Press, 1973).

190   "violent outbursts": Andrew H. Malcolm, "Deaths on the Iowa Prairie," *New York Times,* December 11, 1985.

191   there are accounts: *Iowa City Press-Citizen,* as reprinted in the *New York Times,* December 15, 1985.

Writing the News (By Telling the "Story"), BY ROBERT KARL MANOFF

197   "Nature of Reality": Cited by "TRB" in "Don't Stop the Presses," *New Republic,* June 2, 1986, p. 41

198   few days before: For an account of the report, see Peter Samuel, "SDI Got Top Pre-Summit Priority," *Defense Week,* March 10, 1986, pp. 15ff.

"the Oval Office": Morton Kondracke and Jim [James] McCartney, "Pool Report—Air Force One—Washington to Geneva," November 16, 1985, p. 1.

199   "when Helen asked him": Telephone interview with Michael Putzel, January 22, 1986.

   "thought about it": Interview with Helen Thomas, Geneva, November 17, 1985.

   "senior American official": Kondracke and McCartney, "Pool Report," p. 1.

199–200   "received such attention": Telephone interview with Charles J. Lewis, January 17, 1986.

200   TREATY VIOLATIONS: Slugged "Reagan-Salt II-16," the transmission of wire ZCZC NLE 158 was concluded at 19:02 GMT.

202   "put the two together": Interview with Jack Nelson and Richard Cooper, Geneva, November 19, 1985.

   forty-eight hours away: Jack Nelson and Eleanor Clift, "Advisers' Discord Clouds Reagan's Arrival in Geneva," *Los Angeles Times,* November 17, 1985, p. 1.

   the pool report: Interview with Bernard Weinraub, Geneva, November 20, 1985.

203   of their readers: Bernard Weinraub, "Reagan Aides Upset by Disclosure of Weinberger's Letter on Arms," *New York Times,* November 17, 1985, p. 1; Lou Cannon, "Reagan Hopeful for Geneva," *Washington Post,* November 17, 1985, p. 1.

206   at the summit: Cooper interview.

207   several days earlier: Although the *Post* reported that the White House received the letter on Wednesday, Speakes told the pool it had been Tuesday. Kondracke and McCartney, "Pool Report," p. 2.

   top of the page: Michael R. Gordon, "Weinberger Urges U.S. to Avoid Vow on 1979 Arms Pact," *New York Times,* November 16, 1985, p. 1; "Weinberger Letter to Reagan on Arms Control," *New York Times,* November 16, 1985, p. 7.

   text of the letter: Walter Pincus, "Avoid SALT II Pledge, Weinberger Bids Reagan," *Washington Post,* November 16, 1985, p. A11.

   "some agreement": Michael R. Gordon, "Weinberger Urges U.S. to Avoid Vow," p. 7. "The Media seem, in this play of extratextual quotation, to make reference to the world, but in effect they are referring to the contents of other messages sent by other media. . . . Any difference between knowledge of the world (understood naively as a knowledge derived from an extratextual experience) and intertextual knowledge has practically vanished." Umberto Eco, "Innovation and Repetition: Between Modern and Post-Modern Aesthetics," *Daedalus* 114, no. 4 (Fall 1985): 172.

   summit-related articles: The five other summit articles in the *Washington Post* of November 16, 1985, were: David Hoffman, "President's Offstage Style Could Be a Factor in Geneva," p. A1; Lou Cannon and David Hoffman, "Joint Ceremony to Cap Summit," p. A1; Don Oberdorfer,

"More Regular Meetings of U.S., Soviets Expected," p. A10; Gary Lee, "Soviets Court World Press in Geneva," p. A12; and Karlyn Barker, "Groups Rally in Presummit Protests," p. A14.

page A3: George C. Wilson, "Reagan Urged to Preempt Cuts," *Washington Post,* November 16, 1985, p. A3.

"as previously reported": Walter Pincus, "Avoid SALT II Pledge," p. A11.

Pincus and the *Post*.: Pincus subsequently saw an eleven-page summary of the report which the letter accompanied and concluded that although the "general contents of Weinberger's findings" had already been reported, the summary itself contained "a number of new points." The judgment about the letter itself remained as previously rendered. See Walter Pincus, "Weinberger Urges Buildup Over Soviet 'Violations,' " *Washington Post,* November 18, 1985, p. A1.

208 **SS-19 ICBMs:** Michael R. Gordon, "Weinberger Urges U.S. to Avoid Vow," p. 7.

"arms control positions": Michael R. Gordon, "Weinberger Urges U.S. to Avoid Vow," pp. 1, 7.

with the Allies: Robert Karl Manoff, "Covering the Bomb: The Nuclear Story and the News," *Working Papers,* Summer 1983, pp. 19–27. For an account of this period, see Gregg Herken, *The Winning Weapon: The Atomic Bomb in the Cold War, 1945–1950* (New York: Random House, 1982), pp. 1–42.

"on the specifics": Evan Thomas, "Mixed Signals from America's Team," *Time,* November 18, 1985, p. 24; Rowland Evans and Robert Novak, "Policy Shift Endangers SDI," *San Diego Union,* October 22, 1985, p. B6; Leslie H. Gelb, "U.S. Officials Reveal Disunity on Arms Goals," *New York Times,* October 25, 1985, p. A1.

209 **"are not new":** The White House, Office of the Press Secretary, "Press Briefing by Larry Speakes," November 17, 1985, p. 3.

Monday's *New York Times*: R. W. Apple, Jr., "Weinberger Note Seen as Opposing Softness at Talks," *New York Times,* November, 18, 1985, p. A8.

"games in town": Lewis interview.

with the president: William R. Doerner, "Lobbying Through Leaks," *Time,* December 2, 1985, p. 37.

he failed: Walter Pincus, "Pentagon to Probe Staff for Leak," *Washington Post,* November 19, 1985, p. A22.

210 **agent in its creation:** Compare Roland Barthes, "Introduction to the Structural Analysis of Narratives," in *Image-Music-Text,* trans. Stephen Heath (New York: Hill & Wang, 1977), p. 116. It should also be said that the canon prescribes occasions when it should be "broken," as when the paper goes to the aid of a citizen in distress or reports government efforts to

PAGE

manage or suppress the news. (Reporting of the Pentagon Papers is a principal example; more recently see Bob Woodward and Patrick E. Tyler, "Eavesdropping System Betrayed," *Washington Post,* May 21, 1986, p. A1.) Such ruptures of the code are, of course, controlled by another code.

212   **different speeches entirely:** Bill Gertz, "McFarlane Says More Effort Needed to Put Down Spying," *Washington Times,* December 10, 1985, p. 3A; Lou Cannon, "McFarlane Optimistic on Arms Control," *Washington Post,* December 10, 1985, p. A7.

213   **the story wrong:** "Notebook," *New Republic,* June 2, 1986, p. 10.

215   **"Disarray Under Regan":** Lou Cannon, "Disarray Under Regan," *Washington Post,* December 16, 1986, p. A2.

216   **earlier in the day:** Walter V. Robinson, "Reagan Cool on Prospects for Arms Progress," *Boston Globe,* November 13, 1985, p. 1.

       briefing on the summit: Jack Nelson, "President Is Upbeat on Summit," *Los Angeles Times,* November 13, 1985, p. 1.

217   **"statement of policy":** Lou Cannon and Don Oberdorfer, "U.S. Offers to Extend SALT II Compliance," *Washington Post,* November 13, 1985, p. A1.

219   **was nothing new:** Fred Kaplan, "Weinberger Says 45 Soviet Missiles Violate SALT II," *Boston Globe,* January 10, 1986, p. 14.

       yet to be written: Johanna Neuman, "Arms Talks to Start Amid New Charges," *USA Today,* January 10, 1986, p. A4.

       "budget-struggle story": James Gerstenzang, "45 New Soviet ICBMs Now Deployed, Weinberger Says," *Los Angeles Times,* January 10, 1986, p. A5.

       secretary himself: Mark Thompson, "Arms Pact Linked to Pentagon Boost," *Philadelphia Inquirer,* January 10, 1986, p. 7A.

220   **also echoed here:** Bill Keller, "Weinberger Says Military Budget Cuts Would Imperil Arms Talks," *New York Times,* January 10, 1986, p. A11. The leak of the secretary's letter to the president had provided the occasion for a number of stories in the "influence" genre. See Walter Andrews, "Weinberger Won't Step Down Under a Cloud, Officials Say," *Washington Times,* November 19, 1985, p. 3A; George C. Wilson, "Weinberger Surrounded by Snipers," *Washington Post,* November 19, 1985, p. A22; Patricia O'Brien and David Hess, " 'Cap the Knife' is Losing His Edge in Washington," *San Jose Mercury News,* November 20, 1985, p. 12.

223   **"treatment of Sakharov":** Celestine Bohlen, "Gorbachev Will Not Let Sakharov Go," *Washington Post,* February 8, 1986, p. A14.

       Gorbachev's accusation: "From News Services," "Gorbachev Says Sakharov Will Not Be Allowed To Leave," *San Diego Union,* February 8, 1986, p. A2.

PAGE

224 **"approved the launch"**: Boyce Rensberger and Kevin Klose, "Thiokol Engineers Tell of Being Overruled," *Washington Post,* February 26, 1986, p. A1.

225 **an editorial:** "The Frailties of Machines and Men," *New York Times,* March 2, 1986, Week in Review section, p. 22.

    possible at all: Compare Tzvetan Todorov, "Introduction to Verisimilitude," in *The Poetics of Prose,* trans. Richard Howard (Ithaca: Cornell University Press, 1977), pp. 80–88.

226 **"a wide berth"**: William E. Geist, "About New York," *New York Times,* February 22, 1986, p. 26.

227 **"noche obscura"**: Joan Didion, *Salvador* (New York: Simon & Schuster, 1983), pp. 35–36.

    "as it finds it": Northrop Frye, *Anatomy of Criticism* (Princeton: Princeton University Press, 1957), pp. 40ff.

228 **" 'appeared amusing' "**: Wayne C. Booth, "The Empire of Irony," *Georgia Review* 37, no. 4 (Winter 1983): 719–37.

THE CONTRIBUTORS

JAMES W. CAREY is dean of the College of Communications at the University of Illinois, Urbana-Champaign. Formerly the George Gallup Professor of Journalism at the University of Iowa and a past president of the Association for Education in Journalism and Mass Communication, he writes on communication and cultural studies, the history of media technologies, and communication theory.

DANIEL C. HALLIN teaches communication and political science at the University of California, San Diego. He is the author of *"The Uncensored War": The Media and Vietnam,* and many articles on the politics of news. He is currently writing a book on news coverage of Central America, and collaborating with European researchers on a study of television coverage of the Reagan-Gorbachev summit in the United States, Italy, Britain, and Sweden. Professor Hallin received his Ph.D. in political science in 1980 from the University of California, Berkeley.

ROBERT KARL MANOFF is the cofounder and codirector of the Center of War, Peace and the News Media at New York University. He has been the managing editor of *Harper's* magazine, the editor of the *Columbia Journalism Review,* and senior editor of *MORE.* He is working on a book about press coverage of nuclear issues and Soviet-American relations, about which he has written widely. He has taught at the Massachusetts Institute of Technology, Columbia University, and New York University. In 1985, he won an Olive Branch Award for excellence in the reporting of nuclear issues.

CARLIN ROMANO is the literary editor and critic of the *Philadelphia Inquirer.* Before becoming editor of the *Inquirer*'s Sunday book review section, he worked as a reporter for the *Inquirer,* the *Washington Post, New York Daily News,* and *Flatbush Life,* a weekly newspaper in Brooklyn, N.Y. He has also written for the *Village Voice, Wall Street Journal,* and *USA Today.* Mr. Romano received his law degree from Columbia University, and also holds an M. Phil. in philosophy from Yale. As a lecturer at Yale, he taught a seminar entitled "Philosophical Problems of Journalism."

MICHAEL SCHUDSON is chairman of the Department of Communication and a professor in the Department of Sociology at the University of California, San Diego. He is the author of *Discovering the News: A Social History of American Newspapers* and *Advertising, the Uneasy Persuasion: Its Dubious Impact on American Society* as well as articles on the news media in both popular and professional journals. He is currently working on a study of communication and collective memory.

LEON V. SIGAL teaches government at Wesleyan University. He is the author of *Reporters and Officials* as well as *Alliance Security: NATO and the No-First-Use Question,* and *Nuclear Forces in Europe,* both published by the Brookings Institution, where he has been a guest scholar. He has written numerous articles in such periodicals as the *Christian Science Monitor, Foreign Policy,* and *Political Science Quarterly.*